MEDIEVALIA ET HUMANISTICA

MEDIEVALIA ET HUMANISTICA

New Series

Paul Maurice Clogan, Editor
University of North Texas

EDITORIAL BOARD

MEDIEVALIA ET HUMANISTICA

STUDIES IN MEDIEVAL & RENAISSANCE CULTURE

NEW SERIES: NUMBER 17

EDITED BY
PAUL MAURICE CLOGAN

ROWMAN & LITTLEFIELD PUBLISHERS, INC.

ROWMAN & LITTLEFIELD PUBLISHERS, INC.

Published in the United States of America
by Rowman & Littlefield Publishers, Inc.
8705 Bollman Place, Savage, Maryland 20763

**The Library of Congress has cataloged this serial publication
as follows:**

Medievalia et humanistica. fasc. 1– jan. 1943– ;
 new ser. no. 1– 1970–
 Totowa, N.J. [etc.] Rowman and Littlefield [etc.]
 no. 26 cm.
 Annual, 1943–
 "Studies in medieval and renaissance culture."
 Vols. for 1970-72 issued by the Medieval and neo-Latin Society;
 1973– by the Medieval and Renaissance Society.
 Key title: Medievalia et humanistica, ISSN 0076-6127.
 1. Middle Ages—History—Periodicals. 2. Civilization,
Medieval—Periodicals. 3. Renaissance—Periodicals.
I. Medieval and Neo-Latin Society.
II. Medieval and Renaissance Society.
D111.M5 940.105 47-36424 CIP
                    MARCS-S

ISBN 0–8476–7658–7
Library of Congress {8101}

5   4   3   2   1

Printed in the United States of America

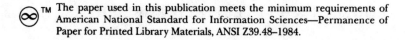

Contents

REVIEW NOTICES

Editorial Note

Since 1970, this new series has sought to promote significant scholarship, criticism, and reviews in the several fields of medieval and Renaissance studies. It has published articles drawn from a wide variety of disciplines and has given attention to new directions in humanistic scholarship and to significant topics of general interest. This series has been particularly concerned with exchange between specializations, and scholars of diverse approaches have complemented each other's efforts on questions of modern interest.

Medievalia et Humanistica is sponsored by the Modern Language Association of America, and publication in the series is open to contributions from all sources. The Editorial Board welcomes scholarly, critical, or interdisciplinary articles of significant interest on relevant material and urges contributors to communicate in a clear and concise style the larger implications, in addition to the material of their research, with documentation held to a minimum. Texts, maps, illustrations, diagrams, and musical examples will be published when they are essential to the argument of the article. In preparing and submitting manuscripts for consideration, potential contributors are advised to follow carefully the instructions given on page xi. Articles in English may be submitted to any of the editors. Books for review and inquiries concerning *Fasciculi* I-XVII in the original series should be addressed to the Editor, *Medievalia et Humanistica*, P.O. Box 13348, North Texas Station, Denton, Texas 76203.

Inquiries concerning subscriptions should be addressed to the publisher.

Articles for Future Volumes Are Invited

Articles may be submitted to any of the editors, but it would be advisable to submit them to the nearest or most appropriate editor for consideration. A prospective author is encouraged to contact his editor at the earliest opportunity to receive any necessary advice and a copy of the style sheet. The length of the article depends upon the material, but brief articles of notes are normally not considered. The entire manuscript should be typed, double-spaced, on standard 8½" × 11" bond paper with ample margins, and documentation should be held to a minimum. Endnotes, prepared according to *The Chicago Manual of Style,* thirteenth edition (University of Chicago Press), should be doubled-spaced and numbered consecutively and appear at the end of the article. All quotations and references should be carefully verified before submission. The completed article should be in finished form, appropriate for printing. Only the original manuscript (not photocopy or carbon) should be submitted, accompanied by a stamped, self-addressed manuscript envelope.

The addresses of the American editors can be determined by their academic affiliations. The addresses of the editors outside the United States are:

Mr. Peter Dronke, Faculty of Modern and Medieval Languages, University of Cambridge, Sidgwick Avenue, Cambridge CB3 9DA, England (Medieval Latin Poetry and Thought).

Professor Ian D. McFarlane, Wadham College, Oxford OX1 3NA, England (Renaissance French and Neo-Latin Literature).

Professor Jean-Claude Margolin, 75 Bld Richard-Lenoir, 75011 Paris, France (Humanism, Renaissance Philosophy and Neo-Latin Literature).

The Just War as Concept and Motive in the Central Middle Ages

JOHN R. E. BLIESE

The concept of the just war is an ancient one. The idea that some wars are morally acceptable but others are not was inherited by the Christian West; it was developed and adapted as Christian doctrine during the age of the church fathers, especially by St. Augustine. In the intellectual flowering of the central Middle Ages, one of the concerns of legal scholars and theologians was to define more precisely this concept of the just war. Modern discussions of medieval theories focus almost exclusively on their intellectual efforts. The most complete account, Frederick Russell's *The Just War in the Middle Ages,* deals strictly with canon law and theology.[1]

However, the belief that one is right, that one has a worthy cause to fight for, is not only a legal and theological concept. It is also a motive to fight and a motivational instrument in war. A leader can stir up war fever by the righteousness of his cause, whether it be to recover the Holy Sepulcher or to make the world safe for democracy. The cause for which an army is to fight can be an important element in morale and therefore an important factor in victory.[2]

The use of the just cause as a motivator shows what things a society thinks are worth fighting for, and for which it is right and proper to fight. These will typically be popular ideas rather than abstract philosophical concepts. But the commonly held notions are surely more efficacious in the world of action, especially in questions of war and peace, than are the theories of scholars. To understand the mentality of the medieval man-at-arms, it is therefore important to discover what these popular beliefs were.[3] The just cause as a stimulus for knights to fight, however, is a largely overlooked aspect of medieval ideas of the just war, and one that deserves further attention.

The chroniclers of the central Middle Ages offer us an approach for studying morale and motivation in war. They tell us that before committing their troops to battle, commanders often exhorted their men. Frequently the chroniclers include more or less detailed versions of these

Medievalia et Humanistica, New Series, Number 17 (Paul Maurice Clogan, ed.) Rowman & Littlefield Publishers, Inc.

orations. In such speeches, the leaders must rouse their troops so that they will fight to the utmost of their ability and give up their lives if necessary. To build up their courage the speakers must use those lines of appeal which they think strike at the core of their warriors' motives.

Of course, these speeches are not verbatim reports of orations actually given on the field of battle, nor are they simply borrowed from the classics. The chroniclers were writing in a tradition of historiography heavily influenced by rhetoric.[4] They were expected to spice up their narratives by putting appropriate speeches into the mouths of their characters. The battle speeches are their own rhetorical inventions.[5] As would any other rhetorical devices, however, the speeches had to meet the tests of plausibility for their readers.[6]

The chroniclers had ample opportunity to learn about the mentality of the knights. Several authors were knights themselves; others accompanied armies on the Crusades. Even the monastic writers had considerable opportunity to learn about the psychology of the knights. The monks came from the same social background as the warriors, and converted knights often lived in monasteries. As Keen concludes, "Knights and clerks . . . understood each other's worlds better than is often allowed for."[7] The battle speeches are, therefore, valuable sources of information. They contain those appeals that the authors, with more or less detailed knowledge of the psychology of combat, thought would be most appropriate and effective with their contemporaries in building courage and morale. Thus, they are useful in helping us understand the mentality of medieval man in war.[8]

The analysis here is based on battle speeches from chronicles written in western Europe in the eleventh, twelfth, and early thirteenth centuries. I have found in 92 chronicles accounts of 360 battle orations that are detailed enough to show us something of what the speakers supposedly said.[9]

In these speeches, the leaders use a number of recurrent motive appeals, rhetorical *topoi,* to build up the courage of their men.[10] One of the most important has the speaker exhort the knights by telling them they are fighting for a worthy cause. Fully 109 speeches develop this appeal directly, claiming in some way that they have right on their side and that the enemy is evil. The speakers sometimes specifically claim that they are fighting for a just cause. Usually, however, they simply dwell on the terrible crimes their enemies have committed, in contrast to their own righteousness. Some speakers, especially in chronicles of the Crusades, invoke concepts of holy war, often claiming that the foes are infidels and enemies of God.

Overall, the just-cause *topos* is second in frequency; only appeals to the martial virtues, such as prowess and valor, are more numerous. In addition, in a separate category of their own, in twenty-three orations the speakers claim that their men are fighting for Christ or the Holy Sepulcher, and these may be added to the just-cause *topos*. Also, in forty-six speeches the knights are asked to defend themselves or their families or country. A few of these are directly relevant to the just-war concept, and all may be. (A few speakers state that self-defense is just, but most claim only that it is necessary.) Thus, the belief that they were fighting a just war was, according to the chroniclers, a major element in morale for a medieval army.

The ways in which the speakers develop the justice of a war in order to stimulate fighting spirit, however, are significantly different from the discussions of the legal scholars and theologians. Many theoretical issues do not occur at all in the military harangues; some are developed in quite different ways in the speeches; and some motive appeals are directly contradictory to the legal and theological concepts. The chroniclers give no indication that the knights thought these discrepancies from doctrine made their wars morally wrong. Consequently, if the rhetoric is compared with the theory, a very different concept of the just war emerges, and an important aspect of medieval mentality is disclosed.

In making these comparisons, the nuances and individual differences in the ways in which the theoretical concept of the just war was developed by numerous medieval scholars cannot be detailed here.[11] This study, rather, will focus on several of their primary, common themes to compare and contrast with the battle rhetoric. It will rely primarily on the concepts developed by three of the most important theorists: Augustine, who formulated the basis for the medieval theory; Gratian, who established its place in canon law; and Thomas Aquinas, who reinforced the basic Augustinian concepts in systematic theology.[12]

The scholars who were concerned with just-war theory developed the concept largely around three major criteria and a number of satellite issues. The criteria which determined whether a war was just were (1) authority (was the war waged by orders of one who had proper authority to declare war?), (2) cause (was the war being fought for a legitimate reason?), and (3) intention (were those fighting the war doing so with the proper motives?) Necessity was sometimes added as a fourth criterion. War is so terrible that it is to be avoided whenever possible. Even if the other three criteria are met, war is to be waged only if there is no other means of redressing a wrong.[13]

Other issues that received considerable attention from the scholars cluster around such questions as: What could clerics do in a war? What obedience does a warrior owe to his superiors? What are the legal consequences of a just war?

The theorists believed that most feudal wars were unjust.[14] But the chroniclers clearly show that the knights who fought them believed that they were right and proper. Moreover, the chroniclers testify that it was very important to those knights to believe that their wars were just. The ways in which the motive appeals were developed in the speeches therefore had to be quite different from the scholars' concepts. In general, the speeches omit all the secondary issues because there would be no reason to deal with them in a battle harangue. Of the three major criteria for justifying a war, the speakers ignored the first one; they developed the second in their own ways; and they often flatly contradicted the third. Each of these criteria will be considered in turn.

The most important question for the theorists concerned the authority for waging a just war.[15] Who had the right to declare a war? The theorists were virtually unanimous in claiming that only a prince had the right to declare war; private individuals did not. Augustine set the standard when he insisted that only the ruler or God himself had the right to wage war.[16] A war fought by divine command was just, because it was waged on the highest possible authority. The Old Testament contains stories of instances when the Israelites fought by God's command. For example, God ordered Joshua to conquer the city of Ai.[17] The medieval theorists all thought these wars were just, following Augustine, who declared that "when war is undertaken in obedience to God, who would rebuke, or humble, or crush the pride of man, it must be allowed to be a righteous war."[18]

After God, only a public authority could declare a war to be just. Gratian contended that for a war to be just, it had to be "waged by an authoritative edict."[19] Likewise, Thomas Aquinas argued that only "the authority of the sovereign" could declare a war; a private person could not.[20] Exactly who had public authority in the Middle Ages was, of course, subject to some dispute. Was it only the emperor? Could a king legally declare war? Could a duke or a lesser authority? Sometimes the resolution was based on the principle that if one had a superior, he could not settle quarrels by waging war but must appeal to the judgment of his lord. Only one who had no superior could legitimately declare war.[21] However the theorists might resolve that question, the implication clearly was that the private warfare so common in the Middle Ages was illegal and unjust.

As a morale-booster, on the other hand, the notion of proper authorization for a war appears in only one battle speech. Frederick Barbarossa assured his men before attacking Milan that "the war is just, and waged at the command of a higher power."[22] Proper authority may be implied in one other oration. Aelred of Rievaulx related the story of King Alfred and the Battle of Edington in 878. Alfred had retreated from the Danes into the marshes at Athelney. He gathered a few warriors around him and exhorted them to take the war to the enemy. In his harangue he claimed that they had been called together by God himself.[23] But that is as close as Aelred came to claiming that the war on the pagan Danes was authorized or declared by God.

One might expect to find references to God's authority in the battles of the Crusades. At the Council of Clermont in 1095, when Pope Urban II proclaimed the Crusade, the audience shouted, "God wills it."[24] They apparently believed that this particular war was ordained by God. If God willed the Crusade, one might expect his command to be used to enhance morale in battle. Many of the battle speeches on the Crusades, and indeed on other occasions as well, claimed that the warriors were about to fight *for* God or Christ, but not a single battle oration claimed that the war was being waged *by order* of God.[25] Thus, the authority behind a war—the most important element of the just-war theory—played virtually no role in motivation for combat.

On the other hand, both theorists and chroniclers were concerned about the second criterion: the specific cause for which the army was about to fight. For a war to be just, the cause for which it was fought must be legitimate. The theorists developed several categories.

Much of the theorists' discussion was conducted at the most general level, at which Augustine had established the basic definition of a just war: "Just wars avenge injuries (*iusta autem bella ea definiri solent quae ulciscuntur iniurias*)."[26] This definition became "the single most important statement of the later medieval theories."[27] Gratian proposed as his definition: "A just war is waged by an authoritative edict to avenge injuries."[28] According to Thomas Aquinas, "Secondly, a just cause is required, namely that those who are attacked are attacked because they deserve it on account of some wrong they have done."[29] In general, a legitimate cause for war was to coerce the wicked or to punish evildoers.

To the extent that much of the theory remained at that high level of abstraction, it was relatively unhelpful in determining whether a particular war was just. Indeed, the theorists seem to have spent relatively little effort on determining exactly what factors constitute a just cause. What, exactly, would constitute an "injury"? What kind of "wrong" would deserve a war? Within this very vague and broad concept of injury or wrong, if anywhere, the vast majority of the chroniclers' motive appeals would fit.

Sometimes the speeches are equally general. For example, according to William of Poitiers, Duke William told his men before the Battle of Hastings that they were fighting for a just cause.[30]

The speeches, however, are usually quite specific. The speakers fre-

quently detailed the evil deeds of their opponents as a means of enraging
their men and bolstering their fighting spirit. In Henry of Huntingdon's
version of William the Conqueror's address to his men at Hastings the
duke referred to Harold's perjury, his breach of faith, and the earlier
murder of Alfred, brother of Edward the Confessor.[31] In Wace's version
of this speech, William dredged up crimes of the English against the
Normans and Danes going back even further. "They have done much ill
to our kindred, as well as to other people, for they do all the treason and
mischief they can. On the night of the feast of St. Bryce, they committed
horrible treachery; they slew all the Danes in one day. . . . You have all
heard of Alfred, and how Godwin betrayed him, . . . tore out his eyes and
afterwards killed him. He had the men of Normandy . . . decimated."[32]
In the Mahdia campaign of 1087, Bishop Benedict exhorted the Pisan
army. He stressed that the enemy are foes of God, "they capture Christians," they "afflict the people of God and hold them in prison."[33] King
Arthur, according to Geoffrey of Monmouth, exhorted his men to battle
against "these perjured villains and robbers."[34] Odo Borleng exhorted
the other knights at the Battle of Bourgthéroulde: "See, the king's
enemies are running wild over his lands with impunity, and are carrying
off into captivity one of the nobles to whom he entrusted the defence of
his realm. . . . Are we to permit them to devastate the whole province
unchallenged?"[35] At the Battle of Lincoln in 1141, Henry of Huntingdon
had three speakers—two for Matilda's side and one for King Stephen's—
dwell at great length on the weaknesses, moral depravities, and evil deeds
of their foes.[36] In all these cases, the speakers stress that their enemies
are evil people who clearly deserve to be punished, but the notion of
punishment is usually only implied. The speaker merely claims that "we
are good and they are bad."

Although the theoretical treatment of the second criterion was often
left highly abstract, a few specific causes were almost universally accepted
as justifying a war. Here are some notable differences in emphasis and
development between the theorists and the historians. Of the specific
causes, two were dominant: defense and the recovery of stolen goods.

The clearest case in which the use of violence was acceptable was for
defense. In spite of Jesus' injunctions—such as to turn the other cheek
and not to return evil for evil—a war to defend one's family, country, or
church was believed to be justified in virtually all theological and legal
thought.[37] St. Ambrose set the standard, for he believed it legitimate to
defend the country against invading barbarians.[38] For Augustine, "a
defensive war is obviously a just war, since it aims only to prevent or to
punish the unjust actions of the aggressor."[39] Gratian declared that a war
waged to repel an enemy attack was just.[40] Aquinas thought that a prince

could lawfully defend his territory and "use the sword of war to protect the commonweal from foreign attack."[41]

As a motive to fight, defense was indeed very important. It appears in forty-six orations, which places it eighth among the seventeen recurrent themes. In a few cases, defense was used explicitly to claim that a war is just. In Aelred of Rievaulx's account of the Battle of the Standard, Walter Espec said: "Certainly none will deny the justice of our cause since we take up arms for our country *(patria);* because we fight for our wives, for our children, for our churches, driving back imminent danger."[42] At Hevenfeld, Oswald told his soldiers that God "knows that we undertake a just war for the safety of our nation."[43]

The plea for defense, however, usually does not even mention justice; it only stresses necessity. A typical instance comes from Helmold's *Chronicle of the Slavs.* The speaker said simply, "The most certain destruction of our fatherland demands recourse to battle."[44] Of course, a call for defense may imply that a war is just, especially when the speaker asks his men to defend the holy church.[45] Leo of Ostia described a bishop calling on the Roman people to defend the apostolic see.[46] William the Breton depicted a speaker exhorting his men to defend the law of Christ, saying that if the enemy won, the land would return to heresy and Christianity would perish there.[47] But the speakers did not explicitly state that these factors made the battle just.

Much of the theoretical discussion of self-defense involved such questions as: How much force can legitimately be used in defense? How much time may elapse between the attack and the defense? These issues never appear in the speeches.

War was also justified when it was fought to recover stolen goods. For the Romans, if some neighboring people stole something and refused a request to return it, a war could justly be waged to recover the lost goods *(rebus repetitis).*[48] The canonists and theologians adopted this notion. Isidore of Seville, for example, accepted the Roman premise in its entirety: A war waged upon formal declaration to recover lost goods was just.[49] Ivo of Chartres adopted this statement, and so, in turn, did Gratian.[50]

In the speeches, by contrast, it seldom occurs as a motive. There are only two clear cases. According to Aelred of Rievaulx, King Alfred exhorted his men against the Danes: "We do not seek what belongs to others, but we demand our own back. They have taken our possessions from us." He even came close to the technical formula: *"Praeterea non aliena petimus, sed nostra repetimus."*[51] John of Wallingford also had Alfred tell his men that "our possessions which the Danes seized unjustly will revert to us."[52] The Crusades were often perceived as wars to recover the rightful inheritance of Christians from the infidels who had usurped it.[53] Yet that idea is not reflected in the battle rhetoric. Thus, of the specific just causes identified by the theorists, the two most important and venerable ones played little role in motivation.

Several other, less prominent causes appear, if only infrequently, in the battle rhetoric. Perhaps most important in this secondary group, it was thought legitimate to fight in order to put down rebellions.[54] Frederick Barbarossa exhorted his troops against the Milanese: "It is not a lust for domination that drives us to battle but a fierce rebellion. . . . Milan has given us just cause for war, since it stands revealed as rebellious against lawful authority."[55] In the accounts of the rebellion against Henry II in 1173, this cause was used to justify the war on his side. In the chronicle attributed to Benedict of Peterborough, William, Earl of Arundel, exhorted Henry's forces: "The king of France unjustly, against the precept of God, supports the rashness and error of the sons of our Lord, the most invincible king of England, against him and his will."[56] In Jordan Fantosme's account, Henry said that King Louis of France and his own eldest son were stripping him of his rightful possessions and that some of his barons were in revolt.[57]

Some theoretically important causes for war never appear in the speeches. Perhaps the most outstanding example concerns the right of innocent passage. The question stems from the Old Testament story in which the Israelites were denied rights to pass through the country of the Amorites, so they conquered them.[58] This case gave the lawyers of the central Middle Ages what seems to have been a largely academic problem to wrestle with.[59] It never appears as a motive appeal in the military harangues. Nor does the case of a negligent judge who refuses to render justice or who is corrupt and renders a false judgment.[60]

The ultimate in just wars, of course, were the Crusades and other holy wars.[61] Yet Russell concludes that there was a great reluctance on the part of the theorists to formulate a specific doctrine for these wars.[62] Likewise, it is surprising to note how few of the many speeches in the chronicles of the Crusades stress the justice of the cause. A few do so explicitly. William of Tyre had a speaker explain to his men the situation they were in and then conclude, "Since our cause is just, let us cherish a confident hope of victory."[63]

When the speakers did stress that righteousness was on their side, they normally used two claims, separately or together. First, they could tell their knights that they were fighting for God, Christ, or the Holy Sepulcher. Bohemond exhorted his standard-bearer, Robert Fitz Gerard, to "fight valiantly for God and the Holy Sepulchre."[64] On the Crusade against the Albigensians, Count Simon reminded his men that "the cause of Christ depends entirely on this battle."[65] Even in a minor territorial dispute far from the Holy Land, Archbishop Albero told his men that they were about to fight "for God and righteousness."[66]

Second, they could say simply that they were fighting against infidels, and that was justification enough. The enemy are "impious and unbelievers".[67] They are "enemies of the living God."[68] They "defile the sanctuary of God" and "crucify Christ anew."[69] They are pagans and "enemies of the cross of Christ."[70] The crusaders are fighting a war of "faith against treachery"; the Moslems "do not fight against you, but against Christ."[71] The crusaders are fighting to "exalt everywhere the name of Christ whom these degenerate ones always vigorously revile."[72]

The theorists discussed the conditions and situations in which Christians could justly wage war on the Saracens, and often placed restrictions on such warfare. Innocent IV, for example, argued that Christians could not make war on Moslems merely because they were infidels; Moslems could be attacked only when they polluted Christian territory or attacked Christians.[73] The opinion emerged that peaceful infidels and those outside the Holy Land were to be left in peace.[74] By contrast, the chroniclers seem to have thought that infidels could always be attacked.[75]

Still in the realm of the holy war, in what seems to be a special case of avenging injuries, the theorists thought it was just to punish an enemy for God.[76] In several speeches such a motive appeal occurs. Riley-Smith notes that the call for the first Crusade was perceived in part as being a call for vengeance.[77] Perhaps the best example of this *topos* is in the form of an *a fortiori* argument to the first crusaders: "If some foreigner were to strike any of your kin down, would you not avenge your blood? How much more ought you to avenge your God, your father, your brother, whom you see reproached, banished from his estates, crucified; whom you hear calling, desolate, and begging for aid."[78] King Baldwin called on his men at Jaffa to "take arms boldly to do vengeance for God." He then listed the enemies' dastardly deeds against the crusaders and named their comrades who had been killed.[79] (The call for vengenace in these texts raises a serious problem which will be considered in more detail below.)

Punishing for God was not limited to the Crusades. Robert Guiscard justified his invasion of Sicily "to avenge the injustice to God."[80] At the Battle of the Standard, both Henry of Huntingdon and Aelred of Rievaulx used this *topos*. According to Henry, Bishop Ralph of Orkney said: "Those who in this land have violated the temples of the Lord, polluted his altars, slain his priests, and spared neither children nor women with child, shall on this same soil receive condign punishment for their crimes. This most just fulfillment of his will God shall this day accomplish by our hands."[81] According to Aelred, Walter Espec described in graphic and gory detail the atrocities committed by the invading Scottish army. He then called on the men: "Consecrate your hands in the blood of the sinners; blessed are the hands of those Christ chooses today to avenge his injuries."[82]

In sum, of the theoretically legitimate causes for going to war, some of the major ones do not appear as motive appeals at all. Others occur only seldom. The chroniclers for the most part simply had the commanders tell their men that the enemy are evil people, usually going into detail to explain just how bad they are. These appeals seem to fit, if somewhat loosely, in the abstract category of avenging injuries and punishing the wicked.

But when we turn to the third criterion, intentions, we find motives and practices diverging far from the just-war theories. The motives of the knights would have rendered virtually all medieval warfare unjust in theory, for all three criteria had to be met. If the intentions of the warriors were not right, neither was the war, even if a legitimate authority had declared it for a good reason.

Augustine established the basis for this criterion when he wrote that a just war could be fought only out of Christian love for the enemy; hatred, revenge, and desire for plunder were specifically ruled out. "The real evils in war are love of violence, revengeful cruelty, fierce and implacable enmity, wild resistance, and the lust for power, and such like."[83] He illustrated the proper motivation in war by using the analogy of a father punishing his son, out of love, to correct him.[84] Gratian adopted Augustine's transformation of Christian love and patience into motivation for war, and he likewise condemned the inward vices listed by Augustine.[85] Thomas Aquinas explained, with support from Augustine: "Thirdly, the right intention of those waging war is required, that is, they must intend to promote the good and to avoid evil." He then quoted the passage from Augustine given above.[86] One of the reasons so many of the theorists wanted to limit the right to declare war to a proper authority was that a public official would, presumably, be moved by considerations of policy and not by personal feelings.[87] The war would then be waged with acceptable intent.

The theorists ruled out not only hatred but desire for plunder as well. Augustine condemned military service for the purpose of acquiring booty.[88] Gratian condemned wars motivated by desire for private gain.[89] Likewise, Alexander of Hales argued that just intention "demands that the soldiers do not fight from cupidity or a desire for booty."[90]

The motives the chroniclers show us in their battle rhetoric are quite different on all three counts. The speeches contain not a single reference to charity or love for the enemy.[91]

On a few occasions, the speeches do show concern that the army should have proper intentions and motives. King Alfred exhorted the English before they fought the Danes, "Following the teaching of the blessed Cuthbert, flee from avarice, envy, long anger, adultery, perjury, homicide, and all evils." Rather, they should "be faithful to God, patient, humble, hospitable, give alms, be merciful and modest."[92] Henry, bishop of S. Agata dei Goti, spoke to the papal army before the battle of Nocera in 1132, saying that "they should fight not for their own revenge or for money or booty, but in defence of the Church and of their shared freedom."[93] Sometimes the commander claimed that his men did have righteous intentions, especially when compared with the enemy. According to Giraldus Cambrensis, Diarmait exhorted his men and told them of their virtues, concluding, "Humility will fight for us against arrogance . . . modesty and restraint against arrogance and license."[94]

But usually the whole purpose of dwelling on the evil deeds of the enemy was to rouse hatred. Thus, in Henry of Huntingdon's account William the Conqueror asked his men explicitly to "set no bounds to your merited rage."[95]

Moreover, the knights frequently (in thirty-nine speeches) were exhorted to wreak vengeance on their foes. Both Wace and Henry of Huntingdon treated the Norman invasion of England as a just war *and* as a search for revenge for crimes of the English against their ancestors. In Henry's version, William concluded, "Be the avengers of the noble blood which has been spilled."[96] Wace went even further and said that God himself may offer the warriors the opportunity for vengeance, which seems quite inconsistent with the theories of the canonists and theologians. William said, "These felonies, and many others which they have done to our ancestors, and to our friends . . . we will revenge on them, if God so please."[97] Likewise, Earl Robert exhorted his men at the Battle of Lincoln. He reminded them that King Stephen had humbled and disinherited them. He then called on them to "take the vengeance which [God] offers you on these iniquitous men."[98]

It is possible that at least part of the contradiction between theory and rhetoric is due to a fundamental ambiguity in the terms *ultio* and *ulcisor*, used by Augustine and repeated by Gratian and others. They can mean repulsion or punishment as well as vengeance, and the theoretical differences are critical.[99] Repulsion of injuries is simply defense. Punishment is a penalty exacted for the benefit of the victim, to correct him for his own good. Augustine, as noted earlier, used the analogy of a father who punishes his child out of love. Defending onself or punishing an enemy, of course, were acceptable reasons for fighting. Revenge, on the other hand, is exacted for the psychological benefit of the avenger. It is an entirely impermissible motive for Christian warriors, for it is based on hatred, not on love for one's enemies. In his fundamental definition, when Augustine claimed that just wars "avenge injuries," he presumably used this term in the sense of punishing those responsible.

When a commander, in haranguing his troops, used these words (or, less commonly, some form of *vindicare*, which bears the same ambiguity), he theoretically could have meant only that they were punishing the enemy. Especially if a speaker exhorted an army to take vengeance for God, he presumably could be limiting his motive appeal to the permissible sense of punishment for the good of the enemy. But in most cases it is clearly the sense of personal revenge which the speaker had in mind.[100] There is absolutely no indication that the knights or chroniclers thought that personal vengeance was an improper motive or that seeking revenge for themselves would render an otherwise just war morally culpable. Quite to the contrary, a desire for vengeance was seen as a reason that justified fighting against an enemy at whose hands one had suffered some injustice. Indeed, they thought it would have been a moral failure not to seek revenge.

Naturally, one of the major inducements to combat was the hope of plunder. The speeches (forty-eight of them) unabashedly demonstrate this, regardless of what the theorists may have said. At the Battle of Hastings, Duke William promised his men, "When we have conquered them, we will take their gold and silver, and the wealth of which they have plenty, and their manors, which are rich."[101] Even in the Crusades, material gain played an important role in the motivation of the Christian armies. The *Gesta Francorum* contains a marvelously luminous line that shows the mixture of motives of the first crusaders. At the Battle of Dorylaeum the knights encouraged one another by passing a message along their line: "Stand fast all together, trusting in Christ and in the victory of the Holy Cross. Today, please God, you will all gain much booty."[102] As Jerusalem fell, Raymond of St. Gilles addressed his men: "Why do you delay here? Don't you see that the Franks are already in the city and are taking the best of the spoils?"[103] There is absolutely no indication that the knights thought the desire for booty tainted their wars, not even the holy ones.[104]

Here, again, the theorists made a distinction which is surely too subtle to have been useful in the real world of medieval warfare. Desire for plunder, as previously noted, was not an acceptable motive for fighting. As with all other impermissible motives, if the intentions of the warriors were corrupted by lust for booty, the entire war was unjust. On the other hand, at least the later scholars decided that if a war was just, the knights were permitted to plunder the enemy and keep the booty, but they could not fight for the purpose of getting it.[105] Aquinas, for example, "supported the right of just warriors to retain their plunder without sin provided their pillaging was motivated by justice rather than cupidity."[106] Hostiensis contended that it was acceptable to take booty in a just war but not in an unjust one.[107]

The battle speeches demonstrate how unrealistic the theory of right intention was as a criterion for a just war. Regardless of what the theorists may have wished, the warriors of the central Middle Ages were motivated by hatred, desire for revenge, and lust for booty. Moreover, there is no indication that the knights or the chroniclers thought that hatred of their foes or desire for riches or revenge would make their otherwise righteous wars morally culpable. Nor do the chroniclers seem to be trying to take advantage of potential loopholes offered by ambiguous technical terminology. The *topoi* seem to be used in a perfectly straightforward way.

The chroniclers' concerns were very different from those of the theologians and canonists. The theorists, operating largely in an academic environment, were attempting to define a philosophical concept. The chroniclers, on the other hand, were trying to characterize contemporary knights and to show what stimulated them to fight. Whereas the theorists were conceptual in their approach, the chroniclers were rhetorical—that is, they were interested in depicting plausible motives.

Analysis of the chroniclers' battle rhetoric does not simply establish that the knights did not live up to the theoretical standards of the just war. That is certainly true, and it would be easy enough to demonstrate by comparing the theories with the chroniclers' descriptions of the knights in battle. But the battle rhetoric contains something much more important than that. It shows that the chroniclers believed that the warrior class in the central Middle Ages had its own, very different idea of what justified a war.[108] And the frequency of these ideas in the rhetoric demonstrates that these notions were very important to the knights.

The chroniclers thought that several factors justified war in the minds of the knights. Most significant for the medieval warriors was the simple claim that they themselves were good and their enemies were evil. Frequently, they had in mind some specific dastardly deeds their enemies had committed. If the foes were infidels, that was quite sufficient to justify attacking them. If they were in rebellion, it was likewise just to put them in their proper places. To fight in defense was just, but that does not seem to have been a major concern; the necessity of defending one's family and country was motive enough. The knights were clearly motivated by hatred and lust for revenge. The chroniclers believed that the knights thought these motives were quite right; they in no way detracted from the justice of their cause. Indeed, personal vengeance and hatred for a foe who was evil were acceptable and desirable motives. It was, of course, always good to get rich by plundering an enemy. And the knights simply did not care who had declared the war.

As Russell indicates, the legal and theological theory of the just war was in many ways inadequate for the times and did not deal with many of the realities of medieval warfare.[109] Contrasting the battle speeches with the theories underlines Russell's conclusion. The motives of the medieval warriors were far removed from the conceptual criteria of just-war theory, and their own notion of what was right and proper in war surely had much more impact on conduct in the real world than did the concepts of lawyers and theologians.

Notes

(Full citations for the sources of the speeches may be found in the bibliography of battle orations.)

1. Frederick H. Russell, *The Just War in the Middle Ages* (Cambridge, 1975). The same is true of the other leading summaries: Stanley Windass, *Christianity versus Violence* (London, 1964); Alfred Vanderpol, *La Doctrine Scolastique du Droit de Guerre* (Paris, 1919); Robert Regout, *La Doctrine de la Guerre Juste de Saint Augustin à Nos Jours* (Paris, 1935); Franziskus Stratmann, *The Church and War, A Catholic Study* (New York, 1971); John W. Baldwin, *Masters, Princes and Merchants*, 2 vols. (Princeton, 1970), chapter 10.

2. The psychological elements of morale and courage have been largely overlooked by historians of medieval warfare. There are two notable exceptions, but neither devotes significant attention to a medieval army's belief in the cause for which it was fighting. Philippe Contamine's *War in the Middle Ages*, trans. Michael Jones (Oxford, 1980) includes a short chapter on courage (chapter 9), but it focuses largely on the theological definition of courage as a virtue and on an assessment of risk in the wars of the later Middle Ages. In chapter 10, his discussion of the just war deals primarily with the legal and theological concepts. He indicates that popularization of the canonists' teaching occurred only late in the Middle Ages, beginning in the fourteenth century (280).

   J. F. Verbruggen analyzes fear in medieval armies and some of the factors that helped to overcome it. He does not consider belief in a just cause to be an element in morale, except for a very brief mention of the support of the church that commanders sometimes obtained. *The Art of Warfare in Western Europe During the Middle Ages*, trans. Sumner Willard and S. C. M. Southern (Amsterdam, 1977), 249–50.

   Detailed study of the psychology of ordinary soldiers in battle only begins with the wars of the twentieth century. Commitment to a cause has been variously estimated as an element in morale in the modern army. See the evidence from many sources summarized by Anthony Kellett, *Combat Motivation, The Behavior of Soldiers in Battle* (Boston, 1982), 169–99. S. L. A.

Marshall's conclusion is perhaps best: "Men who have been in battle know from first-hand experience that when the chips are down, a man fights to help the man next to him. . . . An ideal does not become tangible at the moment of firing a volley or charging a hill. . . . Yet above and beyond . . . are all of the ideas and ideals which press upon men, causing them to accept a discipline and to hold to the line even though death may be at hand.

"If any man doubts that these values have a place in hardening the resolve of an army, let him answer the question: What happens when an army loses faith in its cause? It is in fact defeated and wholly submissive to the enemy. Its will is defeated. . . . Belief in a cause is the foundation of the aggressive will in battle." *Men Against Fire* (New York, 1947), 161–62.

3. S. B. Chrimes has argued: "By studying political ideas in close relation to actualities and as understood by practical men and the people at large, [the historian] avoids the unfortunate abstraction and academic character which pervades almost all Histories of mediaeval Political Thought. Here we find the assumptions and ideas not of philosophers and scholastics, but of the men who governed and were governed—notions of far greater importance to all students except historians of Philosophy than learned systems of political doctrine." Introduction to Fritz Kern, *Kingship and Law in the Middle Ages* (New York, 1956), xvii. He perhaps overstates his case to make a valid point.

4. See, for example, R. W. Southern, "Aspects of the European Tradition of Historical Writing: 1. The Classical Tradition from Einhard to Geoffrey of Monmouth," *Transactions of the Royal Historical Society*, 5th ser., 20 (1970): 173–96. Roger D. Ray, "Medieval Historiography Through the Twelfth Century: Problems and Progress of Research," *Viator* 5 (1974): 33–59. John O. Ward, "Classical Rhetoric and the Writing of History in Medieval and Renaissance Culture," in *European History and Its Historians*, ed. Frank McGregor and Nicholas Wright (Adelaide, 1977), 1–10. John O. Ward, "Some Principles of Rhetorical Historiography in the Twelfth Century," in *Classical Rhetoric and Medieval Historiography*, ed. Ernst Breisach (Kalamazoo, 1985), 103–65.

5. Frequently, however, medieval chroniclers borrowed wholesale from earlier medieval works, which they then continued into their own times. Whenever the later chroniclers borrowed battle speeches, they were at least reinforcing the appropriateness of the orations they adopted. All such cases can, therefore, be treated as separate speeches.

6. Plausibility was a primary criterion by which rhetorical strategies were judged. Nancy Partner even refers to it as a "rhetorical imperative"; "The New Cornificius: Medieval History and the Artifice of Words," in Breisach, ed., *Classical Rhetoric and Medieval Historiography*, 12. See also in the same source the essay by Roger Ray, "Rhetorical Scepticism and Verisimilar Narrative in John of Salisbury's *Historia Pontificalis*," 66 and 83–84. For relevant precepts from the two most popular texts for the study of rhetoric at the time, see Cicero, *De Inventione,* 1.7.9; 1.19.27–1.20.28; 1.21.30. *Rhetorica ad Herennium*, 1.2.3; 1.8.11–1.9.16.

7. Maurice Keen, *Chivalry* (New Haven, 1984), 32.

8. For the value of rhetoric in studing the mentality of an age, see Joseph L. Blau, "Public Address as Intellectual Revelation," in Thomas R. Nilsen, ed.,

Essays in Rhetorical Criticism (New York, 1968), 18–28. Ernest J. Wrage, "Public Address: A Study in Social and Intellectual History," *Quarterly Journal of Speech* 33 (1947): 451–57. Edwin Black, "The Second Persona," *Quarterly Journal of Speech* 56 (1970): 109–19.

9. I have used only speeches attributed to Western leaders addressing Western armies. The few speeches by Byzantine or Moslem commanders to their respective armies are excluded. I have, however, included a few speeches in which Roman commanders address Roman legions, because the chroniclers do not seem to have thought that the Romans were different from their contemporaries.

10. Seventeen different *topoi* recur with some frequency in these speeches. All of these motive appeals are analyzed as evidence for the psychological structure of morale in the medieval army in my article "Rhetoric and Morale, A Study of Battle Orations from the Central Middle Ages," *Journal of Medieval History,* 15 (1989) 201–26. Theology and canon law, however, are not considered there.

11. For these details see especially Russell, *Just War,* and Regout, *La Doctrine de la Guerre Juste.*

12. The literature on the theory of the just war is vast. In addition to the secondary sources listed in note 1, the following were particularly helpful for this study.

   For St. Augustine: Yves de la Brière, "La Conception de la Paix et de la Guerre chez Saint Augustin," *Revue de Philosophie,* nouvelle sér., 1 (1930): 557–72. Herbert A. Deane, *The Political and Social Ideas of St. Augustine* (New York, 1963), chapter 5. Richard Shelly Hartigan, "Saint Augustine on War and Killing: The Problem of the Innocent," *Journal of the History of Ideas* 27 (1966): 195–204. R. A. Markus, "Saint Augustine's Views on the 'Just War,'" *Studies in Church History* 20 (1983): 1–13. Frederick H. Russell, "Love and Hate in Medieval Warfare: The Contribution of Saint Augustine," *Nottingham Medieval Studies* 31 (1987): 108–24.

   For Gratian: G. Hubrecht, "La 'Juste Guerre' dans le Décret de Gratien," *Studia Gratiana* 3 (1955): 161–77. Stanley Chodorow, *Christian Political Theory and Church Politics in the Mid-Twelfth Century, The Ecclesiology of Gratian's Decretum* (Berkeley, 1972).

   For Thomas Aquinas: Joan D. Tooke, *The Just War in Aquinas and Grotius* (London, 1965).

13. De la Brière, "La Conception de la Paix et de la Guerre chez Saint Augustin," 565. Hubrecht, "La 'Juste Guerre' dans de Décret de Gratien," 168.

14. Russell, *Just War,* 141.

15. Russell, *Just War,* 68: "The most crucial issue in any just war theory is the locus of authority capable of waging war."

16. Russell, *Just War,* 22. Augustine, *Contra Faustum Manichaeum,* 22.74: "God or some lawful authority"; 22.75: "the monarch, king," in *Corpus Scriptorum Ecclesiasticorum Latinorum,* vol. 25 (Vienna, 1891); trans. R. Stothert in Philip Schaff, ed., *A Select Library of Nicene and Post-Nicene Fathers of the Christian Church,* vol. 4 (Grand Rapids, Mich., 1956 reprint).

17. Joshua 8:1–2.

18. Augustine, *Contra Faustum* 22.75. See also Augustine's *City of God* 1.21, in

Corpus Scriptorum Ecclesiasticorum Latinorum, vol. 40 (Vienna, 1899), trans. Marcus Dods (New York, 1950).

19. Gratian, *Decretum* C. 23 q. 2 d. p. c. 2, in *Corpus Iuris Canonici,* vol. 1, ed. A. Friedberg (Graz, 1955 reprint); trans. Russell, *Just War,* 64.

20. Thomas Aquinas, *Summa Theologiae,* 2-2, q. 40, art. 1. I have used the text and translation in the Dominicans' New English *Summa.* Quaestio 40, On War, appears in vol. 35, ed. and trans. Thomas R. Heath (Oxford, 1972).

21. For example, Russell, *Just War,* 139 for Alanus Anglicus, 146 for Innocent IV, and 222–23 for Peter the Chanter.

22. Rahewin 203 *MGH;* 206 Mierow and Emery, trans. This is a most remarkable, and unique, oration in which Mierow and Emery note "the emperor's appeal to canon law in support of his advocacy of a 'just war' " 206. It explicitly incorporates all three criteria to justify the war.

23. Aelred of Rievaulx, *Genealogia Regum Anglorum,* 721.

24. Robert the Monk, *Historia Hierosolymitana, Recueil des Historiens des Croisades: Historiens Occidentaux,* 3: 729.

25. "God wills it!" was, however, taken up as the battle cry used by the crusaders; see Carl Erdmann, *The Origin of the Idea of Crusade,* trans. Marshall W. Baldwin and Walter Goffart (Princeton, 1977), 343.

26. Augustine, *Quaestiones in Heptateuchum,* 6.10, in *Corpus Scriptorum Ecclesiasticorum Latinorum,* vol. 28 (Vienna, 1895). I have adopted Russell's shortened form of the basic definition; *Just War,* 18. See also Augustine, *City of God,* 19. 7: "For it is the wrong-doing of the opposing party which compels the wise man to wage just wars."

27. Russell, *Just War,* 18.

28. Gratian C. 23 q. 2 d. p. c. 2.

29. Thomas Aquinas, *Summa Theololgiae* 2-2, q. 40, art. 1.

30. William of Poitiers, 184.

31. Henry of Huntingdon, 202 RS; 211 Forester, trans.

32. Wace, *Roman de Rou,* 2: 159–60 Holden, ed.; 160–61 Taylor, trans.

33. *Carmen in victoriam Pisanorum,* 26.

34. Geoffrey of Monmouth, 277 Faral, ed.; 260 Thorpe, trans.

35. Orderic Vitalis, 6: 348–49.

36. Henry of Huntingdon, 268–73 RS; 274–78 Forester, trans.

37. The way in which the lawyers and theologians got around those clear precepts of Jesus is interesting. Augustine decided that they refer to the inner disposition rather than to overt acts. He observed that neither Jesus nor Paul acted on them. When Christ was struck on the face, he replied: "If I have spoken evil, give testimony of the evil, but if well, why strikest thou me?" (John 18:23). "If we look at the words literally, He obviously did not fulfill His own precept, for He did not offer His other cheek to the striker." Likewise, "Paul apparently did not keep the command of his Lord and Master either, when he was also struck on the face, and said to the chief priest: 'God shall strike thee, thou whited wall. Thou sittest to judge me according to the law, and contrary to the law, thou commandest me to be struck.' (Acts 23:3) . . . Therefore, those precepts of patience are always to be preserved in the heart. . . . But, we often have to act with a sort of kindly harshness"; *Epistle* 138.2.13, in *Corpus Scriptorum Ecclesiasticorum Latinorum,* vol. 44, (Vienna, 1904); Saint Augustine, *Letters,* vol. 3, trans. Sister Wilfrid

Parsons (The Fathers of the Church, vol. 20; New York, 1953), 45–46. Gratian adopted this reasoning; C. 23 q. 1 c. 2.

38. Regout, *La Doctrine de la Guerre Juste,* 39–40. Russell, *Just War,* 13. Ambrose, *De Officiis Ministrorum* 1, 27, 129, in *Patrologia Latina* 16: 61.
39. Deane, *Political and Social Ideas of St. Augustine,* 160. Augustine, *Epistle* 47. 5, in *Corpus Scriptorum Ecclesiasticorum Latinorum,* vol. 34; Saint Augustine, *Letters,* vol. 1, trans. Sister Wilfrid Parsons (The Fathers of the Church, vol. 12; Washington, D.C., 1951), 230.
40. Gratian C. 23 q. 2 c. 1.
41. Thomas Aquinas, *Summa Theologiae* 2–2, q. 40, art. 1.
42. Aelred of Rievaulx, *Relatio de Standardo,* 187.
43. Roger of Wendover, in Matthew Paris, *Chronica Majora,* 1: 279 RS; 1: 82 Giles, trans.
44. Helmold of Bosau, 127 *MGH;* 185 Tschan, trans.
45. As in Baldericus, 256.
46. Leo of Ostia, 864–65.
47. William the Breton, *Philippidos,* 234–35.
48. Cicero, *De Officiis,* 1.11.36, and *De Republica* 3.23.35.
49. Russell, *Just War,* 27. Isidore of Seville, *Etymologiarum sive Originum Libri xx,* 18.1.2–4, ed. W. M. Lindsay, vol. 2 (Oxford, 1911).
50. Ivo of Chartres, *Decretum* 10.116 and *Panormia* 8.54, in *Patrologia Latina* 161: 727 and 1315. Gratian C. 23 q. 2 c. 1.
51. Aelred of Rievaulx, *Genealogia Regum Anglorum,* 721.
52. [John of Wallingford], 35.
53. Russell, *Just War,* 253. Jonathan Riley-Smith, "Crusading as an Act of Love," *History* 65 (1980): 180.
54. Russell, *Just War,* 99 for Huguccio. Aquinas says that a prince can lawfully defend his commonwealth against "domestic disturbance"; *Summa Theologiae* 2–2, q. 40, art. 1.
55. Rahewin 203 *MGH;* 205 Mierow and Emery, trans.
56. [Benedict of Peterborough], 1: 52.
57. Jordan Fantosme, 12–13. Recovery of lost goods is also implied here as cause for war.
58. Numbers 21:21–25.
59. For example, Russell, *Just War,* 21 for Augustine, 64 for Gratian, 91 and 100 for the Decretists, 221 for Robert Courzon.
60. Russell, *Just War,* 138.
61. For the development of the concept of holy war see Erdmann, *Origin of the Idea of Crusade.*
62. Russell, *Just War,* 294–95. For the canon lawyers see also James Brundage, *Medieval Canon Law and the Crusader* (Madison, 1969), and James Brundage, "Holy War and the Medieval Lawyers," in Thomas Patrick Murphy, ed., *The Holy War* (Columbus, Ohio, 1976), 99–140.
63. William of Tyre, 201 *RHC;* 1: 231 Babcock and Krey, trans.
64. *Gesta Francorum,* 37.
65. Pierre of Vaux Cernay, 1: 268.
66. Baldericus, 256.
67. Albert of Aix, 381.
68. Albert of Aix, 320.

69. Baldric of Bourgueil, 101.
70. [Benedict of Peterborough], 2: 191.
71. Guibert of Nogent, 177.
72. Fulcher of Chartres, 392 *RHC;* 157 Fink, ed.
73. Russell, *Just War,* 199.
74. Russell, *Just War,* 201.
75. The underlying notion is expressed clearly in the *Song of Roland:* "Pagans are wrong and Christians are right"; v. 1015. Matthew Paris, however, placed a speech in the mouth of the sultan of Egypt which expresses a critical view of the Crusade of Saint Louis in 1250: "For what rash madness excites them to attack and endeavour to deprive us of our inheritance, who have inhabited this noble country since the Flood? Do they wish us to believe in their Christ against our will? Who can be converted or believe against his will? A certain motive, however slight, urges the Christians to covet the land which they call Holy; but what have they to do with Egypt?" Matthew Paris, 5: 156–57 RS; 2: 375 Giles, trans.
76. For example, Gratin C. 23 q. 5 cc. 27–29. Russell, *Just War,* 59.
77. Jonathan Riley-Smith, *The First Crusade and the Idea of Crusading* (Philadelphia, 1986), 47–49.
78. Baldric of Bourgueil, 101.
79. Orderic Vitalis, 5: 348–49.
80. Amatus of Monte Cassino, 234.
81. Henry of Huntingdon, 262 RS; 268 Forester, trans.
82. Aelred of Rievaulx, *Relatio de Standardo,* 187–88.
83. Augustine, *Contra Faustum* 22.74.
84. Augustine, *Epistle* 138. See also William R. Stevenson, Jr., *Christian Love and Just War* (Macon, Ga., 1987), esp. 104–13.
85. Gratian C. 23 q. 1 c. 4. Although Gratian rejected improper attitudes in war, he did not use the specific term *"recta intentio";* Russell, *Just War,* 64–65. See also Russell's discussion of Gratian's justification for corporal punishment; *Just War,* 57–60.
86. Thomas Aquinas, *Summa Theologiae* 2–2, q. 40, art. 1.
87. Russell, *Just War,* 68.
88. Russell, *Just War,* 27. Augustine *Epistle* 138, 2.15. This is a fairly weak statement, although the implication is there. Augustine is quoting, in support of a different point, the advice of John the Baptist to some soldiers who had asked him what they should do. He advised them to "rob no one by violence or by false accusation, and be content with your wages"; Luke 3:14.
89. Gratian C. 23 q. 1 c. 2 para 5, and C. 23 q. 1 cc. 4–6. Russell, *Just War,* 61.
90. J. Barnes, "The Just War," *The Cambridge History of Later Medieval Philosophy,* ed. Norman Kretzmann, Anthony Kenny, Jan Pinborg, Eleonore Stump (Cambridge, 1982), 774.
91. Riley-Smith notes that the crusaders were often asked to fight for love of their fellow Christians in the East, but never out of love for the enemy; "Crusading as an Act of Love," 190.
92. *Historia de Sancto Cuthberto,* 206.
93. Henry, bishop of S. Agata dei Goti, Letter 259.
94. Giraldus Cambrensis, 46–47.
95. Henry of Huntingdon, 202 RS; 211 Forester, trans.

96. Henry of Huntingdon 202 RS; 211 Forester, trans.
97. Wace, *Roman de Rou* 2: 160 Holden, ed; 161 Taylor, trans.
98. Henry of Huntingdon 270 RS; 276 Forester, trans.
99. Russell, *Just War,* 66–67.
100. Russell indicates that the later canonists, recognizing the semantic problem, avoided these terms whenever possible and shifted the emphasis explicitly to "repulsion of injuries"; *Just War,* 133, 221.
101. Wace, *Roman de Rou* 2:161 Holden, ed.; 161 Taylor, trans.
102. *Gesta Francorum,* 19–20.
103. Guibert of Nogent, 227.
104. Several speakers warned their men not to grab for booty, but except for the one case cited in note 93, the reasons did not have anything to do with preserving the justice of their war. The commanders were concerned only with fighting the battle. A typical speech is Peter Tudebode's account of the Patriarch addressing the first crusaders the night before the Battle of Ascalon. He ordered "that no man should turn to any booty until the battle's end and the defeat of God's enemies. But afterwards they could return happily because of their good luck and great victory and seize whatever God had alloted to them"; *Historia de Hierosolymitano Itinere,* trans. J. Hill and L. Hill (Philadelphia, 1968), 123.
105. Russell, *Just War,* 245–46, and Brundage, "Holy War and the Medieval Lawyers," 116.
106. Russell, *Just War,* 278. *Summa Theologiae* 2–2, q. 66, art. 8.
107. Russell, *Just War,* 164–65.
108. Analysis of the battle rhetoric thus leads to a conclusion rather different from that drawn by Raymond H. Schmandt in his study of the deliberations over the three moral crises during the course of the fourth Crusade; "The Fourth Crusade and the Just War Theory," *Catholic Historical Review* 61 (1975): 191–221. He concludes: "These particular crusaders were well aware of the same currents of opinion that found a place in the scholarly treatises, and . . . they instinctively used the same norms by which to assess the options open to them in making their decisions as did the theoreticians functioning in the realm of abstraction"; 197. Rather, the battle rhetoric leads to a conclusion similar to Riley-Smith's analysis of crusading ethics. He contends that "one can see attitudes to violence being expressed on several levels. . . . we find the ideas of the theologians drastically modified as they were expressed in terms the laity could understand. And below them, among the laity themselves, there seethed emotions, prejudices and a medley of Christian, semi-Christian and pre-Christian beliefs, varying from class to class and region to region, growing more sophisticated as time progressed, but remaining even at the end of the thirteenth century, the products almost of another world to that of the theologians"; "An Approach to Crusading Ethics," *Reading Medieval Studies* 6 (1980): 4, 6. Contamine, we have seen (note 2), contends that the theory of just war was not popularized before the fourteenth century.
109. Russell, *Just War,* e.g., 92–93, 293, 303–5.

Bibliography of Battle Orations
(Accounts written between c. 1000 and 1250.)

In the following speeches, the speakers claim in some way (or clearly imply) that their cause is a just one.

Aelred of Rievaulx. *Genealogia Regum Anglorum. Patrologia Latina.* 195: 721.

———. *Relatio de Standardo. Chronicles of the Reigns of Stephen, Henry II and Richard I,* vol. 3, Rolls Series, edited by Richard Howlett, 185–89.

Aimoin of Fleury. *Miracula Sancti Benedicti. Les Miracles de Saint Benoît,* edited by E. De Certain, 117–18. Paris, 1858.

Albert of Aix. *Historia Hierosolymitana. Recueil des Historiens des Croisades: Historiens Occidentaux,* 4:320, 363, 381, 509.

Amatus of Monte Cassino. *Storia de'Normanni,* edited by Vincenzo de Bartholomaeis, 234, 241–42. Rome, 1935.

Ambroise, *L'Estoire de la Guerre Sainte,* edited by Gaston Paris, lines 6,395–6,402. Paris, 1897. *The Crusade of Richard Lion-Heart,* translated by Merton Jerome Hubert, notes by John La Monte, lines 6,395–6,402. New York, 1941.

Baldericus. *Gesta Alberonis Archiepiscopi. Monumenta Germaniae Historica, Scriptores,* 8:256.

Baldric of Bourgueil. *Historia Hierosolymitana. Recueil des Historiens des Croisades: Historiens Occidentaux,* 4:100–1.

[Benedict of Peterborough]. *The Chronicle of the Reigns of Henry II and Richard I,* 2 vols., Rolls Series, edited by William Stubbs, 1:52–53; 2:163, 191.

Brevis Relatio de Origine Willelmi Conquestoris. Scriptores Rerum Gestarum Willelmi Conquestoris, Regis Angliae, edited by J. A. Giles, 7. Caxton Society, 1845.

Capitula de Miraculis et Translationibus Sancti Cuthberti. Simeon of Durham. *Opera Omnia,* vol. 1, Rolls Series, edited by Thomas Arnold, 242.

The Carmen de Hastingae Proelio of Guy Bishop of Amiens, edited and translated by Catherine Morton and Hope Muntz, 16–19. Oxford, 1972.

Carmen in victoriam Pisanorum. H. E. J. Cowdrey. "The Mahdia Campaign of 1087." *English Historical Review* 92 (1977): 25–26.

Fulcher of Chartres. *Historia Hierosolymitana. Recueil des Historiens des Croisades: Historiens Occidentaux,* 3:392.

A History of the Expedition to Jerusalem, edited by Harold S. Fink, translated by Frances Rita Ryan, 157–58. Knoxville, Tenn., 1969.

Geoffrey Malaterra. *De Rebus Gestis Rogerii Calabriae et Siciliae Comitis et Roberti Guiscardi Ducis fratris eius. Rerum Italicarum Scriptores,* edited by L. A. Muratori, 5, 1:43–44, 50.

Geoffrey of Monmouth. *Historia Regum Britanniae. La Légende Arthurienne,* vol. 3, edited by Edmond Faral, 232, 232–33, 266–67, 277. Paris, 1929.

The History of the Kings of Britain, translated by Lewis Thorpe, 216 (1), 216 (2), 249–50, 260. Baltimore, 1966.

Gervase of Canterbury. *Chronica. The Historical Works of Gervase of Canterbury,* vol. 1, Rolls Series, edited by William Stubbs, 113–14, 114–15, 115–16.

Gesta Alberonis Metrica. Monumenta Germaniae Historica, Scriptores, 8:242.

Gesta Consulum Andegavorum et Dominorum Ambaziensium. Chroniques d'Anjou, edited by Paul Marchegay and André Salmon, 107–8, 146–47. Paris, 1856.

Giraldus Cambrensis. *Expugnatio Hibernica,* edited and translated by A. B. Scot and F. X. Martin, 42–45, 44–47, 46–49. Dublin, 1978.

Guibert of Nogent. *Gesta Dei Per Francos. Recueil des Historiens des Croisades: Historiens Occidentaux,* 4:177.

Henry of Huntingdon. *History of the English (Historia Anglorum),* Rolls Series, edited by Thomas Arnold, 200–2, 262–63, 268, 268–71, 272–73.

The Chronicle of Henry of Huntingdon, translated by Thomas Forester, 210–11, 267–69, 274, 274–76, 277–78. London, 1853.

Henry of Valenciennes. *Histoire de l'Empereur Henri de Constantinople,* edited by Jean Longnon, 43–44. Paris, 1948.

L'Histoire de Guillaume le Maréchal, comte de Striguil et de Pembroke, Régent d'Angleterre de 1216 à 1219, 3 vols., edited by Paul Meyer, 2: Lines 16137–16196, 16277–16400, 17313–17328. Paris, 1891–1901.

William the Marshal, translated (in part) by Jessie Crosland, 121, 122–23, 133. London, 1962.

Historia de Sancto Cuthberto. Simeon of Durham. *Opera Omnia,* vol. 1, Rolls Series, edited by Thomas Arnold, 206, 214.

Hugo Falcandi. *Storia (1146–1169). Cronisti e Scrittori Sincroni Napoletani,* vol. 1, edited by Giuseppe Del Re, 332. Naples, 1845.

John of Marmoutier. *Historia Gaufredi Ducis Normannorum et Comitis Andegavorum. Chroniques d'Anjou,* edited by Paul Marchegay and André Salmon, 302–3, 303–4, 305–7. Paris, 1856.

[John of Wallingford]. *The Chronicle Attributed to John of Wallingford,* Camden, 3d series, edited by Richard Vaughan, 90:35. London, 1958.

Jordan Fantosme. *Jordan Fantosme's Chronicle,* edited and translated by R. C. Johnson, 12–13, 14–15, 16–19, 92–93. Oxford, 1981.

Lambert of Ardre. *Chronicon Ghisnense et Ardense, 918–1203 (Chronique de Guines et d'Ardre),* edited by Godefroy de Ménilglaise, 129. Paris, 1855.

Leo of Ostia. *Chronicon Casinense. Patrologia Latina,* 173:677–78, 838, 864–65.

Matthew Paris. *Chronica Majora,* 7 vols., Rolls Series, edited by Henry Richards Luard. The first part of this chronicle was written or compiled by Roger of Wendover. The speeches cited here are from Matthew's part of the work. 3:408; 5:154–55, 219–20, 646.

English History, 3 vols., translated by J. A. Giles, 1:65, 2:373, 429; 3:243–44. London, 1853.

———. *Historia Anglorum (Historia Minor),* 3 vols., Rolls Series, edited by Sir Frederic Madden, 1:259.

Nicolas de Bray. *Gesta Ludovici VIII Francorum Regis. Recueil des Historiens des Gaules et de la France,* edited by M. Bouquet et al., 17: lines 677–99.

Orderic Vitalis. *The Ecclesiastical History,* 6 vols., edited and translated by Marjorie Chibnall, 3:314–15; 5:348–49; 6:348–51. Oxford, 1969–80.

Otto of Freising and Rahewin. *Gesta Friderici Imperatoris. Monumenta Germaniae Historica Scriptores Rerum Germanicarum in Usum Scholarum,* 46:202–4.

The Deeds of Frederick Barbarossa, translated by Charles Mierow and Richard Emery, 205–6. New York, 1953.

Rangerius. *Vita Anselmi Lucensis Episcopi. Monumenta Germaniae Historica, Scriptores,* 30:1292.

Richard of Devizes. *The Chronicle of Richard of Devizes of the Time of King Richard the First,* edited and translated by John T. Appleby, 23. London, 1963.

Richerus. *Gesta Senoniensis Ecclesiae. Monumenta Germaniae Historica, Scriptores,* 25:294.

Robert of Clari. *La Conquête de Constantinople,* edited by Philippe Lauer, 72. Paris, 1956.

The Conquest of Constantinople, translated by Edgar Holmes McNeal, 94. New York, 1936.

Roger of Hoveden. *Chronica,* 4 vols., Rolls Series, edited by William Stubbs, 1:193–94, 199, 200–1, 202–3; 3:106–7.

The Annals of Roger of Hoveden, 2 vols., translated by Henry T. Riley, 1:231–33, 238, 239–40, 241–43; 2:201. London, 1853.

Roger of Wendover. *The Flowers of History,* 3 vols., Rolls Series, edited by Henry G. Hewlett. This is the conclusion of Roger's chronicle, starting with 1154. The first part, which he compiled from earlier histories, appears in the Rolls Series edition of Matthew Paris' *Chronica Majora.* The speeches cited here are the ones Roger adopted or wrote himself. Matthew Paris, 1:216, 279; 2:168. Roger of Wendover, 2:213; 3:84.

Flowers of History, 2 vols., translated by J. A. Giles, 1:17, 82, 488–89; 2:392–93, 589. London, 1849.

Saxo Grammaticus. *Gesta Danorum,* vol. 1, edited by J. Olrik and H. Raeder, 53–61, 218, 410. Copenhagen, 1931.

The History of the Danes, vol. 1: English Text (books 1–9), edited by Hilda Ellis Davidson, translated by Peter Fisher, 56–63, 241. Cambridge, 1979.

Danorum Regum Heroumque Historia, Books X–XVI, 3 vols., translated by Eric Christiansen, 414. Oxford, 1980–81.

Stephen of Rouen. *Draco Normannicus. Chronicles of the Reigns of Stephen, Henry II and Richard I,* vol. 2, Rolls Series, edited by Richard Howlett, 617–18, 643–45, 682–84.

Wace. *Roman de Brut,* 2 vols., edited by Ivor Arnold, 404, 491–92, 662–63. Paris, 1938–40.

Arthurian Chronicles, translated by Eugene Mason, 20–21, 48, 104–5. London, 1962.

———. *Le Roman de Rou de Wace,* 3 vols., edited by A. J. Holden, 2:159–62. Paris, 1971.

Chronicle of the Norman Conquest, translated (in part) by Edgar Taylor, 159–62. London, 1837.

Walter the Chancellor. *Bella Antiochena,* edited by Heinrich Hagenmeyer, 73, 87, 113–14. Innsbruck, 1896.

William of Apulia. *La Geste de Robert Guiscard,* edited by Marguerite Mathieu, 178–80. Palermo, 1961.

William of Newburgh. *Historia Rerum Anglicarum. Chronicles of the Reigns of Stephen, Henry II and Richard I,* vol. 1, Rolls Series, edited by Richard Howlett, 326–27.

The History of William of Newburgh. The Church Historians of England, vol. 4, pt. 2, translated by Joseph Stevenson, 574. London, 1856.

William of Poitiers. *Histoire de Guillaume le Conquérant,* edited by Raymonde Foreville, 182–84. Paris, 1952.

"The Deeds of William, duke of the Normans and king of the English," translated (in part) in *English Historical Documents,* vol. 2, edited by David C. Douglas and George W. Greenaway, 225. London, 1953.

William of Tyre. *Historia Rerum in Partibus Transmarinis Gestarum. Recueil des Historiens des Croisades: Historiens Occidentaux,* 1, 1:132–33, 200–1, 455–56.

A History of Deeds Done Beyond the Sea, 2 vols., translated by Emily Atwater Babcock and A. C. Krey, 1:172, 231, 465–66. New York, 1943.

William the Breton. *Gesta Philippi Augusti. Oeuvres de Rigord et de Guillaume le Breton, Historiens de Philippe-Auguste,* vol. 1, edited by H.-Francois Delaborde, 273. Paris, 1882.

―――. *Philippidos Libri XII. Oeuvres de Rigord et de Guillaume le Breton, Historiens de Philippe-Auguste,* vol. 2, edited by H.-Francois Delaborde, 81–82, 167, 234–36, 310, 313–14. Paris, 1885.

In the following speeches, the speakers specifically claim that the army is about to fight for God, Christ, or the Holy Sepulcher.

Albert of Aix. 382, 401–2, 509.

Baldericus, 256.

Baldric of Bourgueil. 100–1.

Carmen in victoriam Pisanorum. 25–26.

Ekkehard of Aura. *Chronica. Patrologia Latina* 154:982.

Gesta Francorum et Aliorum hierosolymitanorum, edited and translated by Rosalind Hill, 36–37. London, 1962.

Guibert of Nogent. 161, 178.

Henry of Valenciennes. 37–38.

Historia Peregrinorum. Quellen zur Geschichte des Kreuzzuges Kaiser Friedrichs I, edited by A. Chroust, 168. Berlin, 1928.

Lisiardus Turonensis clericus. *Historia Hierolosymitana. Patrologia Latina,* 174:1603.

Nicolas of Bray. Lines 1186–98, 1501–12, 1763–80.

Orderic Vitalis. 6:498–501.

Pierre of Vaulx Cernay. *Historia Albigensium,* 3 vols., edited by Pascal Guébin and Ernst Lyon, 1:268. Paris, 1926–30.

[Ralph of Coggeshall]. *Libellus de Expugnatione Terrae Sanctae per Saladinum. Radulphi de Coggeshall Chronicon Anglicanum,* Rolls Series, edited by Joseph Stevenson, 211.

Walter the Chancellor. 87, 113–14.

William the Breton. *Philippidos*. 234–36, 313–14.

In the following speeches, the speakers ask the knights to defend themselves or their country, families, property, churches, and the like.

Aelred of Rievaulx. *Genealogia Regum Anglorum*. 721.

———. *Relatio de Standardo*. 185–89.

Aimoin of Fleury. 117–18.

Baldric of Bourgueil. 34.

Encomium Emmae Reginae, Camden, 3d series, edited and translated by Alistair Campbell, 72:26–27. London, 1949.

Florence of Worcester. *Chronicon ex Chronicis*, 2 vols., edited by Benjamin Thorpe, 1:174, 177; 2:25. London, 1848.

   The Chronicle of Florence of Worcester, translated by Thomas Forester, 128, 130, 190. London, 1854.

Geoffrey Malaterra. 96.

Geoffrey of Monmouth. Faral, ed., 206, 207, 213, 232–33, 265–266, 272.

   Thorpe, trans., 189, 190, 197, 216, 248–49, 255.

Gesta Consulum Andegavorum. 146–47.

Giraldus Cambrensis. 42–45, 44–47.

Guibert of Nogent. 160.

Helmold of Bosau. *Cronica Slavorum*. *Monumenta Germaniae Historica Scriptores Rerum Germanicarum in Usum Scholarum*, 32:127.

   The Chronicle of the Slavs, translated by Francis Joseph Tschan, 185. New York, 1935.

Henry, Bishop of S. Agata dei Goti. Letter to Pope Innocent II, July 1132. *Monumenta Bambergensia*, edited by Philip Jaffe, letter number 259. Berlin, 1869.

L'Histoire de Guillaume le Maréchal. Meyer, ed., lines 16137–16196, 16277–16400.

   Crosland, trans., 121, 122–23.

Jordan Fantosme. 92–93.

Leo of Ostia. 864, 864–65.

Matthew Paris. *Chronica Majora*, Rolls Series, 5:646.

   Giles, trans., 3:243–44.

Nicolas of Bray. Lines 1798–1800.

Orderic Vitalis. 6:236–37.

Otto of St. Blasien. *Chronica*. *Monumenta Germaniae Historica Scriptores Rerum Germanicarum in Usum Scholarum*, 47:23–24.

Rahewin. *MGH*, 202–4.

   Mierow and Emery, trans., 205–6.

Richard, Canon of Holy Trinity, London. *Itinerarium Peregrinorum et Gesta Regis Ricardi*.

Chronicles and Memorials of the Reign of Richard I, vol. 1, Rolls Series, edited by William Stubbs, 268.

Itinerary of Richard I, attributed to Geoffrey of Vinsauf. *Chronicles of the Crusades,* translated by J. A. Giles, 238. London, 1903.

Richer. *Histoire de France, 888–995,* 2 vols., edited by Robert Latouche, 1:66. Paris, 1967.

Richerus. 294.

Roger of Hoveden. Rolls Series, 1:82, 84.

Riley, trans., 1:98, 101.

Roger of Wendover. Rolls Series (Matthew Paris), 1:222, 279, 495, 497.

Giles, trans., 1:23, 82, 288, 289.

Saxo Grammaticus. Olrik and Raeder, ed., 185, 218.

Fisher, trans., 205, 241.

Simeon of Durham. *Historia Regum. Opera Omnia,* vol. 2, Rolls Series, edited by Thomas Arnold, 150, 152.

William the Breton. *Philippidos.* 186, 320.

Martial and Seneca: A Renaissance Perspective

JOYCE MONROE SIMMONS

It is widely accepted that the Senecas were among the prominent Spanish families from whom Martial sought patronage when he first came to Rome in A.D. 64, a notion based on Martial's few, remote references to Seneca in the epigrams.[1] Some have even suggested that it was Seneca who first encouraged Martial to write epigrams.[2] Yet at the same time the possibility of a relation between the works of Martial and Seneca is a matter that has been largely ignored today. While the association between Martial and other poets and prose writers has received regular attention, interest in literary correspondences between Martial and Seneca has not been sustained.[3]

Friedlaender included thirteen sets of correspondences between the two in the notes to his 1886 edition of the epigrams.[4] These accompanied references to Catullus, Horace, Vergil, Ovid, and others, which marked the advances in turn-of-the-century scholarship on Martial.[5] Of Friedlaender's thirteen references to Seneca, two are drawn from the tragedies, one from the epistles, and the rest from the Senecan epigrams of the *Anthologia Latina*.[6] Gustav Friedrich expanded upon Friedlaender's work in 1910, identifying thirty-four additional sets of correspondences, this time drawing from a broader base of the Senecan corpus.[7] Except for Hammer's note in 1926 relating a single epigram to a Senecan passage, Friedrich's inquiry is the last of its kind to date, evidence in support of a hypothesis that has won little acceptance in the intervening years.[8]

The presence of Seneca in the epigrams of Martial, however, is a subject that humanists of the sixteenth and seventeenth centuries had already explored and preserved in a body of neo-Latin literature long since forgotten. Except for the references to the Senecan epigrams, Renaissance commentators on Martial had already identified virtually all the correspondences noted by Friedlaender and Friedrich, and many more correspondences as well. The frequency and regularity with which Seneca is cited in Renaissance commentaries on Martial suggest that it

Medievalia et Humanistica, New Series, Number 17 (Paul Maurice Clogan, ed.)
Rowman & Littlefield Publishers, Inc.

was commonplace for humanists to associate the two. But Friedlaender and before him Schneidewin—whose chief interest lay in charting advances in textual criticism—ignored those commentaries which stressed interpretation instead of emendation. Their accounts of significant editions of Martial pass directly from the 1602 Gruter to the 1619 Scriverius.[9]

The history sketched by them fails to evaluate, or in some cases even to mention, the interpretive commentaries that appeared separately or as part of editions during this period. When commentaries of interpretation are included in the tally of editions, however, the first quarter of the seventeenth century emerges as a high point in Martial scholarship. At least twenty-six separate editions of Martial appeared between 1600 and 1620, with a total of at least sixty-one editions between 1600 and 1670—figures which do not include the many popular works on Martial as a subject of translation and imitation in the vernacular.[10]

Among the works of interpretation to come forth in this period, three neo-Latin commentaries in particular provide an excellent record of the association between Martial and Seneca. Together, these works yield more than two hundred sets of correspondences between the two. First, the work of the Spanish lawyer and man of letters Lorenzo Ramirez de Prado contains the text of the epigrams, with a commentary on the *Liber Spectaculorum* and the first four books of epigrams.[11] Ramirez was only twenty-two when he composed this work, and in it he displays both the enthusiasm and brashness of his youth. His readings are always bold, independent, and marked by a sensitivity to Martial's wit and elegance which permits him to explicate unabashedly even the most obscene of the epigrams. He defends himself in a short digression, expressed in Martialian idiom:

Amo Poetam hunc multis de causis, sed praecipue quod urbanitatis magister sit diligentissimus. Odi superciliosos qui existimant hominem obscenum esse. Dispeream si quid in eo obscenum offendi. Omne enim eo fine scribit, ut nos risu et subsannatione a vitiis & a rusticitate morum deterreat. . . .[12]

Ramirez never hesitates to challenge the readings of more established scholars, a characteristic which placed him at the center of more than one critical controversy and earned him the disdain of other scholars.[13] His commentary appeared only once: in Paris in 1607.

Such was not the fate of the commentaries of the indefatigable Matthew Rader, whose "gelded" texts of Martial passed through three editions between 1601 and 1627. In the preface to the 1627 edition, more than one thousand pages long, Rader outlines his threefold plan for the work: to reach the mind of the poet ("mentem poetae"); to illustrate the poet's ideas with parallel passages ("geminis dictis") by other writers; and to fortify his own readings with other evidence.[14] Likening himself to Servius or Porphyrion, Rader declares Martial a poet in need of greater illumination ("maiore face") because he is so learned ("doctus") and more riddling ("aenigmatodes") and obscure ("tenebricosus") than others.[15] The commentaries of Matthew Rader, monuments to his erudition, remained popular, being reprinted throughout Europe in various forms as late as 1784.

Finally, there is the three-volume composite edition of Peter Scriverius. In his preface, Scriverius acknowledges the ascertainment of the text as his primary interest; and for this achievement, he earned the praise of Schneidewin and Friedlaender.[16] But the work's 950 pages contain more than the text and Scriverius's own emendations and readings, which comprise the first two volumes. The third volume presents a collection of readings on Martial by other scholars, including those of Scriverius's own circle at Leiden: Joseph Scaliger, Janus Rutgers, the Jesuit Johan Pontanus (Spanmüller), Janus Gruter, and Justus Lipsius.[17] Gruter, who was Scriverius's student at Leiden, contributes two collections of readings, the second of which, *Appendicula ad Martialem,* is interpretive and yields some correspondences between Martial and Seneca. Each of these contributions is accompanied by a letter to Scriverius, in effect bringing to life again the circle of foremost classical scholars of the early seventeenth century. From an earlier age, there are the readings of Joannes Brodaeus (Jean Brodeau); excerpts from the *Adversaria* of Hadrian Turnebus; and as a final ornament, excerpts on Martial from the *Miscellanea* of Angelo Politian, one of the earliest *umanisti.*[18]

Scriverius calls the *Miscellanea* "aureolo libello" and declares that to omit the work of this Italian would be a crime because his readings were "elegantissima et plena nimirum bonae frugis."[19] This commentary pays tribute to the unbroken tradition of serious critical attention to Martial, preserving the claim to immortality that the humanists felt Martial deserved. In this commentary, Scriverius, Gruter, Brodaeus, Lipsius, and Turnebus identify correspondences between Martial and Seneca, although the total number is rather small because their notes address only particular lines of selected epigrams, unlike the works of Ramirez and, especially, Rader, who furnishes the greatest number.

Of the many insights they provide into Renaissance conceptions of Martial and the epigram, these three commentaries make clear that Renaissance humanists well understood the place of Martial in the imitative tradition. Martial might have been condemned for his obscenity, but he was never trivialized in the Renaissance as he has been at intervals in more recent times. The commentators seek to align Martial with other writers of the Golden and Silver Ages, of which Seneca is but one prominent example. While Friedlaender was restrictive and even negative in his approach to Martial's literary debt, limiting his cross-references to those expressions and idioms in which Martial was not original, the commentators display an understanding of imitation and an enthusiasm for intertextuality that more closely approaches our own today. They recognize not only similar words, expressions, and themes, but also whole epigrams as imitations of earlier models.

Poetic models include Catullus, Horace, Vergil, Ovid, Propertius, Tibullus, the Greek Anthology, and collections not so readily associated with Martial today: the *Priapea*, the *Disticha Catonis*, the fables of Publilius Syrus, and the emblems of Alciati. As for prose writers, the commentators cite Tacitus, Suetonius, Pliny the Elder, and Petronius, but mostly to explain points of history or ancient custom. There is a combined total of sixty sets of correspondences showing the imitative debt of Pliny the Younger to his older contemporary Martial, but the attempt to align the style and substance of Martial with Seneca is the single most noticeable element in the commentaries, outweighing citations of any other prose or poetic model. When Friedlaender dismissed the works of Ramirez and Rader as out of date ("veraltet"), however, he in the process obscured the tradition associating Martial and Seneca, those two expositors of wit and elegance.[20]

It is not difficult to imagine what would lead men of the Renaissance to align Martial and Seneca, who were both at the pinnacle of their popularity during this time.[21] Besides their common Spanish heritage and the possibility of direct influence through personal contact, Martial and Seneca come together stylistically in the pith and point of epigrammatic expression and unexpected turn of thought. As Ramirez puts it, "and those things which Seneca the chief of Stoics teaches with a great display of words and sayings Martial shows to us with his most pleasing jests."[22] Both can be seen to manipulate point of view, the perspective on their subjects—Seneca through the Stoic paradox and Martial through the use of comparison in the epigram.[23] Through these manipulations, in the end, the visions of both transcend the common view of manners, morals, and truth.

The pursuit of the uncommon, be it point of view or expression, is the legacy both inherited from the private rhetorical schools of their day. These institutions of declamation oratory undoubtedly influenced both Martial and Seneca and in turn turned the literary tastes of their audiences toward a "rhetorical" declamatory style. By imperial times, the schools' oratorical exercises, once practical and educational, had become a form of recreation and entertainment, delighting in rhetoric more for its own sake. There were two forms of exercises: the *suasoria*, a speech in either the first or second person which details the inner conflict of an historical or mythological figure; and the *controversia*, a speech which applies a Greek, Roman, or sometimes fictitious law to a highly imaginative and often thorny set of circumstances, with the declaimer taking one side of the issue. Some results of such training can be found in the common elements that unite Martial and Seneca: love of rhetorical brilliance, epigrammatic expressions, paradox, *sententiae*, brevity, and a fondness for moralizing and social criticism.[24]

Valued from antiquity onward for their style and substance, Martial and Seneca endured as objects of imitation. Intense interest in Seneca by the church fathers secured his survival through the Dark and Middle Ages, and anywhere that learning survived, so did Martial.[25] One of the great encyclopedias of the Middle Ages, the thirteenth-century *Speculum Quadruplex* of Vincent of Beauvais, contains thirty-five references to Martial, some of which are aligned with the text of Seneca, one of Vincent's favorite authorities.[26] In the early fourteenth century, references to Martial appear in the marginal notes of a work on Seneca by Albertano da Brescia.[27] References of this kind hint at the possibility that the relation between Martial and Seneca was already traditional during the Middle Ages, and prefigure the more systematic work of the commentators on Martial of the sixteenth and early seventeenth centuries.

The collected correspondences in the works of Ramirez, Rader, and Scriverius warrant some introduction because they are diverse in nature. A few are based on what we would now consider to be corrupt readings of Martial. Other references to Seneca serve the more pedestrian purpose of explaining ancient custom. The greater number, however, acquit themselves of the charge of superficiality or mere antiquarianism. They may be classified into the two larger categories of verbal and thematic similarities. The verbal similarities can be further classified. Sometimes a commentator observes in Martial and Seneca the shared use of an unusual word, as when Rader notices their use of *stropha* to mean "trick" or "fraud."[28] Rader again relates their common use of *diripio*, not in the literal sense ("to tear asunder"), but in the unusual figurative sense of contending or struggling for something.[29] Often the shared uses of a single word are even more suggestive when the poetic context in which they appear is considered, as in the use of *deprendi*, as cited by Ramirez. In an address to Lesbia, who conducts her amours with doors open wide, Martial allows her her immorality and forbids her only to get caught.[30] In the epistles, Seneca also associates doorways with the idea of getting caught. He observes that because few people can live with their doors open ("aperto ostio"), being disclosed to view is, in effect, being caught ("deprehendi") in the act. It is our conscience, not our pride, that puts doorkeepers at our doors.[31] Martial's Lesbia, the exhibitionist, is a woman without a doorkeeper, a woman without a conscience.

Again, in their shared use of *fritillus* (the dice box), Ramirez observes that Martial takes the auditory suggestion of Seneca's "resonante fritillo" one step further through personification: "December sonat fritillis."[32] Both also employ *fruor* to express the paradox of delighting in something that is loathsome, as Martial's Mucius enjoys the punishment of his hand in the fire and Seneca's Hercules the wrath of Juno.[33]

Beyond verbal similarities, Martial and Seneca are seen, through their *gemina dicta*, to share one corner of a poetic universe that is full of objects that expose the excesses of human desire and the weaknesses of men. The images they hold in common reveal that world's lust for novelty and the grotesque. The commentators take note of remarkably similar glimpses which Martial and Seneca give us, for example, of faddishly sunlit baths, of the halls of social climbers lined with the busts of their ancestors, of men with a taste for rings on every finger, of crocuses watered by a hidden sprinkler system, of roses in winter, and wine in summer cooled with mountain ice.[34] Martial's "lectulus," from which could be seen more than one body of water, recalls for Rader Seneca's image of guests dining amid flowing waters.[35] And just as Martial carps at Cotta for using a sedan chair drawn by a sweating Libyan ("Libys eques") in a trail of dust ("longo pulvere"), Seneca also condemns the need of sophisticates of the day to be preceded by "Numidarum equitatus" and to announce their arrival "magno pulvere."[36] Chief among these shared images, perhaps, is that of the arena, that microcosm of all that is right and wrong with the Empire, realized in the paradox of the wild beast tamed or the tamer with his head in the lion's mouth.[37]

Many of the correspondences align the substance of the two. The effect is to underscore the conception of Martial as a serious poet or to bestow a philosophical basis to the "points" of the epigrams. For example, Rader associates the epigram on Gellia, who weeps for her dead father only when others are present, with the Senecan idea from the epistles that sorrow ceases when the sorrowful one is not in front of an audience ("sine spectatore cessat dolor"), and the related notion that tears are never so base as when they are feigned.[38]

On another note, Rader recognizes in Martial's famous line "Lasciva est nobis pagina, vita proba" a playful inversion of the proverb cited by Seneca in the epistles: "Talis hominibus fuit oratio qualis vita."[39] In another epigram, Martial admonishes a wealthy friend who, when asked for a loan, advises the poet instead to plead cases. The poet replies, "Quod peto da, Gai: non peto consilium."[40] Ramirez declares the line taken ("desumta") from Seneca, once again by inversion, for in the epistles, advice is precisely what Lucillius wants from Seneca, but to his dismay, he gets books instead.[41] Rader further identifies Seneca's lines on the folly of seeking friends in the atrium and testing them at the dinner table as the foundation of Martial's epigram to the host whose excellent menu, not good company, draws his companions to him.[42]

Often the Senecan context colors the reading of the entire epigram. For example, Rader associates Martial's use of the word "immodicis" in the epigram on the death of Glaucia the slave with Seneca's use of the word in the epistles: "nec umquam immodica durarunt."[43] The effect is to align the epigram with the very heart of Stoic philosophy. Rader associates almost every line of the often-translated "Vitam quae faciant beatiorem" with passages from the *De Beata Vita*, transforming the epigram into a portrait of the ideal Stoic *sapiens*.[44] Rader and Ramirez both explain Martial's distich on Paulus, who buys poetry and recites it as his own, in light of a passage from the *De Beneficiis*. There Seneca distinguishes between the owner of a thing and the owner of the use of a thing. They see Martial playing wittily with this paradox in his line "Nam quod emas possis iure vocare tuum."[45]

The distinction between possession and ownership also figures in the reading of the epigram on Matho, who, after being a frequent guest at Martial's villa, has bought the place for himself.[46] Ramirez associates Martial's conclusion, "Rus tibi vendo tuum," with the Senecan notion that greed alone distinguishes between possession and ownership: "Stulta avaritia mortalium possessionem proprietatemque discernit . . . ," an idea based in turn on the Stoic paradox that men cease to possess all things when they desire to possess them for themselves: "Desierunt enim omnia possidere, dum volunt propria."[47]

Roughly one-fourth of the references to Seneca in the commentaries are made to the *De Beneficiis*. The effect here is to establish a moral philosophical context for those epigrams of Martial that deal with the giving and receiving of gifts and with patronage in general. Rader compares Martial's detailed catalog of Saturnalian gifts that he did *not* receive with Seneca's passage on the ingratitude of those who fail to return a favor.[48] Martial concludes his epigram by calling the ingrate "dissimulator"; Seneca, too, uses *dissimulat* for the ingrate who pretends not to have received any gift.[49] For the epigram on Sextus, who loudly proclaims his financial difficulties expressly to avoid being asked a favor, Ramirez cites a passage from the *De Beneficiis* condemning the ungracious strategies some people adopt when they suspect they might be approached for a favor.[50] In another epigram, in which Martial compares his own meager possessions with the splendor of Candidus's, the commonplace "Koina philon" ("Friends have all things in common") ironically frames the catalog. Rader identifies the two references in the *De Beneficiis* which underscore the irony of the situation.[51]

Renaissance readers of the *De Beneficiis* undoubtedly valued it as a kind of courtesy book, setting down a code of behavior in which Seneca calls for the cultivation and polish of man's raw nature to a state of gracious reciprocity and social harmony. When viewed in this light, Martial's epigrams of complaint about gifts and favors can be seen as legitimate criticisms of a less-than-ideal social order, not as the mere carping of a social parasite. Here, too, as elsewhere, the commentators show that Seneca provides an ethical and stylistic context in which the epigrams may be received and fruitfully explored. The presence of Seneca in the epigrams of Martial deserves to be recognized and preserved once again, as it was by the Renaissance commentators, as part of the imitative tradition in which Martial shared. The work of Seneca is one more light to illuminate the brilliance of Martial, the "doctus," the "tenebricosus," the "aenigmatodes."

Notes

1. Martial 1.61.7; 4.40.1; 7.44.9–10; 7.45.1; 12.36.8, *M. Val. Martialis Epigrammata*, ed. W. M. Lindsay (Oxford, 1929). Friedlaender, for example, maintains this position: *M. Valerii Martialis epigrammaton libri* (Leipzig, 1886), 1:4–5, as do Mario Citroni, *M. Val. Mart. Epigrammaton Liber Primus* (Florence, 1975), xxv, 43, and 321, and J. P. Sullivan, *Literature and Politics in the Age of Nero* (Ithaca, 1985), 21–22. Biographies of Seneca, however, lend little support. See, for example, W. Sorenson, *Seneca: The Humanist at the Court of Nero* (Chicago, 1984), and M. T. Griffin, *Seneca: A Philosopher in Politics* (Oxford, 1976). Discussions of Martial and patronage are equally disappointing. See R. P. Saller, "Martial on Patronage and Literature," *CQ* 33(1983): 246–57; P. White, "*Amicitia* and the Profession of Poetry in Early Imperial Rome," *JRS* 68 (1978): 74–92; and P. White, "The Friends of Martial, Statius, and Pliny and the Dispersal of Patronage," *HSPh* 79 (1975): 265–300.
2. A. G. Carrington, "Martial," *Neronians and Flavians: Silver Latin I*, ed. D. R. Dudley (London, 1972), 247; this conjecture is based on the existence of epigrams attributed to Seneca found in the *Latin Anthology*.
3. There are a number of noteworthy exceptions. First is the single instance of correspondence observed by N. M. Kay in *Martial Book XI: A Commentary* (Oxford, 1985) between Martial 11.56.16 and Seneca *Epist.* 78.2. Kay suggests that Martial "may be deliberately recalling [Seneca's] writing and personality here" (195). Citroni (note 1), xxv–xxvi, observes the greatest Senecan influence in the first two books of epigrams, which award prominence to Stoicism in general and to the Stoic Decianus in particular. Citroni also identifies a number of specific correspondences: Martial 1.39.6 and Seneca *Epist.* 10.5, *Ben.* 2.1.4; 6.38 (126); Martial 1.15.10 and Seneca *Epist.* 1.1 (66); Martial 1.21 and Seneca *Prov.* 3.4, *Ben.* 7.15.2, *Epist.* 24.5, 66.51, 76.20, 98.12 (76); Martial

1.21.7 and Seneca *Epist.* 66.52 (78); Martial 1.79 and Seneca *Tranq. An.* 12.2 (255); and Martial 1.90.9 and Seneca *Epist.* 95.21 (284). See also P. Howell, *A Commentary on Book One of the Epigrams of Martial* (London, 1980), 247, 283, for mention of Seneca.

    In addition, R. J. Tarrant observes a number of possible imitations of Seneca by Martial in his editions of two of the tragedies. The commentary on the *Agamemnon* (Cambridge, 1976) identifies five parallels: Martial 1.117.5 and Seneca *Agam.* 31 (174); Martial 2.41.13f. and Seneca *Agam.* 707 (303); Martial 9.101.9 and Seneca *Agam.* 835f. (329); Martial 14.75 and Seneca *Agam.* 670ff. (298–99). The notes to the *Thyestes* (Atlanta, 1985) include three: Martial 9.68.10 and Seneca *Thyes.* 307 (134); Martial 6.86.5 and Seneca *Thyes.* 354 (141); and Martial 5.64. 3–4 and Seneca *Thyes.* 947–48 (224).

4. Friedlaender (note 1) records the following correspondences: Martial 1.114.1 and Seneca *Epigr.* 45.1; Martial 2.41.13 and Seneca *Epigr.* 19.1; Martial 2.91.2 and Seneca *Epigr.* 24.2–4; Martial 5.74 and Seneca *Epigr.* 10–14, 64–66; Martial 6.11.10 and Seneca *Epist.* 9.6; Martial 7.69.2 and Seneca *Epigr.* 15.8; Martial 8.3.2 and Seneca *Epigr.* 39.2; Martial 8.23.1 and Seneca *Epigr.* 41.1; Martial 9.18.1 and Seneca *Epigr.* 43.1; Martial 9.90.11 and Seneca *Thyes.* 357; Martial 9.101.7 and Seneca *Herc. Oet.* 1241; Martial 10.47.13 and Seneca *Epigr.* 5.12; Martial 10.96.13 and Seneca *Epigr.* 18.7. References to the works of Martial and Seneca in this paper follow the numbering of the texts of the standard modern editions as follows: *M. Val. Martialis Epigrammata*, ed. W. M. Lindsay (Oxford, 1969), *L. Annaei Senecae Opera Quae Supersunt*, 3 vols., ed. C. Hosius, O. Hense, E. Hermes, A. Gercke (Leipzig: Teubner, 1905–14); *Tragoediae*, ed. R. Peiper and G. Richter (Leipzig: Teubner, 1902); and *Naturales Quaestiones*, ed. A. Gercke (Stuttgart: Teubner, 1970, reprint 1907). Friedlaender refers to the edition of Seneca's epigrams by Emil Baehrens in vol. IV of *Poetae Latini Minores*, 5 vols. (Leipzig: Teubner, 1879–83).

5. See, for example, R. Paukstadt, *De Martiale Catulli imitatore* (Halis, 1876); A. Zingerle, *Martialis Ovidstudien* (Innsbruck, 1877); and E. Wagner, *De M. Val. Martiale poetarum Augusteae* (Konigsberg, 1880).

6. For a review of the scholarship on the Senecan epigrams, see M. Coffey, "Seneca Tragedies, including pseudo-Seneca *Octavia* and Epigrams Attributed to Seneca: Report for the years 1922–1955," *Lustrum* 2 (1957): 113–89. A. L. Motto, *Seneca* (New York, 1973), 137 n., asserts that only three epigrams have manuscript authority, while H. Bardon, "Les épigrammes de l'Anthologie attribuées à Sénèque le philosophe," *REL* 17 (1939): 63–90, can accept none with confidence. Citroni, however (note 1), 58, 129, 137, 237, 277, discusses their relation to Martial.

7. "Zu Seneca und Martial," *Hermes* 45 (1910): 583–94.

8. J. Hammer, "Seneca *De Beneficiis* 3.26.1 and Martial 10.48.18–22," *CW* 22 (1929): 200. G. M. W. Harrison III rejects Friedrich's correspondences, which were offered with little discussion, as "superficial," but finds Hammer persuasive, "Martialis 1901–1979," *Lustrum* 18 (1975): 533. A. Bourgéry, *Sénèque prosateur* (Paris, 1922), who admits the possibility of "une imitation directe" between Seneca and Juvenal, denies a correspondence with Martial on the suspect belief that "le genre qu'il avait adopté ne permettait guère l'imitation du philosophe tant vanté" (158). P. Faider, *Etudes sur Sénèque* (Ghent, 1921), finds the influence of the elder Seneca on Martial greater than that of the

younger (29–30). More recently, G. M. Ross finds the case for "direct Senecan influence" on Martial "tenuous" in the realm of philosophy and morals, in "Seneca's Philosophical Influence," *Seneca*, ed. C. D. N. Costa (London, 1974), 120.

9. Friedlaender (note 1), 1:120–1, and *M. Val. Martialis epigrammaton libri*, ed. F. G. Schneidewin (Leipzig, 1881), xliii–lv.

10. Information concerning Renaissance editions of Martial was compiled from descriptions listed in the *National Union Catalog: Pre-1956 Imprints* (London, 1968–); *the British Museum General Catalogue of Printed Books: Photolithographic Edition to 1955* (London, 1965); and the *Catalogue général des livres imprimés de la Bibliothèque Nationale* (Paris, 1924–).

11. *Hypomnemata ad Librum Spectaculorum et quator primos epigrammaton M. Valerii Martialis collecta ex schedis succisiviis Domini Laurentii Ramirez de Prado* (Paris, 1607). For biographical and bibliographical accounts, see Joaquin de Entrambasaguas, *La Biblioteca de Ramirez de Prado* (Madrid, 1943), vii–xxxx, and the *Catalogus Translationum et Commentariorum: Mediaeval and Renaissance Latin Translations and Commentaries*, ed. F. E. Cranz and P. O. Kristeller (Washington, 1980), 4:290–92.

12. Ramirez de Prado (note 11), 53.

13. For example, in his own notes to Martial, *Animadversiones in Martialem*, Peter Scriverius makes several unflattering references to Ramirez: *M. V. Martialis nova editio: Ex museo P. Scriverii* (Leiden, 1619), 2:77, 84, 113. The same edition also contains an undated letter from Joseph Scaliger to Scriverius. It presumably accompanied Scaliger's contribution to the edition, his *Diatribe Critica* on Martial, and perhaps even a copy of Ramirez's *Hypomnemata*. In the letter Scaliger declares Ramirez a bright young man ("praeclarum ingenium"), but one rather taken with himself and his own ideas ("depravere posset philautia"), especially in his youthful scorn for great men, particularly Janus Gruter, and in his misrepresentation of the work of older scholars. Scaliger charges Scriverius to correct the mistaken impression of Gruter, but with restraint, by increased praises of Gruter rather than condemnation of Ramirez—an admonition not heeded by Scriverius. Scaliger further observes that Ramirez had been declared *doctissimus* in France and that, if Ramirez would heed these warnings, his work would one day be worthwhile (3:167).

Cranz and Kristeller (note 11), 291, accept Ramirez as the author of the *Hypomnemata*, but from time to time the very authorship of the work has been challenged, largely because of Ramirez's youth at the time of its publication. The *Hypomnemata* has also been attributed to the famed grammarian Baltasar de Cespedes, Ramirez's teacher at the University of Salamanca. It is thought that Baltasar might have sold his rights to the bright young Ramirez, who was wealthy enough to have it published. Later, Ramirez was to do exactly this with another work attributed to him but actually composed by another former teacher. The responses of Scaliger, Scriverius, and Rader to the *Hypomnemata*, however, make it clear that his contemporaries certainly accepted Ramirez as the author, and he paid dearly for the pleasure of having his name (rightly or wrongly) affixed to the commentary. First, according to Cranz and Kristeller (290), the manuscript had been stolen from Ramirez by William Bichon, a French librarian who printed it in 1607. Its controversial relish for obscenity and its criticism of J. J. Scaliger, Justus Lipsius, and Janus Gruter prompted a full-scale refutation by Theodorus Marcilius in 1607 (Cranz and Kristeller, 281). Then, Matthew Rader, in the second edition of his commentary on Martial (1611), charged Ramirez with plagiarism, perhaps because the *Hypomnemata* was printed without any prefatory acknowledgements. Ramirez responded with an unauthorized broadside against Rader which is still preserved in the National Historical Archives in Madrid. Because the work was unauthorized, Spanish officials prosecuted Ramirez in 1612 and punished him with eight years' banishment and a fine, both of which penalties were later rescinded (Cranz and Kristeller, 291; and Entrambasaguas, note 11, xi). Ramirez had the last laugh on the authorities, however, by finally succeeding, after two years of petitions, in being named to the Office of the Inquisition in 1626 (Entrambasaguas, xii). With the appointment came a papal dispensation to read anything he wished, a privilege which he apparently valued. Although Ramirez devoted his public life to law, politics, and diplomacy, a posthumous catalog of his huge library—made in 1662, presumably to purge forbidden books before the collection was dispersed—reveals Ramirez to be a man equally devoted to letters and scholarship. It also reveals his apparent lifelong interest in Martial. The library included the complete works of Politian (1553), the *Adversaria* of Hadrian Turnebus (1581), and the works of Justus Lipsius (1637), excerpts of all of which are included in the Scriverius Martial (1619). Ramirez also owned the Perotti *Cornucopia* commentary on Martial (1526), a 1560 text of the epigrams, with the commentaries of Merula and Calderino, another 1617 edition from Paris, and even the Marcilio refutation of the *Hypomnemata*. He also owned the 1602 and 1627 Rader editions and the 1619 Scriverius (Entrambasaguas, *passim*.).

14. *Mattaei Raderi de Societate Jesu ad M. Valerii Martialis epigrammaton libros plenis commentariis novo studio confectis, explicatos, emendatos, illustratos, rerumque et verborum lemmatum item et communium locorum variis et copiosis Indicibus auctos, curae tertiae plurimis locis meliores* (Mainz, 1627), preface n. p. For a biographical and bibliographical account of Rader, see Cranz and Kristeller (note 11), 284–87, and C. Sommervogel, *Bibliothèque de la Compagnie de Jésus* (Brussels-Paris, 1890–1919), 4:1007–8. While neither Rader nor the Jesuits were the first to purge Martial of obscenity, John Donne, who perceived the gelding of texts as a Jesuit effort to manipulate learning, attacked Rader and his edition of Martial directly, first in an unsavory epigram and then in an anti-Jesuit tract, *Ignatius His Conclave* (1611). See *John Donne: The Satires, Epigrams and Verse Letters*, ed. W. Milgate (Oxford, 1967), 54, and *Complete Poetry and Selected Prose of John Donne*, ed. C. M. Coffin (New York, 1952), 544. I am most grateful to Evelyn Hart, director of the Peabody Library, Baltimore, for making the very rare Ramirez and Rader volumes available to me and for countless other acts of assistance during my stay there.

15. Rader, preface, n. p.

16. Scriverius (note 13), preface, n. p. Cranz and Kristeller (note 11) give an account of Scriverius and the edition, 4:293–95, as does J. E. Sandys, *A Companion to Latin Studies*, 3d ed. (Cambridge, 1925), 2:307.

17. On Scaliger (1540–1609), see Cranz and Kristeller (note 11), 4:289–90; Sandys (note 16), 2:199–204; and J. Hutton, *The Greek Anthology in France: And in the Latin Writers of the Netherlands to the Year 1800* (Ithaca, 1946), 152–57. The Jesuit Pontanus is cited by Rader in the prefatory index to the sources

used in the 1627 edition. Pontanus also wrote a treatise on the epigram; see J. Hutton, *The Greek Anthology In Italy to the Year 1800* (Ithaca, 1935), 60, 65. Accounts of Janus Gruter (1560–1627) may be found in Cranz and Kristeller, 4:287–89; Hutton, *France*, 246–47; and Sandys, 2:359–362. Both Lipsius and Scaliger were dead by the time the long-delayed edition came forth in 1619, and in his notes Scriverius mourns their loss (2:49).

18. On Brodaeus, see Cranz and Kristeller (note 11), 4:275–76, and Hutton, *France* (note 17), 98–101. For Turnebus, see Cranz and Kristeller, 4:278; Sandys (note 16), 2:185–86; and Hutton, *France*, 97–98. For Politian, see Cranz and Kristeller, 4:271–72; L. D. Reynolds and N. G. Wilson, *Scribes and Scholars: A Guide to the Transmission of Greek and Latin Literature* (Oxford, 1968), 117–20.

19. Scriverius (note 13), 3:266.

20. Friedlaender (note 1), 1:125. Friedlaender's inclusion of the early work of Paukstadt et al. (note 5), reviving interest in Martial's poetic models, undoubtedly paved the way for its general and easy acceptance by scholars today. See the recent commentaries of Citroni (note 1), Kay, and Howell (note 3). See also J. Ferguson, "Catullus and Martial," *PACA* 6 (1963): 3–15; H. H. Huxley, "Martial and the Epodes of Horace," *Proceedings of the Pacific Northwest Conference on Foreign Languages* 23 (1972): 36–38; G. Donini, "Martial I, 49: Horatius in Martiale," *AJP* 85 (1964): 56–60; J. W. Spaeth, "Martial and Vergil," *TAPA* 61 (1930): 19–28; D. Martin, "Similarities between the *Silvae* of Statius and the Epigrams of Martial," *CJ* 34 (1939): 461–70; L. Hermann, "Martial et les Priapées," *Latomus* 22 (1963): 31–55; and H. Szelest, "Martials satirische Epigramme und Horaz," *Altertum* 9 (1963): 27–37.

21. For example, see T. Whipple, *Martial and the English Epigram from Sir Thomas Wyatt to Ben Jonson* (Berkeley, 1924); A. Giulian, *Martial and the Epigram in Spain in the Sixteenth and Seventeenth Centuries* (Philadelphia, 1930); G. Williamson, *The Senecan Amble: Prose Form from Bacon to Collier* (Chicago, 1966); *"Attic" and Baroque Prose Style: The Anti-Ciceronian Movement: Essays by Morris W. Croll*, eds. J. M. Patrick, R. O. Evans, J. W. Wallace (Princeton, 1969); and G. Braden, *Renaissance Tragedy and the Senecan Tradition: Anger's Privilege* (New Haven, 1985).

22. Ramirez (note 11): ". . . & quae Stoicorum princeps Seneca magna sententiorum et verborum, hic facetiis gratissimis nobis exhibet. . . ." (53).

23. Comparison in the epigram here refers to perspective—the perception of an object in terms of one or more other objects. The epigrammatist may be said to achieve his ends by witty manipulation of the perspective on his subject. A number of Renaissance treatises on the epigram identify comparison as the structural basis of the genre. Foremost among them is the *Poetices libri septem* of J. C. Scaliger (Lyons, 1561), whose chapters on the epigram are the first elaborate treatment of the genre as a discrete form. Scaliger, influenced by Aristotle's *Rhetoric*, declares that the epigram's argument, its structured collection of arguments, will deduce "some thing that is either greater than, less than, equal to, other than, or contrary to, the thing signified" ("idque aut maius, aut minus, aut aequale, aut diversum aut contrarium," Book 3, cap. 126, p. 170). In the *Rhetoric*, Aristotle named comparison as the basis of all metaphor: rhetorical figures represent objects by showing them to be either greater or less than, like or unlike, or something other than the object

(3.10.5–3.11.6). It is true that all poets use figures in this way for all kinds of poems. The difference, it appears, is that in the Renaissance epigram, rhetoric is admired for its own sake, not simply as a means to the end of an apt representation of some person or thing: its form is its function. Through comparison an epigrammatist may make an individual seem greater or less than others, or may just as easily overturn common understandings (perceptions) of an event or social custom by providing different perspectives on the subjects at hand. Scaliger's definition of *epigram* is found in subsequent treatises on the genre through the mid-seventeenth century. See T. Correa, *De toto eo poematis genere quod epigrammata vulgo dicitur et de iis quae ad illud pertinent libellus* (Venice, 1569); A. Possevino, *Tractatio de poesi et pictura ethnica* (Leiden, 1595); M. Rader (note 14), 9–12; and Gerardus Vossius, *Poeticarum institutionum libri tres* (Amsterdam, 1647), Book 3, cap. 19–21, pp. 161–67. More recently, Mario Praz interprets wit in poetry and illusionism in painting as manifestations of a single Renaissance phenomenon: "the managing of the point of view from which objects had to be seen," *Mnemosyne: The Parallel Between Literature and the Visual Arts* (Princeton, 1974), 126. He further associates the epigram, "the literary form that most appealed to the mind of a seventeenth-century man," to those architectural innovations of the day that manipulated point of view and suggests that the epigram is the "poetical counterpart" of the false perspective, which, through illusion, can make things seem greater, smaller, or other than they really are (127).

24. For a full discussion of declamation oratory, see S. F. Bonner, *Roman Declamation* (Berkeley, 1949); R. J. Tarrant, *Seneca's Thyestes* (note 3), 19–22; and George Kennedy, *The Art of Rhetoric in the Roman World 300 B.C.–A.D. 300* (Princeton, 1972), 318–37.

25. See Bourgéry (note 8), 150–86, on Seneca, and Reynolds and Wilson (note 18) on Martial *passim*.

26. The work remained popular through the Renaissance. I refer here to a 1624 edition: *Vincenti Burgundi Bibliotheca mundi: speculum quadruplex; naturale, doctrinale, morale, historiale* (Duaci, 1624). Reynolds and Wilson (note 18) call Vincent "the most monumental encyclopedist of the Middle Ages" (97).

27. Cranz and Kristeller (note 11), 4:251.

28. Martial 3.7.6 and Seneca *Ep*. 26.6 (Rader, note 14, 250).

29. Martial 7.76.1 and Seneca *Brev. Vit*. 7.8 (Rader, 529).

30. Martial 1.34.10 (Ramirez, note 11, 66).

31. Seneca *Ep*. 43.4 (Ramirez, 66).

32. Martial 4.14.8 and Seneca *Apoc*. 15 (Ramirez, 310).

33. Martial 8.30.3–4 and Seneca *Her. Fur*. 33–34 (Rader, 566).

34. Martial 1.77.4 and Seneca *Ep*. 86.8 and *Ep*. 108.4 (Ramirez 109–10); Martial 4.40 and 2.90.5 and Seneca *De Ben*. 3.28.2 and *Polyb*. 14.3 (Rader, 240); Martial 5.12 and Seneca *Q. Nat*. 7.31.2 (Rader, 370); Martial 5.25.7 and Seneca *Ep*. 90.15 (Rader, 387); Martial 6.80 and Seneca *Ep*. 122.7–8 (Rader, 476); Martial 5.64.2 and Seneca *Q. Nat*. 4.13.10 (Gruter, Scriv. 3:118).

35. Martial 10.51.9 and Seneca *De Tranq*. 1.8 (Rader, 719).

36. Martial 10.14.2 and Seneca *Ep*. 87.9 and *Ep*. 123.7 (Rader, 687–88). Turnebus 3:246 cites only *Ep*. 123.7.

37. Martial 2.75 and Seneca *De Ben*. 1.2.5 and *Ep*. 85.41 (Ramirez, 204; Rader, 229–30).

38. Martial 1.33.2–3 and Seneca *Ep.* 99.16 and *Ep.* 99.20 (Rader, 110–11).
39. Martial 1.4.8 and Seneca *Ep.* 114.1 (Rader, 84).
40. Martial 2.30.6.
41. Seneca *Ep.* 45.2 (Ramirez, 170).
42. Martial 9.14 and Seneca *Ep.* 19.11 (Rader, 619).
43. Martial 6.29 and Seneca *Ep.* 74.19 (Rader, 448).
44. Martial 10.47 and Seneca *Vit. Beat.* 5, 11, 22, 23 (Rader, 712–13).
45. Martial 2.20 and Seneca *De Ben.* 7.6. (Rader, 200; Ramirez, 163).
46. Martial 4.79.
47. Martial 4.79.2 and Seneca *Ep.* 73.7 and *Ep.* 90.3 (Ramirez, 364).
48. Martial 4.88 and Seneca *De Ben.* 3.1 (Rader, 356).
49. Martial 4.88.10 and Seneca *De Ben.* 3.1.3 ("Dum. . . dissimulat") (Ramirez, 370).
50. Martial 2.44 and Seneca *De Ben.* 1.1.5 (Ramirez, 181).
51. Martial 2.43 and Seneca *De Ben.* 7.4 and 7.12 (Rader, 214).

"As thynketh yow": Conflicting Evidence and the Interpretation of The Franklin's Tale

DAVID M. SEAMAN

The Franklin's Tale concludes with a question about the relative generosity of its characters: "Which was the mooste fre, as thynketh yow?" (1622).[1] This suggests, at first, that there is a single answer to be discovered in the text. In the attempt to deduce this answer, however, one realizes that key pieces of evidence have been constructed to support conflicting solutions. Several of the promises contain ambiguous or contradictory terms; the tale provides evidence for very different answers to the problem with which the Franklin leaves us. Rather than challenging the reader to uncover a single intended reply to its final question, *The Franklin's Tale* compels the reader to examine how one's own literary prejudices and preconceptions impinge upon an assessment of conflicting evidence. In thinking about "Which was the mooste fre" one is made to realize both that any single answer needs to give priority to certain pieces of evidence in the text and that the choice will be dictated not by the tale but by the reader's expectations and desires, by "as thynketh yow."

One needs to know something about the Franklin in order to understand the motivation behind his question at the end of the tale. This information is not in short supply. In addition to the implications of his *estate*,[2] the Franklin is described in the General Prologue, and we have "The wordes of the Frankeleyn to the Squier," the Franklin's Prologue, and portions of the *The Franklin's Tale* to give us the impression of a character who is deeply concerned with displays of *gentil* deeds. In *The Franklin's Tale*, however, Chaucer does not show an overriding interest in the creation of a consistent *individual* narrative presence. It is not reasonable to assume, as some readers have, that we should consider every narratorial statement to be an expression of the Franklin's personality.[3] The first-person narratorial speech in *The Franklin's Tale* is most often generic rather than individual; regularly it consists of the commonplaces

Medievalia et Humanistica, New Series, Number 17 (Paul Maurice Clogan, ed.) Rowman & Littlefield Publishers, Inc.

of Middle English fictional narration: "And shortly, if the sothe I tellen shal" (935), or "And thus in joye and blisse I lete hem dwelle, / And of the sike Aurelius wol I telle" (1099–1100), for example.[4] The passages of first-person narration that can be most easily attributed to the Franklin cluster most noticeably near either end of the poem. For example, there is the passage discussing marriage early in the tale (761–816);[5] at the end are the Franklin's attempt to close down discussion of the marriage of Dorigen and Arveragus (1550–56) and his stress on the question about *gentillesse* (1621–24). Even these passages are replete with the formulaic (and nonindividualizing) first-person narrative phrases that constitute much of the first-person speech in *The Franklin's Tale*.[6] As David Lawton has observed, "The Franklin's Tale is a vintage performance of the standard high-style narrator."[7] Speaking of *The Miller's Tale* and *The Reeve's Tale*, Lawton points out that the narrative voice in these tales "is [for the most part] conceived not dramatically but rhetorically and stylistically."[8] The same must be said of *The Franklin's Tale*. Interpretations of *The Franklin's Tale* that rely on the consistent dramatic presence of the Franklin are likely to be inaccurate. Those passages in which the narrative voice is unambiguously that of the Franklin occur less frequently than many readers have assumed.[9]

Critics who hear the Franklin's voice throughout the tale suggest that certain passages of third-person narration are significant to our understanding of the psychological composition of the Franklin–narrator. Consider, for example, the following passage:

> But sodeynly bigonne revel newe
> Til that the brighte sonne loste his hewe;
> For th'orisonte hath reft the sonne his lyght—
> This is as muche to seye as it was nyght—
> And hoom they goon in joye and in solas . . . (1015–19)

This passage is often said to indicate either that the Franklin feels the need to explain an aureate expression to part of his audience or that he is inept in his use of rhetoric not natural to his *estate*.[10] Editors of Chaucer have long treated these lines as a comical treatment of a "colour of rethoryk": Gilman notes that "The Franklin was no poet",[11] and Skeat believes the passage to be "A humorous apology for a poetical expression" (whether the apology is from Chaucer or the Franklin is unclear).[12] Manly is more explicit: "Most editors have taken it as the Franklin's jocose apology for using language too ornate for his character and education; but Chaucer was poking fun at the rhetorical figure called *circumlocutio*,"[13] and Robinson supports this: "The astronomical mode of defining times and persons, here satirized, was very characteristic of Chaucer and his times."[14]

Whatever Chaucer's editors have decided, the construction used in this passage was not interpreted as humorous or satirical by two of Chaucer's near contemporaries, judging from their own use of it. As Harrison pointed out fifty years ago, it is twice used as a straightforward rhetorical "colour" by Lydgate in Book 4 of the *Troy Book*:[15]

> Þe longe day þus went he to and fro,
> Til Phebus char lowe gan declyne
> His golden axtre, þat so cler doth shine,
> —Þis to seyne, þe sonne went[e] doun—(626–29)

> And Espirus gan his liȝt to shede
> —Þis to seyn, for it drowe to nyȝt,—(3582–83)

and by King James in the *Kingis Quair*:[16]

> The longe day thus gan I prye and pour
> Till Phebus endit had his bemes bryght,
> And bad go farewele euery lef and flour,
> This is to say, approchen gan the nyght,
> And Esperus his lampis gan to light, . . . (498–502)

Fifteenth-century admirers and imitators of Chaucer were certainly capable of misinterpreting Chaucer's intentions. The passage, however, also looks much less parodic when compared to Chaucer's use of this construction—in which a description is repeated in less aureate or less technical language—in his other romances. See, for example, the description of Arcite's funeral pyre in *The Knight's Tale*:

> And twenty fadme of brede the armes straughte—
> This is to seyn, the bowes weren so brode. (I.2916–17)[17]

or the description of the marvelous steed in *The Squire's Tale*:

> This steede of bras, that esily and weel
> Kan in the space of o day natureel—
> This is to seyn, in foure and twenty houres—
> Wher-so yow lyst, in droghte or elles shoures,
> Beren youre body . . . (V.115–19)[18]

and it occurs once more in *The Franklin's Tale*:[19]

> This subtil clerk swich routhe had of this man
> That nyght and day he spedde hym that he kan
> To wayten a tyme of his conclusioun;
> This is to seye, to maken illusioun . . . (1261–65)

Chaucer also uses "this is to seyn" throughout *Boece* when incorporating glosses or commentaries into his translation. At one point he explains an aureate description of daybreak, which recalls the description of day's end in *The Franklin's Tale*:

Whan Phebus, the sonne, bygynneth to spreden his clernesse with rosene chariettes, thanne the sterre, ydymmed, paleth hir white cheeres by the flambes of the sonne that overcometh the sterre lyght. (*This to seyn, whan the sonne is rysen, the day-sterre waxeth pale, and leeseth hir lyght for the grete bryghtnesse of the sonne.*) Book II, Metrum 3:1–8.

Lines 1015–19 of *The Franklin's Tale* demonstrate the impact that editorially imposed punctuation can have on the way one reads the text.[20] Despite Skeat's conviction that the line is "a humorous apology," his punctuation does not enshrine this as the only possible reading:

> For th'orisonte hath reft the sonne his lyght;
> This is as muche to seye as it was nyght.

Hopper (1948) adopts Skeat's punctuation exactly, and the editions of Donaldson (1958; 1975), Fisher (1977), and Blake (1980) adopt the period after "nyght," using either a dash (Donaldson and Fisher) or a comma (Blake) after "lyght." Manly's 1928 edition is the first (to my knowledge) to insert an exclamation point after "nyght," in addition to emphasising line 1018 by marking it off with a pair of dashes:

> For th'orisonte hath reft the sonne his lyght—
> This is as muche to seye as it was nyght!—

Manly's exclamation point and pair of dashes are adopted by Robinson, in the most influential of all twentieth-century editions of Chaucer (1933; 1957), and by Baugh (1963) and Pratt (1966). The present standard text, the third edition of the *Riverside Chaucer* (1987), retains the dashes from Robinson's text but removes the exclamation point and refers in an explanatory note to Harrison's argument against a humorous reading of this passage. Tyrwhitt (1775), Morris (1882), and Burrell (1908) enclose line 1018 in parentheses, denying it the emphasis given in those twentieth-century editions whose editors believe it to be parodic. Freed from the assumption that the Franklin is a consistent narrative presence in his tale, and freed from Manly and Robinson's exclamation point and dashes, the passage is far from an obvious satire on a rhetorical device. In *The Franklin's Tale*, Chaucer is not consistently concerned with an examination of the psychological workings of the Franklin's mind. The Franklin's voice dominates the earlier and later parts of the tale, but its occasional appearance in the body of the tale should not mask the fact that much of the romance is told in the voice of a generic, rather than an individual, narrator.[21]

*   *   *

The Franklin's Tale begins unequivocally as a courtly romance. Despite the problems associated with a definition of the genre, the events and the vocabulary of the first fifteen lines of *The Franklin's Tale* are thoroughly familiar to a reader of medieval romance.[22] The knight is a worthy one, and he performs "many a greet emprise" (732) before he wins a lady who is "oon the faireste under sonne" (734); eventually, the lady consents "To take hym for hir housbonde and hir lord, / Of swich lordshipe as men han over hir wyves" (742–43). Elements later in this opening passage, however, complicate the expectations raised by the highly stylized behavior of these anonymous romance characters. That their love is mutual, enduring, and existing within marriage is common in Middle English romance. Gervase Mathew points to *Sir Degrevant, Sir Eglamour of Artois*, and *Sir Partenope of Blois* as Middle English romances that assume a harmonious relationship between love and marriage, although he could have chosen many another.[23] This is overlooked by critics who are eager to prove that the medieval mind would inevitably see Dorigen and Arveragus's love as being sinful and opposed to the theory and reality of marriage.[24] The discussion of equality within marriage, however, is much less common and is an early indication that this is an unusual romance.

Immediately after the marital pledges have been exchanged between the knight and his lady, the narrative voice shifts from a third-person romance narrator to a first-person interpreter of the tale. This interpretative voice draws attention to equality in marriage, passes favorable judgment on it, and discusses the nature of love and the need for *pacience* therein (761–86). Following this passage the narrative voice modulates back and forth for another nineteen lines between the role of storyteller and that of a commentator on the story being told. These first-person asides prompt the reader to judge the marriage by realistic, human criteria, and this encouragement is continued by the letters that Arveragus sends home while he is in England (837–40). This is a delightful domestic detail; I know of no other instance in medieval literature of a serious courtly knight writing home to his wife while on a knightly adventure.

In addition, Dorigen displays at moments a psychological depth not usually found in the women of medieval romance: as a Chaucerian romance heroine she is more akin to Criseyde than to Canacee or to Emelye.[25] One learns of Dorigen's fears—for example, those centered on the rocks of the Brittany coastline (865–93)—through her own lengthy discussion of them, and the effect of this is to encourage the reader to empathize with her situation in human terms.[26] The artlessness of her weeping when she tells Arveragus of her oath to Aurelius evokes in the reader pity for her suffering, not censure for her mistake (1462–65). As

The Franklin's Tale progresses, there is much in it that is familiar from romance, but by the time that Arveragus returns from England the tale is already firmly established as a romance that in places demands to be treated as a "domestic tragedy," as Pearsall has made clear:

Chaucer . . . [takes] a conventional form of story and [renders] it with an intense quality of imaginative engagement, so that the enigmatic nature of the story as a representation of the matter of experience and reality is brought into sharp focus, and the reader is stimulated to unexpected feats of perceptual tolerance. What he does here is to give to a romantic fairy-tale a degree of dramatic realisation which takes us at least momentarily out of the realm of romance into that of domestic tragedy.[27]

This compels us to question what value system, or systems, we need to employ in order to answer the questions raised by the tale.

It is against the background of a romance that at times asks us to judge it according to the values and expectations of everyday life that we have to assess the actions of the characters in *The Franklin's Tale*. This task is further complicated by the ambiguities inherent in several of the promises made by these characters. There is a marked tendency for the promises of *The Franklin's Tale* to end with a qualifying clause, a restatement designed to clarify or to limit the terms of the pledge being made.[28] This form of contract is familiar from the pledge made at the Tabard Inn, before the company of pilgrims begin their journey:

> "And which of yow that bereth hym best of alle—
> That is to seyn, that telleth in this caas
> Tales of best sentence and moost solaas—
> Shal have a soper at oure aller cost." (I.796–99)

Apart from those in *The Franklin's Tale*, Chaucer's aristocratic romance characters tend not to make qualified promises. For example, the knight's pledge to the hag in *The Wife of Bath's Tale* is emphatically unequivocal: " 'Have heer my trouthe,' quod the knyght, 'I grante' " (III.1013). The qualified nature of the promises in *The Franklin's Tale* might pass without comment if all the additional clauses clarified the terms of their promises, as they do in the following two examples: Arveragus wants the marriage to be a partnership of equals, but in a qualification of this he adds the wish to maintain a public impression of mastery: "Save that the name of soveraynetee, / That wolde he have for shame of his degree" (751–52); Dorigen's pledge to be faithful to Arveragus ends with the clause "til that myn herte breste" (759), a common Middle English romance euphemism for "until I die."[29] In these instances the additional clause clarifies the contract, either by making a qualification explicit or by emphasizing that the contract is binding for life. In Dorigen's pledge to love the squire

Aurelius, and in Arveragus's promise never to exert mastery over Dorigen, however, it is precisely the qualifying clause that creates ambiguity. This ambiguity has important consequences for an interpretation of *The Franklin's Tale*.

After the initial marriage pledges have been exchanged, Dorigen and Arveragus exist for a while isolated from the inevitable uncontrollable elements of everyday life (799–806). This "blisful lyf" (806) is brought to an end by the departure of Arveragus for England, at which point Dorigen is forced back into the world and back into the companionship of other people. Dorigen's sorrow and fear become focused on the "grisly feendly rokkes blake" (868) of the Brittany coastline,[30] and these rocks become the subject for the task that Dorigen sets Aurelius, who expresses his love to her while Arveragus is in England.

In the speech that Dorigen makes to Aurelius shortly before she gives him his impossible task she pledges the following:

> "By thilke God that yaf me soule and lyf,
> Ne shal I nevere been untrewe wyf
> In word ne werk, as fer as I have wit;
> I wol been his to whom that I am knyt." (983–86)

This is clearly intended by Dorigen to be an unambiguous statement of her intention to remain faithful to her absent husband. Subsequent events give it, in retrospect, a fuller meaning. We see later in the tale that it is the confounding of Dorigen's *wit*, by an illusion, that leads to the dilemma of *trouthe*-keeping; this dilemma comes about precisely because she considers herself to be *knyt* to both Arveragus and Aurelius.[31]

Dorigen seeks to reinforce her statement of marital fidelity by offering Aurelius an impossible task: she promises to love him only after he has removed all the rocks from the Brittany coast "stoon by stoon" (993). Dorigen first outlines the terms of this task (989–94), then gives what she intends to be a restatement of the pledge designed to prevent ambiguity (995–97). It is precisely this additional clause (italicized below), however, that makes the oath ambiguous:

> "Looke what day that endelong Britayne
> Ye remoeve alle the rokkes, stoon by stoon,
> That they ne lette ship ne boot to goon—
> *I seye, whan ye han maad the coost so clene*
> *Of rokkes that ther nys no stoon ysene,*
> Thanne wol I love yow best of any man;
> Have heer my trouthe, in al that evere I kan." (992–98)

Dorigen's words do not convey only the meaning she intends. *The Franklin's Tale* suggests that like the rocks on the Brittany coastline, words can be a "foul confusion" (869); they are not simply a fair creation, perfect and stable. It is with the second clause—"That ther nys no stoon *ysene*"— that Aurelius can be said to comply when he arranges for the rocks to be out of sight. It is precisely the inclusion of lines 995–96 that provides the evidence to support this competing interpretation.

Dorigen obviously intends the task to be impossible for Aurelius to fulfill. She is explicit about this—"For wel I woot that it shal never bityde" (1001)—and Aurelius realizes the superlative difficulty of the task: " 'Madame,' quod he, 'this were an inpossible!' " (1009). For Alan Gaylord, Dorigen's intention invalidates the whole pledge; he argues that "a promise is made with some kind of expectation of fulfillment; Dorigen's thoughts run all the other way. Where, then, does Aurelius get the right to assume she has really promised him anything at all?"[32] One answer is that Aurelius gets the right from Dorigen, whose pledge uses the language of promissory declarations already established in the tale. The phrase "Have heer my trouthe" occurs both in Dorigen's promise to Arveragus (759) and in her later promise to Aurelius (998); Dorigen's vow never to be an untrue wife and her vow to be Aurelius's love (if he fulfills the task she sets) are made "By thilke God" (983) and "by heighe God" (989), respectively. Gerald Morgan concludes that this "verbal parallelism is a means of fixing in our minds a sense of the moral equality in the making of the two promises."[33] Certainly, all of the characters in the tale behave as though Dorigen's pledge to Aurelius is binding, and the rest of the action depends on its being interpreted as such.

Although the language of Dorigen's oath to Aurelius echoes other binding pledges in *The Franklin's Tale*, this promise was made, the narrator tells us, "in pley" (988). Again, Chaucer is presenting the reader with conflicting evidence. The oath made "in pley" inevitably leads one to question whether a contract is made binding by its words or by its underlying intention. Chaucer addresses this question in *The Friar's Tale*, when in anger a carter pledges his "hors and cart and hey" (III.1547) to the Devil. Despite this, the Devil decides that the pledge is not binding because "The carl spak oo thing, but he thoghte another" (III.1568), indicating that intention gives legitimacy to an oath. The situation in *The Franklin's Tale*, however, is not directly comparable to that of *The Friar's Tale*. *The Franklin's Tale* is primarily a romance, and promises in romances tend to be binding however they are made, whether or not common sense or legal precedent allows them to be seen as otherwise.[34] A well-known example of this occurs in *Sir Gawain and the Green Knight*, where a pledge made as part of a Christmas game (377–412), and made to a character who uses magic to fulfill his side of the contract (430–66), causes Gawain to set out a year later to seek what he must believe to be certain death.[35]

It should not surprise us, then, that there is no challenge from within *The Franklin's Tale* to the validity of Dorigen's oath to Aurelius. Dorigen does not attempt to argue the invalidity of her pledge, despite being aware that the disappearance of the rocks "is agayns the proces of nature" (1345). Similarly, Aurelius's actions suggest that he believes a pledge was made, albeit one intended to be impossible to fulfill, and he reminds Dorigen of the serious form of her oath when he announces that he has fulfilled its terms: "And in myn hand youre trouthe plighten ye / To love me best—God woot, ye seyde so" (1328–29). Furthermore, Arveragus considers neither the intention behind Dorigen's oath nor the prior claim of her marriage-*trouthe* to him in his assessment of Dorigen's dilemma. Such considerations are of little relevance to this *gentil* romance knight.

Twenty-five years ago, Gaylord surveyed a selection of medieval moral treatises, as part of a discussion of the validity of rash promises, and (not surprisingly) found that their overwhelming judgment was that "rash promises are not to be kept."[36] Gaylord's survey is impressive, if a little incongruous in an essay which maintains that "in the world of courtly romance behavior is not always calibrated by the fine scale of the Church's canons; the characters of *The Franklin's Tale* are situated in Brittany, not Rome, and the sea by which Dorigen complains is not the Vatican's."[37] Gaylord also draws attention to Chaucer's *Tale of Melibee* and its judgments on the justifiable breaking of a *trouthe*.[38] In this tale, Prudence proclaims that it is permissible to break a promise when "the thyng semeth ootherweyes than it was biforn" (VII.1064) and that it is morally mandatory to break one that "be inpossible, or may nat goodly be parfourned or kept" (VII.1229). In a recent book David Aers has made use of Melibee in a discussion of Dorigen's rash promise, suggesting that "Chaucer's romance invites us, in this very different mode, to move towards a similar moral understanding."[39] The key word in Aer's judgment is *invites*; there is room in *The Franklin's Tale* to move to a position in which our values are those of the moral commentaries,[40] but we are certainly not compelled to adopt this viewpoint, and doing so does not solve the problematic aspects of the poem.

Recourse to Boccaccio's *Filocolo*, which contains a source tale of *The Franklin's Tale*, does not help to settle conclusively the degree to which Dorigen's oath to Aurelius is binding.[41] Unlike *The Franklin's Tale*, the tale that Menedon tells is followed by a debate in which a judgment is given by Fiammetta: the marriage pledge takes legal precedence over the lady's promise to the lover, which is judged to be invalid; and the lady's husband, who was prepared to give up his honour, is the most *fre*. It is not reasonable, however, simply to import judgments on the validity of oaths from Boccaccio's tale and apply them to Chaucer's work. Chaucer may have taken the question from Boccaccio, but he did not take the answer; for the reader to supply the answer from *II Filocolo* provides a possible solution, but not the definitive one. Even if a rash promise is invalid in the *Filocolo* or in the medieval legal system, it does not simply follow that it is equally invalid in *The Franklin's Tale*.

The Franklin's Tale does not allow one to prove conclusively that Dorigen's oath to Aurelius is invalid because it was made "in pley"; it was also made "by heighe God above," and the former statement does not automatically cancel out the latter. The reader is certainly encouraged to question the validity of this oath, but in doing so one realizes that the answer will vary according to the value system that informs one's judgment, and the tale supports several. Encouragement can be found in the text for readings from viewpoints informed by the dictates of Church doctrine, or legal theory, or common sense, or the generic expectations of romance tales. Chaucer deliberately does not allow any one of these value-systems to have overbearing authority, however, and the reader should not be lured into doing so against the directive of the tale. To deal with this problematic situation by denying the ambiguous potential of Dorigen's pledge to Aurelius, by making Aurelius the villain of the piece, or by deciding that Dorigen and Arveragus are fools is to resort to a simplification of the text.

* * *

In order to fulfill the task that Dorigen has set, Aurelius hires a clerk who creates the illusion that the rocks have been removed. Dorigen is faced with a dilemma that she has to deal with alone, because Arveragus is "out of towne" (1351). She is caught between an idealistic impulse toward choosing death over dishonor and her unwillingness to commit suicide. Her anguish is poignantly described, and again one is encouraged to react to her as to a human character.[42] Her lament takes the form of a list of *exempla*, consisting mostly of noble women who committed suicide in the face of a threat to their honor.[43] We see that as a wife in a domestic tragedy, it would be stupid of Dorigen to commit suicide because of a pledge she intended to be impossible to fulfill; yet as a woman living by the dictates of a courtly ideal she realizes that it is an expected course of action. Her behavior reflects this tension; instead of committing suicide Dorigen simply talks about it, lamenting for "a day or tweye, / Purposynge evere that she wolde deye" (1457–58). Chaucer gives Dorigen a characteristically courtly mode of expression with which to forestall the need to act in the way that her interpretation of the courtly code insists that she ought to behave.[44]

Dorigen makes no decision, and her helplessness results in Arveragus's imposition of mastery. When she tells Arveragus of the dilemma, he quickly decides that Dorigen must honor her pledge to Aurelius because, as he says, "Trouthe is the hyeste thyng that man may kepe" (1479). As Arveragus speaks these words the regular rhythm of his speech is fractured by a sudden outburst of weeping, and he forbids Dorigen—on pain of death—to tell anyone about her contract with Aurelius (1480–86). Arveragus no longer calmly expounds an ideal; now he is fearful that his wife's adultery will become public knowledge. Arveragus's concern that his wife keep her word (1472–79) is replaced by language in which *his* suffering and welfare are the principal concerns; one has "I wol my wo endure" (1484) where, before his outburst, one may have expected him to say to Dorigen, "Ye shul youre wo endure."[45]

Arveragus can easily be criticized for imposing mastery despite his earlier promise not to do so. *The Franklin's Tale*, however, provides evidence that can excuse Arveragus from the charge of *trouthe*-breaking. His promise to Dorigen—"That nevere in al his lyf he, day ne nyght, / Ne sholde upon hym take no maistrie" (746–47)—has appended to it the qualifying clause" Agayn hir wyl" (748). By refusing to make a decision, Dorigen can be seen to *wyl* a transfer of responsibility and power to her husband. She adopts the position of a subservient wife, and Arveragus takes on the role of master with her (unspoken) consent.[46] Dorigen clearly desires to be told what to do at this point in the tale; thus, by making a decision for her, Arveragus follows "hir wyl in al" (749), as he has pledged. To recognize that the text provides evidence which allows Arveragus to be excused from the charge of *trouthe*-breaking is not, of course, to discover *the* way to interpret Arveragus's actions. It is crucial to accept, however, that the tale deliberately provides us with support for two contrary positions. Whichever reading we favor, we need to be conscious that we are making a choice between a pair of options. *The Franklin's Tale* allows one to criticize Arveragus for breaking his *trouthe*, but it also allows one to decide that Dorigen wishes him to adopt *maistrie* as a way of overcoming her inability to make a decision.

Arveragus's emotional outburst draws attention to the existence of different kinds of *trouthe*, and Stephen Knight rightly identifies this moment as a watershed in the poem:[47] it is the point where the consequences of the *trouthe*-pledgings come home to roost. Although "Trouthe is the hyeste thyng that man may kepe" is a noble sentiment, it is predicated on the assumption that there is only a single *trouthe* and that one knows what it is. The situation in *The Franklin's Tale* is more complicated than this. In order for Dorigen to keep her pledge to Aurelius and remain faithful to her husband's conception of *trouthe*, she would have to break her vow to be a faithful wife; for Arveragus to remain true to his interpretation of *trouthe*, he will have to compel his wife to be an unwilling adulteress. It is a delightfully constructed paradox: in an effort to keep *trouthe* they would have to break *trouthe*; to avoid dishonor they would have to suffer dishonor.

Having demonstrat d that the truth of the situation depends on the viewpoint from which one approaches it—and the tale allows several viewpoints—Chaucer brings the tale to a conclusion in which no one is punished. Dorigen and Aurelius had arranged to meet in a garden, a common romance setting strongly associated with idealized love relationships. Instead, they meet in a crowded street, a setting much more closely allied with the world of everyday experience and one which makes a human response to the romance dilemma more appropriate. Impressed by Arveragus's *gentillesse* and moved by Dorigen's distress, Aurelius decides to release Dorigen from her pledge. In turn, the Clerk frees Aurelius from his promise to pay one thousand pounds for the illusion, making the point that a clerk can perform a *gentil* deed as well as a knight or a squire. Whatever mistakes one decides that the various characters make, and whatever degree of ignobility or sinfulness one attaches to them, the tale does not finally censure any of the characters. The forgiving nature of this closure echoes the Franklin's earlier opinions that man must inevitably "dooth or seith somtyme amys" (780) and that "On every wrong a man may nat be wreken" (784).

The Franklin's voice reemerges as the dominant one at the end of the tale, and it is clear that for him, the important question raised by the narrative concerns a definition of *fredom* and the nature of *gentillesse*. The Franklin's final question—"Which was the mooste fre, as thynketh yow?" (1622)—asks the reader to make a decision about relative degrees of *fredom*, although the question is insufficient as a conclusion to the problems of the tale. If *The Franklin's Tale* had no question posed at its end, there is nothing in it to point inevitably to the central issue being "Which was the mooste fre." There is, for example, a strong case for claiming that the center of attention is Dorigen and Arveragus's marital relationship and the test to which it is put.[48] The concluding question could just have easily have been asked about that. What has happened to the relationship of Dorigen and Arveragus is of interest to the Franklin only insofar as it is essential to a demonstration of *gentillesse*. The Franklin signals that he is giving nothing more on the marriage of Dorigen and Arveragus by the question "What sholde I lenger of this cas endyte?" (1550) and the statement "Of thise two folk ye gete of me namoore" (1556). We recognize that the question about *fredom* is an obvious one for the Franklin to ask, given the emphasis on *libertee* earlier in the tale, but we see too that this question ignores much that is problematic in the poem.

The Franklin's final question has no single answer, which becomes clear as one tries to answer it. A case can be made for each of the principal characters being the one who is the most *fre*, although Aurelius or the Clerk tend to receive more support than do Dorigen or Arveragus. For example, Huppé has argued that only the Clerk displays unambiguous generosity,[49] but the tale does allow the Clerk to be seen as less than totally *gentil*. He was hired "To remoeven alle the rokkes of Britayne, / And eek from Gerounde to the mouth of Sayne" (1221–22), but what he actually does is to create the illusion that they are gone, although Huppé is adamant that the Clerk completes his side of the contract because "the Squire is perfectly aware that he is hiring an illusionist."[50] Huppé goes on to argue that Aurelius's generosity is qualified because his claim to have fulfilled his task is knowingly based on a deception, a temporary illusion. This is true, but there is evidence in the text which tempts one to decide that Aurelius is in compliance with Dorigen's demand that "ther nys no stoon ysene."[51] *The Franklin's Tale* encourages finally a generous response to its characters. Whoever one decides is the most *fre* does not need to triumph at the cost of the harsh condemnation of the other characters.

It is the *second* part of the Franklin's question—"as thynketh yow"—that is most important to the operation of *The Franklin's Tale*. This poem is much less concerned with settling problems of comparative generosity than with the decision-making process itself and with the bearing that "as thynketh yow" has on one's assessment of evidence. *The Franklin's Tale* ends with a question, but it provides contradictory evidence with which to arrive at an answer. There is a temptation to cope with this situation by explaining away all dissenting evidence, but to do this is to simplify the poem instead of facing its contradictions and attempting to understand why they exist. The Franklin's concern with *gentillesse* is clearly reflected in what he decides the tale is about, but the text also makes the reader conscious that his or her own reading is filtered through a set of personal desires and interpretative methods. *The Franklin's Tale* forces one to consider the process by which readers, both in the tale and of the tale, draw their conclusions.[52] It can lead the reader to consider what persuades one to favor a particular set of evidence from the text over another; in this sense, the tale becomes a mirror that can reflect the reader's own literary, social, and moral value systems as surely as the concluding question exposes those of the Franklin.

The principal questions generated by *The Franklin's Tale* center on the testing of relationships: between *gentil* and non-*gentil*; between the intention of a *trouthe* and the unintended form it can take when put into words; between the ideal and the practical; between the public and the private; and, perhaps most important, between the reader and the text.

In attempting to understand these relationships one recognizes that the evidence in the tale allows for different readings to be made. A reading of *The Franklin's Tale* that attempts to solve its problematic elements by applying the dictates of a single value system—be that canon law, or civil law, or the expectations of the romance genre—is never completely satisfactory.[53] Instead, *The Franklin's Tale* makes one aware of the evaluation and selection of information that occurs in an interpretative process and of the crucial bearing that "as thynketh yow" has on the conclusions at which one finally arrives.

Notes

I have benefited greatly from the comments of Professors C. David Benson, Hoyt N. Duggan, Robert M. Jordan, A. C. Spearing, and Derek Pearsall on successive drafts of this article. I would like to thank them for being so generous with their advice and with their time.

1. Unless otherwise noted, quotations from Chaucer's work are taken from Larry D. Benson, gen. ed., *The Riverside Chaucer*, 3d ed. (Boston: Houghton Mifflin, 1987).
2. Until recently the dominant view has been that the Franklin was of non-*gentil* status, that he was aspiring above his station, and that this was central to an understanding of his character and his tale. See, for example, R. M. Lumiansky, *Of Sondry Folk: The Dramatic Principle in the* Canterbury Tales (Austin: University of Texas Press, 1955), 182–93; and D. W. Robertson, Jr., *A Preface to Chaucer* (Princeton: Princeton University Press, 1962), 276, 470–72. For an early affirmation of the Franklin's *gentil* status, see G. H. Gerould, "The Social Status of Chaucer's Franklin," *PMLA* 41 (1926): 262–79; and for a recent one, see Henrik Specht, *Chaucer's Franklin in the* Canterbury Tales: *The Social and Literary Background of a Chaucerian Character* (Copenhagen: Akademisk Forlag, 1981). For a qualification to Specht's position, see Nigel Saul, "The Social Status of Chaucer's Franklin: A Reconsideration," *Medium Ævum* 52 (1983): 10–26.
3. For Robert B. Burlin, the tale contains "the ever-present personality of the Franklin." *Chaucerian Fiction* (Princeton: Princeton University Press, 1977), 202.
4. See also lines 953, 1085–86, 1165, 1243, 1249, and 1466–68. Susan Wittig discusses similar formulaic phrases in *Stylistic and Narrative Structures in the Middle English Romance* (Austin: University of Texas Press, 1978), chapter 2. See especially her comments concerning "motifemes of the *discours*" (61–62). The principal example of first-person narration from the main part of the tale that encourages one to think of the Franklin as the speaker is "I ne kan no termes of astrologye" (1266), said just before a passage full of technical astrological vocabulary. See also the third-person narration at 1129–34 and 1493–98.
5. Stephen Knight points out that lines 761–816 recall the narrative voice of the

Franklin's Prologue. "Rhetoric and Poetry in the Franklin's Tale," *Chaucer Review* 4 (1969): 19–20.

6. Other formulaic first-person narrative phrases can be found at lines 761, 770, 777, 807, 814–15, 1550, 1556, 1621, and 1624.

7. David Lawton, *Chaucer's Narrators* (Cambridge: Brewer, 1985), 98. Earlier in this book Lawton states that "no argument for a dramatically conceived narrator would restrict itself to passages of explicit first-person narratorial activity, but . . . no such argument could possibly be acceptable if it failed to account for all such passages" (8).

8. Lawton, 98. On the rhetorical complexity of *The Franklin's Tale*, see also Benjamin S. Harrison, "The Rhetorical Inconsistency of Chaucer's Franklin," *Studies in Philology* 32 (1935): 55–61. For a more recent treatment of Chaucer's use of rhetoric, see Knight, 14–30.

9. C. David Benson makes a forceful argument against the assumption that the tales are told in the voices of the pilgrims after whom they are named. *Chaucer's Drama of Style* (Chapel Hill: University of North Carolina Press, 1986).

10. See, for example, Robert B. Burlin, "The Art of Chaucer's Franklin," *Neophilologus* 51 (1967): 61–62. See also Knight, for whom this passage is a reminder of the "basically bathetic style" of the teller of the tale (29).

11. Arthur Gilman, ed., *The Poetical Works of Geoffrey Chaucer*, 3 vols. (Boston: Houghton, Osgood, 1879), 2:40.

12. W. W. Skeat, ed., *Complete Works of Geoffrey Chaucer*, 6 vols. (Oxford: Clarendon Press, 1894–1900), 5:390.

13. John Matthews Manly, ed., *The Canterbury Tales by Geoffrey Chaucer* (New York: Holt, 1928), 608.

14. F. N. Robinson, ed., *The Complete Works of Geoffrey Chaucer* (Boston: Houghton Mifflin, 1933), 829; 2d ed. (1957), 724.

15. Harrison, 55–61. References to Lydgate are from Henry Bergen, ed., *Lydgate's Troy Book*, Part III, E.E.T.S. e.s. 106 (London: Oxford University Press, 1910).

16. References are from John Norton-Smith, ed., *The Kingis Quair* (Oxford: The Clarendon Press, 1971).

17. A variation of this, also from *The Knight's Tale*, occurs when Theseus explains a proverb in nonproverbial form:

> "That oon of you, al be hym looth or lief,
> He moot go pipen in an yvy leef;
> This is to seyn, she may nat now han bothe,
> Al be ye never so jalouse ne so wrothe." (I.1837–40)

18. See also *The Squire's Tale*, 160–65.

19. The Prioress also uses "this is to seyn" to amplify a point (VII. 495–501).

20. This survey is not exhaustive. I refer to the following editions: Thomas Tyrwhitt, ed., *The Canterbury Tales of Chaucer*, 5 vols. (London: Payne, 1775–78; rpt. New York: AMS, 1972); Gilman; Richard Morris, ed., *The Poetical Works of Geoffrey Chaucer*, 6 vols., rev. ed. (London: Bell, 1882); Skeat; Arthur Burrell, ed., *Chaucer's Canterbury Tales for the Modern Reader*, Everyman's Library (London: Dent, 1908); Manly; Robinson; Vincent F. Hopper, ed., *Chaucer's Canterbury Tales (selected): An Interlinear Translation* (New York: Barron's, 1948); E. Talbot Donaldson, ed., *Chaucer's Poetry: An Anthology for the*

Modern Reader (New York: Roland Press, 1958; 2d ed., 1975); Albert C. Baugh, ed., *Chaucer's Major Poetry* (New York: Appleton-Century-Crofts, 1963); Robert A. Pratt, ed., *Selections from the Tales of Canterbury and Short Poems* (Boston: Houghton Mifflin, 1966); John H. Fisher, ed., *The Complete Poetry and Prose of Geoffrey Chaucer* (New York: Holt, Rinehart and Winston, 1977); N. F. Blake, ed., *The Canterbury Tales by Geoffrey Chaucer. Edited from the Hengwrt Manuscript* (London: Arnold, 1980); Larry D. Benson.

21. The other principal passages of third-person narration that seem to reveal something about the Franklin are at 1129–34 and 1493–98.

22. For a further discussion of the structure of this opening passage, see Jill Mann, "Chaucerian Themes and Style in the *Franklin's Tale*," *The New Pelican Guide to English Literature, vol. I, Part I, Medieval Literature: Chaucer and the Alliterative Tradition*, ed. Boris Ford (Harmondsworth: Penguin, 1982), 133–40.

23. Gervase Mathew, *The Court of Richard II* (London: Murray, 1968), 192. Mathew further suggests that it "was the fashion at [the court of Richard II] to conceive of marriage in terms of love-service and of *amor courtois*. This had been stressed by the marriages of the Black Prince with Joan of Kent, of John of Gaunt with Blanche of Lancaster, and of Richard II with Anne of Luxembourg" (124).

24. For one such reading, see Paul Edward Gray, "Synthesis and the Double Standard in the Franklin's Tale," *Texas Studies in Literature and Language* 7 (1965): 215–18.

25. For Burlin, the characters of *The Franklin's Tale* are all "elegant but artificial puppets assembled by the Franklin from bits of faded romance, clichés of character, and conventions of courtly manner" (*Chaucerian Fiction*, 202).

26. Knight points out that "Dorigen is the main agent of emotion in the poem and . . . her noble and highly wrought personality is embodied in noble and highly wrought poetry" (22). Gray reduces Dorigen's suffering to a rejection of the virtue of *pacience* for the vice of impatience (218).

27. Derek Pearsall, *The Canterbury Tales* (London: Allen and Unwin, 1985), 152.

28. This characteristic of qualifying and qualified statements also occurs in the "wordes of the Frankeleyn to the Squier": " 'I preise wel thy wit,' / Quod the Frankeleyn, '*considerynge thy yowthe*' " (674–75); " 'ther is noon that is heere / Of eloquence that shal be thy peere, / If that thou lyve' " (677–79) [my italics]. See Marie Neville, "The Function of the *Squire's Tale* in the Canterbury Scheme," *Journal of English and German Philology* 50 (1951): 170.

29. The image of the bursting heart appears many times in Chaucer's work, including twice more in *The Franklin's Tale* (973, 1056).

30. The rocks function both as a physical danger to shipping and as a symbol of all those things that lie outside Dorigen's control. For a fuller treatment of their symbolic potential, see Charles A. Owen, Jr., "The Crucial Passages in Five of the *Canterbury Tales*: A Study in Irony and Symbol," *Journal of English and German Philology* 52 (1953): 295–97.

31. The range of meanings for *knyt* given in the *MED* indicates that it can apply to contracts other than marriage. Aurelius uses *knyt* later in *The Franklin's Tale* to describe the contract between himself and the clerk: "This bargayn is ful dryve, for we been knyt" (1230).

32. Alan T. Gaylord, "The Promises in *The Franklin's Tale,*" *English Literary History* 31 (1964): 347.

33. Gerald Morgan, "Boccaccio's *Filocolo* and the Moral Argument of *The Franklin's Tale,*" *Chaucer Review* 20 (1986): 292. Morgan discusses this parallelism in a passage largely concerned with medieval definitions of a vow, an oath, and a promise, drawn principally from the *Summa Theologiae* of Thomas Aquinas. In brief, a *vow* is a pledge made to God; an *oath* is a pledge "made between man and man by appeal to a greater power"; and a *promise* is a declaration between men, without God being invoked as a witness ("Boccaccio's *Filocolo,*" 290–91; Morgan refers to *ST* 2a 2ae). Under such definitions, two of Dorigen's pledges—to be a true wife to Arveragus and to love Aurelius if he removes the rocks—are oaths, as is the Clerk's refusal to Aurelius to take less than a thousand pounds; Dorigen and Arveragus's marriage pledges are promises, as is Aurelius's pledge to pay the Clerk his requested fee. While Chaucer may not have these specific definitions in mind, they do help to stress that the verbal construction of Dorigen's playful pledge is that of a serious oath.

34. For recent discussions of the legal grounds for nullifying a rash promise, see C. McDonald, "The Perversion of the Law in Robert Henryson's Fable of *The Fox, the Wolf, and the Husbandman,*" *Medium Ævum* 49 (1980): 244–53; and R. J. Blanch and J. Wasserman, "Medieval Contracts and Covenants: The Legal Coloring of *Sir Gawain and the Green Knight,*" *Neophilologus* 68 (1984): 598–610.

35. All references to the *Gawain*-poet are from M. Andrew and R. Waldron, eds., *The Poems of the Pearl Manuscript* (London: Arnold, 1978). See also the second Christmas game, at Bertilak's castle, where the seeming playfulness of the contract belies the seriousness of the test: 1112ff; 1404–9.

36. Gaylord, 352. His sources include the following: Robert of Brunne, *Handlyng Synne*; *Le Manual des Pechiez*; the *Book of Vices and Virtues*; *Agenbite of Inwyt*; Augustine, *Contra Mendacium*; Ambrose, *De Officiis Ministrorum*; the *Somme le Roi*; the *Miroir du Monde*; Cicero, *De Officiis*; John of Salisbury, *Policraticus*; Isidore of Seville, *Sententiae*; Gratian, *Decretum*; Ivo of Chartres, *Decretum*; Hugh of St. Victor, *De Sacramentis*; Peter Lombard, *Sententiae*; Thomas Aquinas, *Summa Theologiae*.

37. Gaylord, 333. More surprising, perhaps, is a substantial discussion of rash promises in an essay which argues that Dorigen does not make a promise of *any* sort (347, 356–57).

38. Gaylord, 355–56.

39. David Aers, *Chaucer* (Brighton: Harvester, 1986), 88.

40. For an example of such a reading, see D. W. Robertson, Jr., "Chaucer's Franklin and his Tale," *Costerus* n.s. 1 (1974): 1–26 (especially 23).

41. All references to Boccaccio's *Filocolo* (Book IV, sections 31–34) are from Donald Cheney, trans., *Il Filocolo* (New York: Garland, 1985), 254–66.

42. Gerald Morgan does not believe that Dorigen's complaint is indicative of "the state of mind of the heroine," and he is adamant that Chaucer has no interest in "the psychological states" of the characters in *The Franklin's Tale*. "A Defence of Dorigen's Complaint," *Medium Ævum* 46 (1977): 77.

43. For a fuller discussion of the composition and purpose of this list, see James Sledd, "Dorigen's Complaint," *Modern Philology* 45 (1947): 36–45. See also

W. F. Bryan and G. Dempster, eds., *Sources and Analogues of Chaucer's* Canterbury Tales (Chicago: University of Chicago Press, 1941), 395–97.

44. See also Aurelius's complaint that he will suffer a "sodayn deeth horrible" (1010) before pining for two years or more, for another example of Chaucer playing with the extravagance of romance rhetoric.

45. Aers has pointed to the self-centered language of Arveragus when faced with his wife's dilemma. *Chaucer, Langland, and the Creative Imagination* (London: Routledge & Kegan Paul, 1980), 166. See also Gaylord, 344. There is a similar occurrence in *Troilus and Criseyde*, Book IV, where Troilus's lament that Criseyde will be exchanged for Antenor shows little pity for her. Troilus says, "O my Criseyde, O lady sovereigne / Of thilke woful soule that thus crieth, / Who shal now yeven comfort to my peyne?" (IV.316–18), where one might expect to find "Who shal now yeven comfort to *youre* peyne?" The Harley 1239 MS does read "youre peyne," and Arch. Selden B.24 reads "thy peyne," indicating perhaps that these scribes were troubled by Troilus's self-centered language; Corpus Christi Coll. 61 and eight other MSS read "the peyne" (see the Textual Note in *The Riverside Chaucer*, 3d ed.).

46. Sledd has also noted that "[Dorigen] has tacitly placed the decision in [Arveragus's] hands" (39–40).

47. Knight, 28.

48. For such a claim, see Robert Kaske, "Chaucer's Marriage Group," in *Chaucer The Love Poet*, ed. J. Mitchell and W. Provost (Athens: University of Georgia Press, 1973), 62–65.

49. Bernard F. Huppé, *A Reading of the Canterbury Tales*, rev. ed. (Albany: State University of New York Press, 1967), 173.

50. Huppé, 173–74.

51. I am not suggesting that one should credit Aurelius with the conscious exploitation of the ambiguity inherent in Dorigen's pledge to him. In fact, he says that the rocks are "aweye" (1338), not no longer "ysene." For the opinion that Aurelius is consciously changing Dorigen's pledge from one made "in pley" to a serious promise, see Judith Ferster, "Interpretation and Imitation in Chaucer's Franklin's Tale," in *Medieval Literature: Criticism, Ideology, and History*, ed. David Aers (New York: St. Martins, 1986): 160.

52. Ferster applies "modern phenomenological hermeneutics" to the interpretation of *The Franklin's Tale* (149) and concentrates on how characters in the tale interpret and sometimes redefine the words and actions of other characters.

53. Several critics have remarked on the air of dissatisfaction surrounding the answers to the tale's final question. See, for example, W. H. Schofield, "Chaucer's Franklin's Tale," *PMLA* 16 (1901): 446–47, and Morton W. Bloomfield, "The Franklin's Tale: A Story of Unanswered Questions," in *Acts of Interpretation: Essays on Medieval and Renaissance Literature in Honor of E. Talbot Donaldson*, eds. Mary J. Carruthers and Elizabeth D. Kirk (Norman: Pilgrim, 1982), 198.

Piety, Politics, and Social Commitment in Capgrave's Life of St. Katherine

KAREN A. WINSTEAD

John Capgrave's *Life of St. Katherine* (c. 1445) is the most complex version of the Katherine of Alexandria legend in vernacular hagiography; indeed, it is one of the most intricate renderings of any saint's life.[1] In five books comprising 8,624 rhyme royal lines, Capgrave provides a comprehensive biography of the saint, from her birth to her death at the hands of the pagan Emperor Maxentius. Not content with merely reporting the events of his protagonist's life, he also furnishes historical background, develops minor characters, and lingers over ceremonies and pageants. In addition, he explores his characters' motivations and dilemmas, using the saint's legend to examine the moral conflicts among political, social, and spiritual obligations. Although several other hagiographers composed lengthy accounts of Katherine's life during the fourteenth and fifteenth centuries, no surviving *vita* approaches Capgrave's detailed embellishment of the legend or his painstaking characterization. His narrative offers invaluable insight into both the private and the public preoccupations of fifteenth-century religious culture.

Surprisingly, Capgrave's extraordinary virgin-martyr legend attracted almost no scholarly attention until the mid-1970s. Before that time, surveys of Middle English literature and studies of hagiography tended to dismiss it as a work of little interest or value. While admitting that the *Life of St. Katherine* was not without merit, G. H. Gerould lamented that Capgrave "had not the power of seizing the great moments of a story in epic fashion and subordinating unnecessary detail."[2] Concurring with F. J. Furnivall, who labeled the *Life* "worthless," H. S. Bennett deplored "the *longueurs* of the narrative, the credulous recital of the impossible, and the long-drawn-out descriptions of torture and mutilation."[3] Fortunately, over the past two decades several critics have offered illuminating discussions of the work's style, sources, structure, and characterization.[4]

Medievalia et Humanistica, New Series, Number 17 (Paul Maurice Clogan, ed.) Rowman & Littlefield Publishers, Inc.

Yet even recent studies have largely ignored the narrative's most revolutionary dimension: its definition of sainthood.

Notwithstanding the *Life of St. Katherine*'s unusual structure and characterization, most critics have not doubted that it upholds the same model of virtue that hagiographers had celebrated since late antiquity. In fact, Thomas J. Heffernan, the only scholar to deal at any length with Capgrave's conception of sanctity, finds nothing innovative about the *Life of St. Katherine*.[5] In his *Sacred Biography*, Heffernan characterizes Capgrave as a nostalgic figure who, during a time of social and intellectual upheaval, used the genre of sacred biography to "nurture ancient cherished ideals which fell about his feet one after another."[6] Citing a number of conventional rhetorical devices and theological commonplaces in the prologue to the *Life of St. Katherine*, he maintains that Capgrave was an old-fashioned hagiographer who, in the tradition of "those revered intellectual ancestors Augustine, Jerome, Benedict, de Voragine, and Tynemouth," promoted a purely conventional ideal of sainthood. "[W]holly nurtured by medieval ideologies despite the great creedal rift begun at the end of the fourteenth century," the Augustinian friar represents for Heffernan "a last burst of bloom from a withered stock."[7]

This study will argue that Capgrave was far from the backward-looking cleric Heffernan envisages. Although he freely uses hagiographical commonplaces, he also transforms or discards many of the time-honored conventions of sacred biography. In so doing, he constructs a radically new kind of saint's life, one which acknowledges the saint's human limitations and endorses her involvement in the world. Unlike most earlier hagiographers, who displayed little interest in the saint's position in society, Capgrave depicts his heroine as a public figure with responsibilities she cannot casually set aside in pursuit of spiritual perfection. The story of her martyrdom unfolds in a world peopled with characters who are motivated by political ambitions and private desires instead of inherent goodness or villainy. Indeed, the saint's own point of view is a limited one, shaped by personal experience rather than divine grace. In the following pages, I will examine the new paradigm of sainthood which emerges in the *Life of St. Katherine*, then consider factors which may have induced Capgrave, along with other fifteenth-century writers, to depart from the modes of representing saints which had become standard in Middle English hagiography. Among the most important of these factors, I will argue, was the hagiographers' need to appeal to the conservative, middle-class women and men who were among the foremost consumers of pious literature in the late Middle Ages.

Traditional Models

Before considering Capgrave's unusual appropriation of hagiographical conventions, it would be useful to review some of the patterns and motifs which medieval English readers probably would have expected to encounter in legends of St. Katherine, in virgin-martyr legends, and in saints' lives generally. A quintessential feature of martyr legends, as Charles F. Altman demonstrated well over a decade ago, is that they are structured around a diametrical opposition between virtue and vice, embodied in the struggle between the saints and their persecutors.[8] From the earliest *passiones* onward, characters fell into two distinct groups—one aligned with the persecutor, the other with the saint—and "[t]he major function of the *passio*," Altman noted, was "to play up the discontinuity between the two groups."[9] Given their standard plots, which revolve around the confrontation between saints and secular authorities, the central conflict of *passiones* was necessarily a public one.[10] Nevertheless, characters and events were rarely described in social, political, economic, or historical terms. This indifference to worldly particulars is by no means surprising, since a plethora of details would only undermine one of the principal goals of hagiography: to demonstrate how the martyr's passion reenacts Christ's own passion and so embodies the archetypal struggle between Good and Evil, God and the Devil, the City of God and the City of Man.

The saint's rejection of society characterized legends of martyrdom throughout the Middle Ages, but it became especially pronounced in legends composed for the edification of the laity during the thirteenth and fourteenth centuries. In Jacobus a Voragine's widely read *Legenda aurea*, legends of confessors and martyrs alike manifested a sharp opposition between saints and the world.[11] By insisting upon his protagonists' detachment from society and their superiority to ordinary mortals, Jacobus was able to edify the laity while simultaneously affirming the preeminence of clerical over secular values and acclaiming the triumph of the church over the secular state. Omnipotent and invulnerable, Jacobus's protagonists were presented to the faithful as puissant intercessors, champions of the church to be admired rather than imitated. Their staunch commitment to celibacy and their contempt for secular institutions provided a powerful endorsement of clerical ideals. Moreover, the spectacular miracles wrought by these charismatic *milites christi* only confirmed the profound chasm which separated God's chosen from ordinary laymen and laywomen. With justice, Alain Boureau has observed, "La *Légende dorée* n'offre pas au fidèle un modèle direct de piété ni de sagesse chrétienne; elle l'invite à admirer l'effort d'une Église militante qui médiatise les desseins providentiels."[12]

The same austere conception of sainthood that characterizes the *Legenda aurea* pervades Middle English hagiography of the late thirteenth and fourteenth centuries, and it finds some of its most extreme expres-

sions in virgin-martyr legends.[13] In relating the stories of women who
choose to die rather than to marry or to sacrifice to the pagan gods,
hagiographers placed particular emphasis on their protagonists' contempt for society.[14] Repeatedly, the virgins admonish those around them
to discard their human modes of perceiving and to set their thoughts on
that "bettre lif in oother place."[15] Sharp-tongued, confident, and miracu-
lously impervious to pain, they handily reduce their bewildered foes to
hapless buffoons. Not only do these obstreperous maidens heap abuse
upon their persecutors but also scorn anyone who is reluctant to embrace
death, and even sympathetic bystanders are not spared their jibes.[16]

Like most Middle English virgin-martyr legends of the time, late-
thirteenth- and fourteenth-century Katherine of Alexandria legends
center on the dramatic encounter between the saint and her persecutor.
Perhaps influenced by the *Legenda aurea* or by other late-medieval *abbrev-
iationes*, most hagiographers simplified the legend as it had evolved in
Latin *passiones* by the eleventh century and as it appeared in the early-
thirteenth-century *Seinte Katerine*.[17] In the process, they divested the story
of all historical and political references. For example, the enormously
popular "Vulgate" *passio* and its derivatives begin by describing the
conflict between Maxentius and Constantine, which ultimately leads to
Maxentius's arrival in Alexandria and Katherine's martyrdom; all surviving Middle English legends of the late thirteenth and fourteenth centuries, however, omit this historical introduction. Whereas in the *passiones*
and *Seinte Katerine* Katherine is the queen of Alexandria, in the adapta-
tions of the *South English Legendary*, the *North English Legendary*, and the
Auchinleck manuscript she is merely a young princess who leaves her
father's palace to challenge Maxentius. The aim of these vernacular lives
is to demonstrate the impotence of evil by showing how a mere girl
frustrates and humiliates her powerful captor: not only does she con-
found the wisest men in his realm with her learning and emerge un-
scathed from a variety of exotic tortures but also converts the emperor's
wife and his dearest friend. Unable to daunt or harm his foe, Maxentius
can only order her execution, conceding his own defeat: "wikked woman,
wo þe be! / No langer sal þou turment me."[18]

Sanctity and Public Responsibility

Capgrave's *Life of St. Katherine* would certainly have surprised medieval
readers whose preconceptions about virgin-martyr legends had been
formed by the *Legenda aurea,* the *South English Legendary,* or such fourteenth-century classics as Chaucer's *Second Nun's Tale.* To begin with,

Capgrave displays an extraordinary interest in the political, historical, and personal frameworks of the saint's martyrdom. Drawing upon a late Latin *vita* instead of the *passiones* used by most previous adapters of the legend, he tells of Katherine's education, conversion by the hermit Adrian, mystical marriage to Christ, and brief reign as queen of Alexandria.[19] Before even introducing his protagonist, however, he describes the popular reign of her father, Costus, and explains the political and economic importance of the two principal cities of Costus's realm, Alexandria and Amalek (1.57–154). Later he offers a lengthy account of the achievements of previous rulers of Alexandria (1.533–693). Detailed descriptions of pageants, historical digressions based on *cronycles* and other *olde bookis,* and references to specific people, places, and local customs further establish the saint's martyrdom as an event in human history as well as in salvation or church history.[20] By supplying such abundant information about people, places, and events Capgrave does not merely furnish a backdrop for his story. As we will see, the narrative's conflicts and characters, both major and minor, are conditioned by the historical and political setting in which the action takes place.

In Capgrave's hands, the two conventional conflicts of virgin-martyr legends—the threat to the saint's chastity and the challenge to her faith—become political and social issues. In dramatizing the first of these conflicts, Capgrave not only blurs the classic opposition between right and wrong but also presents a compelling case against his protagonist. Having been formulated before her conversion, Katherine's resolution to remain celibate reflects her personal preference rather than religious commitment. Medieval readers familiar with the standard themes of virgin-martyr legends might have been predisposed to overlook this and to consider the pressure Katherine's advisers and mother bring upon her to marry to be a form of religious persecution. Accustomed to the diametrical structure of martyr legends, they might have been inclined to look upon anyone who opposes Katherine as being a villain. Capgrave raises the issue, however, in a way which discourages such responses. Having just described the saint's virtues, he abruptly introduces a new topic:

> What is a lond whan it hath non hed?
> The lawes are not kepte, the lond is desolate,
> The hertys hangyng as heuy as leed,
> The commouns grutchynge and euere at debate,
> There is kepte no revle, ne kepte noon astate. (1.848–52)

In an astonishing departure from tradition, Capgrave voices these sentiments—sentiments which any fifteenth-century reader would surely have endorsed—to introduce the complaints of his protagonist's critics. De-

spite his earlier praise of the saint, he presents undeniable evidence in
the parliament, which convenes in Book 2 to urge Katherine to marry,
that all is not well under Katherine's rule. One subject charges that he
has lost a thousand pounds in the short time since King Costus died.
Another claims that people brawl and flout the law in every town. The
queen, her lords lament, does nothing but sit in her gardens and read;
meanwhile, thieves plunder the land and foreign enemies hover about,
waiting for a chance to attack. Katherine, they argue, has a social and
political obligation to set aside her books and marry. A husband would
be able to maintain order and defend the land from invading armies.
Moreover, it is up to her, as an only daughter, to ensure the succession.
Nature, political expediency, and tradition favor marriage; why does she
resist?

Such arguments would not have appeared trivial to a fifteenth-century
audience. They are given additional weight by the fact that Katherine
(silently) acknowledges their validity. Her personal desires, she realizes,
conflict with "my owne lawe, / Whiche I am swore to kepe and to defende"
(2.176–77). Determined to remain single, Katherine argues vigorously
that there is no logical reason why a studious woman should not be a
good monarch; nevertheless, she does not emerge as the clear-cut winner
of the debate. In fact, subsequent events corroborate her opponents'
arguments, as Capgrave reminds us in Book 4. When the Emperor
Maxentius has established himself in the temple of Alexandria and
demands that all citizens make their offerings according to pagan practices, one of Katherine's attendants sadly says:

> Wherfore, madame, now is come that hour
> That was dred tho of youre freendes alle
> Whan that ye wolde receyue no conseillour,
> ffor no thyng that men myght on-to [you] calle.
> I amful soory, for now are lykly to falle
> all tho myshappes whiche that were seyde before.
> Avyse ȝow weel what ye wil doo [þerfore]! (4.463–69)

In this passage, as on many occasions, Capgrave calls attention to the
political repercussions of the saint's decisions. I know of no other Katherine legend which even hints that the saint's martyrdom came about
because her vocation made her an ineffective monarch despite her good
intentions. Instead of rejoicing in the collapse of temporal order, as
hagiographers a century earlier did, Capgrave betrays a certain regret at
the cost of Katherine's heavenly triumph.

To an extent unprecedented in Latin or vernacular versions of the
Katherine legend, Capgrave's *Life of St. Katherine* highlights the political
drama of the saint's martyrdom: "A grete spectacule to the wordly[s] eye,

/ ffor to seen a queen forsake lond and halle, / Soo sodeynly on-to deth for to falle" (5.1748–50). To establish Maxentius as Katherine's political adversary, the extensive introduction to Book 4 (78–357) describes the emperor's ambitions and delineates the series of events which lead to his confrontation with Katherine. In keeping with her public position, Katherine denounces Maxentius on political as well as religious grounds. She acknowledges that his position as emperor entitles him to her respect but declares that he has forfeited it through his behavior (4.555–60). Not only has he offended the "grete[s]t kyng" (4.560) with his pagan ceremonies but also encroached on her authority as queen of Alexandria:

> Sith ȝe arn kyng, and rightwisnesse shulde keepe,
> Whi make ye swiche maystries in other mennes londe,
> Compelle my tenauntes, though þei soore wepe,
> To goo with her offeryngis ryght in her honde,
> With trompes and tabouris be-forn you to stonde,
> With-oute my leue, wyth-oute my licens?
> This is wrong to me, and to god offens. (4.918–24)

With minor details, Capgrave vividly realizes the political world in which the confrontation between emperor and saint takes place. In all previous versions of the legend, Katherine simply stalks up to the imperial throne and denounces Maxentius. Capgrave's Katherine, however, must seek admittance at the temple gates, clear security, and be escorted through the crowds by high-ranking officials, including the emperor's son (4.526–52).

A champion of "ryghtful lawe" (4.511) against an unscrupulous usurper, Capgrave's Katherine presents a striking contrast to the virgin martyrs of thirteenth- and fourteenth-century hagiography, who set themselves against society, denouncing civil authority and reveling in the disintegration of political order. Maxentius, too, is presented in a new light, for the pagan emperor is no longer merely a minion of the devil. Indeed, the *Life of St. Katherine* repeatedly makes a point which was seldom articulated in earlier Middle English legends, namely that the virgin martyr's message of salvation is meant for all people, including her tormentor. For Capgrave, the emperor's actions, though wrong, are by no means damning. What *is* damning is that Maxentius, like Katherine, is a pagan with a choice, and he *chooses* to do wrong. At their first meeting, Katherine insists that the emperor will prosper if he acknowledges God (4.578–881). He responds by arresting her. She beseeches him to convert to Christianity if she wins the debate with his philosophers, but he won't bargain (4.1277–95). She prophesies his imminent defeat at the hands of a Christian leader, his ignominious death, and his eternal damnation, but she insists that these events are not inevitable: "Yet may þou skape al this grete myschauns, / If þou wilt turne the and aske god mercy, / Of thi wikkednesse if þou haue repentauns" (5.1086–88). Again, he ignores her warnings and the miraculous signs corroborating them. Maxentius's wife reiterates this theme, urging the emperor to "Turne thyn bestialte to mannys mynde" and arguing that "The synnes that we dede w[h]il we were ying, / he wil forgeue vs, if we mercy craue; / Aske mercy of hym and thou shal it haue" (5.1447–49). He replies by having her mutilated in his presence and then decapitated. The emperor is given every opportunity to escape the conventional fate of heathen persecutors in hagiography. In the process, the archetypal confrontation between virtue and vice becomes a drama of humans who determine their own fates through moral, political, and religious choices.

Sanctity and Personal Experience

Capgrave's Katherine differs most obviously from conventional virgin martyrs because her point of view is so thoroughly shaped by her personal experience. In Book 2, Capgrave transcends hagiographical issues altogether to explore the private dilemmas of a young woman eloquently depicting her distress at the thought of the changes that marriage would entail: "Shulde I now chaunge my lyf and myn aray, / And trace þe wodes abovte vndir the bow? / I loued it neuere, how shuld I loue it now?" (2.192–94).[21] His Katherine displays a range of ordinary impulses, including confusion and anxiety. As we have seen in the debate over her marriage, she is torn among the conflicting claims of public responsibility, filial obedience, conscience, and personal inclination. Even her conversion is no simple matter, for Capgrave emphasizes that his protagonist stands poised between two grave alternatives: to continue as before or to "leue hir lawe whiche hir lordis alle holde" and "ffalle to a newe for a straunge lordys sake" (3.617–21). Perplexity is not merely a sign of her limited perspective as a pagan. Well after her mystical marriage, when Maxentius arrives in Alexandria and orders her subjects to prove their loyalty to the gods, Katherine is "fful sore astoyned what hir is beste for to doo" (4.498). Although she ultimately decides that commitment to Christ outweighs political expediency, she cannot help wondering why the all-powerful king of heaven would permit his land to be plundered and his people butchered (4.512–13).

In Middle English legends of the late thirteenth and fourteenth centuries, virgin martyrs never suffered doubt or confusion. Even if they received no formal introduction to Christianity, they were illuminated by grace and thus fully conversant in matters of doctrine. Readers might laugh *with* the saints at the simplicity of new converts or the stupidity of pagan persecutors, but they never had the opportunity to laugh *at* them.[22] Capgrave, however, insists that "though god were com as þanne to [Katherine's] herte, / It was fer as yet fro hir knowlechynge" (3.477–78), and he takes advantage of his protagonist's naivete to amuse his readers. A striking example of this occurs at the end of the marriage parliament. After some twelve hundred lines of debate, Katherine's lords are still pestering her to marry; logic has gotten her nowhere, so she changes her tactics and accedes to their demands. She will marry, but, she warns them, "We wil not lyght lower than ye vs layde" (2.1386). Since they themselves have been claiming that she is a perfect woman, she must naturally have a perfect mate (2.1391–93). Her spouse must be the richest, the wisest, the most powerful, handsome, and generous of all men. "I prey yow where dwelleth he," she teases, "So wys, so fayr, so ryche wyth-oute bale, / And of swyche lynage born as we bee?" (1395–97). "[L]ooke weel a-bouthe if ye can fynde swiche oon!" (1414), she challenges them, promising to embrace him gladly (1412)—as long as he is immortal.

> ffor sithe he shal with soo grete labour be sought,
> As me semeth, the game wente sore amys,
> Whan al were weel and al in Ioye and blys
> Sodey[n]ly to fayle and falle fro swiche welthe.
> ⋯⋯⋯⋯⋯⋯⋯⋯⋯⋯⋯⋯⋯⋯⋯⋯
> Therfore ye shul me warrant he shal not deye,
> This lord to whom ye wolde me newe alleye. (1438–41, 1448–49)

Of course Katherine's words mean more than she realizes, and medieval readers would have immediately recognized the queen's ideal spouse as Christ. But to Katherine, the promise is simply a clever ploy designed to defeat her obdurate counselors with their own arguments. She is delighted because she knows that the spouse she has consented to marry will never materialize; readers are delighted because they know that a surprise is in store for her. When a ragged hermit appears out of nowhere one evening and announces that the husband she requested is waiting for her, the joke is on Katherine. It is true that in other renditions of the Katherine legend the saint vows to marry only an immortal, but in these cases she earnestly believes in the spouse she describes.[23] Capgrave stands alone in his playful presentation of his heroine's stipulation.

The hermit Adrian's meeting with Katherine gives Capgrave further opportunity to entertain readers at the saint's expense, for the welcome Katherine accords the Virgin Mary's messenger is far from cordial. She first berates him for intruding into her private quarters (3.415–41). When he tells her that the greatest of all women has sent him to her, she is doubtful: "The wurthyest of alle women we wene þat we bee, / We herd neuere of noon worthiere yit" (3.486–87). Based on her experience, she skeptically muses that Adrian's queen cannot possibly be as mighty as he claims: if she is married she would have to submit to her husband (3.493–95), and if she is single she would still not be free of care, for "Thanne may she make ofte ful moche mone / Right for vexacyon of hir lordes a-bowte— / This knowe we weel, we arn vsed ther-too" (3.497–99). Finally, Katherine asks why such a great queen would send such a shabby messenger (3.526–35); she ought to have sent a delegation. And surely the alleged monarch would require her servants "To clothe more clenly, for wurship of hir hous" (3.578). Even after Adrian tells Katherine about the Virgin Mother of God and lectures her on spiritual clothing, the young queen is full of questions. How can a virgin be a mother? Why would God want to become a man? How is it possible to be man and God at the same time? Capgrave devotes more than a hundred lines to a discussion of these matters (3.635–770).

Knowing more than Katherine, readers might smile at a saint's imperious treatment of a messenger from heaven, at her confident application of human standards to God's mother, and at her confusion over basic articles of the Christian faith. Katherine's bewilderment, however, constitutes a remarkable celebration of ordinary human perceptions within a genre which had long denigrated them. Although Capgrave frequently asserts that human reason cannot comprehend God's designs, by depicting the saint's confusion he acknowledges that human beings cannot be expected to cease thinking as human beings.

Far from challenging readers to transcend their human points of view, Capgrave depicts Katherine's interaction with Christ with a familiarity which affirms the intimacy possible between God and his creatures. Following the tradition of late-medieval affective literature, he presents the Virgin Mary as a fond mother-in-law and her son as an eager suitor.[24] When Christ at first refuses to recognize the unbaptized Katherine, his mother takes the saint by the arm, reassures her, and explains the necessity of baptism in terms that her human charge would surely understand: "It is a goodly vsage, soothly to seye: / ho shal be wedded on-to duke or kyng, / Be-forn her weddyng to haue a bathyng" (3.1069–71). After Katherine has received the sacrament, Christ raises her from the ground, welcomes her warmly, and proposes marriage in the ordinary language of courtship:

> . . . my moder wil heere
> That I shal wedde you; soo wil I saunsfayle;
> Therfore I aske your wil, for to lere
> If ye consente on-to this spousayle.
> With many Ioyes I wil you newely rayle:
> Consente ye, Kataryne? what sey ye now? (3.1226–31)

In keeping with this concrete representation of Christ as an ardent bridegroom, there follows a splendid church wedding with music, vows, and a ring. When he narrates Katherine's passion, Capgrave builds upon the foundation established in this scene, representing the saint's willingness to confront the emperor and ultimately to lose her life as a wife's devotion to her husband (4.501–6).

Virtue in Minor Characters

Capgrave's development of points of view and moral dilemmas is not restricted to Katherine. The saint's servants, anxious for their own safety, waver "be-twix loue and fere" as they wait to see whether their mistress will defy Maxentius (4.523–25). Capgrave even considers the diverse sentiments which entice spectators to Katherine's trial: cruelty, curiosity, and pity (4.1254–62, 5.953–58). In addition to describing the sentiments of groups, he individualizes the legend's secondary characters, delineating their feelings in a manner which complements his representation of Katherine. His most interesting treatments are of the empress and Adrian, and it is worthwhile to devote further attention to these minor protagonists.

Middle English versions of the Katherine legend composed before Capgrave's simply reported that Maxentius's wife took an interest in Katherine and went to visit her in prison. The most intricate delineation of her character is this brief passage from the *North English Legendary:*

> Þe emperise, his wife, herd tell
> How he had done so grete hething
> Vnto Katerin, þat mayden ȝing;
> To speke with hir þan has scho thoght
> & mend hir mischeues, if scho moght.[25]

Capgrave, by contrast, shows "The queen, al in stody, walkyng in the halle, / Thenkynge besyly euere on this mayde" (5.740–41), and he goes to some lengths to describe her dilemma. The empress is disturbed, Capgrave explains, by her husband's cruel treatment of Katherine. From her perspective as an ordinary pagan, Christians are simple, harmless people who just want to be left in peace to worship:

> These cristen foolkis, thei doo noo man wrong;
> Alle that thei beye, truly therfore they pay,
> On-to her god thei synge ful good[ly] song,
> Newe and newe as men seyn euery day;
> Wastful are thei nought in [no] maner of aray,
> Glotones ne drunkelewe wil thei neuere bee—
> This same lyf, ful weel it pleseth mee. (5.743–49)

But much as Christianity appeals to her, she fears the consequences of defying her own laws: "Men shuld seyn that I were a foole" (5.753), and she would be certain to suffer "mekel doole" (754) were the emperor to find out. Though the empress ultimately decides to follow her heart and suffers a brutal death at the hands of her husband, for her, as for Katherine, the "right" choices are difficult, and she is not indifferent to their unpleasant consequences.

The hermit Adrian is perhaps the best example of Capgrave's representation of heroes with human frailties and quotidian concerns. By presenting him as a bumbling old man, an "onlykly" messenger to a queen (3.782), Capgrave juxtaposes even Katherine's mystical marriage with ordinary experience. For example, when Adrian tries to follow the Virgin's instructions and lead Katherine back to his dwelling, he discovers that his hut has vanished. Thus, while Katherine's mind is on heaven, her companion is worrying about where he is going to live from now on. "I must seeke a newe hous, for myn oold is shent. / I had neuere though[t] myn herberwe to chaunge: / Now mote I nedes, and that shal be straunge" (3.845–47), he laments. Though he regrets that he has failed the Virgin Mary and will appear a "fals disseyuere and noon trewe massagere" (3.833) to Katherine, these concerns fade before comparatively mundane matters:

> Shal I now grubbe and make al newe agayn?
> Shal I now delue and make me a welle?
> My myght is I-goo, soothly for to sayn.
> To chaunge my dwellynge was I neuere fayn. (3.863–67)

Similarly, when Katherine returns to earth in a faint, Adrian bewails the inconvenience of having a swooning queen on his hands. He "rubbed hir cheekys, the nose and þe face, / he wepte, he preyed, he cryed ful sore" (3.1358–59). When she awakens, he soundly berates her: "lady, deye no more! / ffor, and ye doo, hens shal I me pak" (3.1361–62).

The empress worries about her reputation, Adrian about his house, Katherine about her political obligations. Capgrave exhibits an understanding of goodness very similar to that which V. A. Kolve observes in the mystery plays. In order to reach the average lay person, Kolve points out, the writers of these dramas present imperfect protagonists who are engrossed in their own problems and material concerns.[26] In so doing, they pay "tribute to every man's right to existence and idiosyncracy, while insisting that he serve God."[27] Perhaps because Capgrave was addressing a similar public, as I will argue, he represents his heroes and heroines in a similar fashion. His conception of virtue, like theirs, acknowledges that "to be man is necessarily to live among men, to enjoy and have place in society, and the good people are as social, as concerned with their kind, as are the evil."[28] Although humans, even saints, are far from perfect, Capgrave's God is a benevolent one with a good deal of patience and relatively modest expectations. Indeed, in his obsession with ordinary experience, Capgrave celebrates God's involvement with humanity in a manner unprecedented in virgin-martyr legends.

It is consistent with the tolerance of human nature which pervades Capgrave's work that Katherine's longing for heaven neither denies the appeal of life on earth nor denigrates human emotions, values, or institutions. Indeed, when Maxentius threatens her with death unless she renounces her faith, Katherine replies,

> Though that my lyf bee ful swete to me,
> Yet had I leuere with a swerd be slayn
> Than that my lyf in ony-maner degree
> Shulde offende the blessed mageste
> Of my lord god. (5.1038–42)

In a virgin-martyr legend, the seemingly innocuous phrase "Though that my lyf bee ful swete to me" is a startling confession. For conventional virgin martyrs, the only consolation life offered was the chance for a spectacular death. But for Capgrave, a radical contempt for the world is no longer a requisite for sanctity. Katherine's mystical marriage lies at the heart of his narrative, thematically as well as structurally; loyalty and devotion to God have become the primary indicators of holiness.

As we have seen, in the *Life of St. Katherine* Capgrave audaciously refashioned formulas which had long governed the representation of virgin martyrs. The most significant of his modifications derive from his careful delineation of the social, political, and personal dimensions of sainthood. As a consequence of this new orientation, a network of oppositions which had traditionally structured the legends of early Christian martyrs disintegrates. No longer does a love of God preclude a love of life; saints are not radically different from ordinary people; protagonists and antagonists are no longer stock characters in the universal struggle between virtue and vice. Though not all people are chosen to be brides of Christ, all people face moral choices, and decisions are no less painful and difficult for saints than they are for anyone else.

The Influence of Lay Piety

Critics have attributed some of the distinguishing elements of the *Life of St. Katherine* to such factors as the influence of other popular genres, Capgrave's aesthetic preferences, or lost Latin sources.[29] These explanations are not altogether satisfying. After all, Capgrave was not the only

writer to reorient traditional hagiographical forms during the first half
of the fifteenth century; at roughly the same time, other Middle English
hagiographers were situating their saints' lives within broader historical
and political frameworks and treating the dilemmas of individuals trying
to pursue a life of holiness in this world. John Lydgate's legends of
Edmund (c. 1433) and Alban (1439), the life of Katherine of Alexandria
in Middle English prose (c. 1420), and a number of saints' lives in the
1438 *Gilte Legende* represent radical departures from traditional models.[30]
All these works appear to have circulated widely during the fifteenth
century. Even Osbern Bokenham, whose saints' lives are more conventional in scope, includes a great deal of information about people, places,
and local customs, and he worries that his readers will be interested in
details of his protagonists' backgrounds that he does not supply.[31] Clearly,
by the middle of the fifteenth century people were reading saints' lives
with different expectations, and writers had new ideas about what details
were appropriate to these narratives. What conditions, we must then ask,
gave rise to this transformation, encouraging writers such as Capgrave to
revise standard paradigms of sainthood and to compose saints' lives so
unlike those produced only decades earlier?

The amplification of saints' lives in Middle English must of course
have been influenced by the more elaborate saints' legends which had
been composed in Latin during the thirteenth and fourteenth centuries.[32]
I contend, however, that the existence of Latin sources and analogues can
only in part account for the developments we have observed. Although
vernacular hagiographers certainly drew upon these works for biographical and historical details, many of them, like Capgrave, went far beyond
any known Latin texts in their treatment of both the private and the
public dimensions of their protagonists' lives. Furthermore, the mere
availability of Latin sources does not explain what made narratives dealing with social responsibility and personal experience so appealing in
fifteenth-century England.

In order to understand saints' lives such as Capgrave's, we must
consider the readers for whom they were intended as well as the social
and cultural context within which they were written and received. Con-
centrating on sources, literary influences, and Capgrave's artistic ability,
studies of the *Life of St. Katherine* have largely ignored Capgrave's audience. Some scholars have taken it for granted that the work was written
for conventual reading, though there is little to warrant this assumption.[33]
Others have very cautiously suggested that Capgrave may have made
"some concessions" to the tastes of a secular public.[34] I believe that the
influence of a lay readership on Capgrave's narrative has been greatly
underestimated. Indeed, I propose that Capgrave's refashioning of the

Katherine legend was motivated by an effort to engage the interests and emotions of the informed, pious lay people who had become enthusiastic readers and patrons of religious literature by the 1440s.

Capgrave clearly assumes that his work will circulate among the laity, for he claims that he undertook his narrative so that the saint's deeds and passion might be known "of man, of mayde, of wyf" (Prol. 66). The *Life of St. Katherine* would most probably have found a receptive audience among members of the East Anglian gentry, who, as Samuel Moore has shown, formed a community of readers which actively encouraged the production of literature during the first half of the fifteenth century.[35] From Osbern Bokenham's prologues, we can deduce that there was an eager audience for vernacular saints' lives within this circle, particularly among women.[36]

Since laywomen were especially avid readers of hagiography in the fifteenth century, it is no surprise that many of Capgrave's changes appear to have been tailored to the special needs and interests of a female audience.[37] The Norfolk friar surely had female readers in mind when he chose so carefully to delineate Katherine's experiences and anxieties. Like the writer of the prose Katherine legend (who claimed to be writing specifically for women), he enhanced the Virgin Mary's presence in his narrative, and he also developed Katherine's mother and the empress as protagonists in his narrative. Thus, he celebrated women acting in a wide range of capacities—as mothers, wives, widows, rulers, and daughters. We have already noted that Capgrave presents the virgin martyr herself as a loyal *wyf* representing her absent husband's interests—a role which fifteenth-century laywomen could readily appreciate.[38]

I have observed that stories of aggressive virgin martyrs who scorned secular values and institutions became common during the thirteenth century, when the clergy was striving to assert its own authority while educating the laity. It seems likely, however, that these legends remained appealing to fourteenth-century readers and writers for other reasons. The middle classes were aggressively challenging traditional conceptions of social order and hierarchy at this time, and many readers may well have found the saint's rebellion against traditional authority figures invigorating. In contrast, contemporaneous hagiographers writing for the generally conservative readers of Anglo-Norman French consistently moderated the contempt for society that was so prominent in Middle English hagiography.[39] Many of their modifications anticipate the changes which occurred in Middle English hagiography a century later, for by the first half of the fifteenth century, the outlook of middle-class readers had shifted. Now more secure in their own position, and perhaps wary of the rising prosperity of the lower class, merchants, professionals, and members of the country gentry tended to look more fondly on the status quo.[40] As readers and patrons of literature, they naturally favored works which affirmed order, security, and traditional social values.[41] They would certainly have preferred a narrative featuring the efforts of a pious laywoman to serve God while fulfilling her secular duties, a subject which spoke to their own experience, to earlier stories of religious radicals locked in combat with a corrupt social order.

A desire for highly personal forms of religious experience was, of course, a hallmark of lay piety during the late Middle Ages. In addressing the religious needs of individuals who craved a more intimate relationship with Christ but could not devote themselves to lives of prayer, clerical writers were seeking ways to reconcile an active life on earth with the pursuit of heaven. Writing in the second half of the fourteenth century, Walter Hilton reminds "a deuout man in temperal estate" that God himself "haþ ordeyned þe & set þe in þe stat of souereynte ouur oþur men . . . and lente þe abundaunce of worldli godes for to rule & susteyne speciali alle þo þat are vnder þi gouernaunce & þi lordschipe in þi miȝt & þi cunnyng."[42] To forsake earthly responsibilities for a life of contemplation, Hilton warns, would actually be sinful:

. . . wite þou wel, ȝif þou leue nedful bisynes of actyf lyf, & be recheles & take no kepe of þi worldly godes, hou þei be kept & spended, ne haue no force of þi soiettes & of þin euencristen, be cause of desyre & wille þat þou hast only for to ȝeue þe to gostly ocupacion, wenyng þat þou art þerbi excused: ȝif þou do so, þou dost not wysli. What are alle þi werkes worþ, wheþer þei be bodili or gostli, but ȝif þei be don riȝtfulli & resonably, to þe worschipe of god & at his biddyng?[43]

He hastens to add, however, that a "worldli lord" need not relinquish the joys of contemplation, for he can still "medle þe werkes of actif lyf wiþ gostly werkes of contemplatyf lyf."[44] Hilton's approbation of the so-called "mixed life" for the laity was echoed by many writers of contemplative literature.[45] We might expect that the changed attitudes toward worldly involvement reflected in so many religious texts should eventually moderate the severe asceticism which had traditionally defined sanctity. As Capgrave's Katherine legend illustrates, by the middle of the fifteenth century even hagiographical genres which had most vehemently denounced worldly interests were being formulated in ways which provided examples of the "medled lyf" of action and contemplation that Hilton and others advocated for the laity.

Lay readers would have found especially appealing the attention paid to the virgin martyr's role as a public figure in Capgrave's *Life of St. Katherine,* for their personal and introspective piety was combined with a consciousness of their place in the temporal world. By the early fifteenth century, these two traits informed virtually all areas of lay religious life. Beautifully illuminated Books of Hours, for example, served both as aids to private devotion and as status symbols. While the prayers and illustrations in many of these works expressed the piety of the men and women who commissioned them, coats of arms, mottoes, and individual or family portraits celebrated the owner's position in society.[46] Likewise, the organization of many late-medieval households into "religious as well as domestic communities" served both social and spiritual ends.[47] As Kate Mertes has pointed out, "magnificent buildings and their accoutrements were one way of advertising one's splendour," and daily services reaffirmed the place of individual members within the social hierarchy of the household.[48] Similarly, the preference among members of the gentry for private pews and enclosed "closetts" in their parish churches both satisfied a desire for greater privacy in their communication with God and suggested to humbler parishioners that "the secular hierarchy was . . . ordained by God and not made by man."[49]

Books of Hours, private chapels, and parish churches all attest to the active role of the laity in shaping the religious culture of late medieval England. At a time when an educated laity was aggressively appropriating so many aspects of clerical culture to its own ends, it is perhaps not surprising that saints' lives should begin to embody—or at least to accommodate—secular values and perspectives. Capgrave's transformation of the virgin martyr from an austere citizen of heaven into a public figure whose perspectives are shaped by her experience in this world represents yet another dimension of the widespread "laicization" of clerical culture which was taking place during the late Middle Ages.

To summarize, I have argued that in his *Life of St. Katherine* Capgrave altered or discarded a number of well-established hagiographical conventions, so producing an essentially new paradigm of sainthood. Unlike the commanding intercessors celebrated in the *Legenda aurea* and in Middle English hagiography of the late thirteenth and fourteenth centuries, his virgin martyr is a naive, indeed fallible, citizen of the world. Instead of emphasizing the monastic ideals, such as celibacy and contempt for the world, which had dominated saints' lives in the past, Capgrave affirmed those qualities that middle-class English people would have prized, such as *besynesse* and respect for *ryghtful lawe*. Indeed, we might recall that what attracts Maxentius's wife to Christianity in the first place are the day-to-day practices of the faithful—their thrift, sobriety, honesty, and piety (5.743–49).

Capgrave was by no means unique in his experimentation with traditional hagiographical forms; rather, his *Life of St. Katherine* represents an extreme expression of tendencies which were evident in the work of several of his contemporaries. During the first decades of the fifteenth century, numerous saints' lives were addressing issues of social morality, endorsing secular pursuits, and reducing the disparity between the experiences of saints and those of ordinary people. The appearance of such saints' legends is best understood as part of the gradual process of accommodation taking place throughout the fourteenth and fifteenth centuries, in which religious culture was being adapted to the needs and values of a growing population of pious, yet sophisticated and highly self-confident, laywomen and laymen.

Notes

1. For all quotations and references, I have used Carl Horstmann's edition of MS. Arundel 396 in *The Life of St. Katharine of Alexandria,* EETS.OS 100 (1893; reprint, Millwood, N.Y.: Kraus, 1987).
2. *Saints' Legends* (Boston: Houghton Mifflin, 1916), 270.
3. *Chaucer and the Fifteenth Century* (1947; reprint, New York: Oxford University Press, 1961), 152.
4. See Jane C. Fredeman, "Style and Characterization in John Capgrave's *Life of St. Katherine,"* *Bulletin of the John Rylands Library* 62 (1979–80): 346–87; Derek Pearsall, "John Capgrave's *Life of St. Katharine* and Popular Romance Style," *Medievalia et Humanistica,* n.s., 6 (1975): 121–37; and Mary-Ann Stouck, "Chaucer and Capgrave's *Life of St. Katharine,"* *American Benedictine Review* 33 (1982): 276–91. The earliest substantial consideration of Capgrave's legend is T. Wolpers, *Die englischen Heiligenlegenden des Mittelalters* (Tübingen: Niemeyer, 1964), 330–42.
5. *Sacred Biography: Saints and Their Biographers in the Middle Ages* (New York: Oxford University Press, 1988), 170–84.
6. Heffernan, 171.
7. Heffernan, 170–71.
8. "Two Types of Opposition and the Structure of Latin Saints' Lives," *Medievalia et Humanistica,* n.s., 6 (1975): 1–11.
9. Altman, 2.
10. Alison Goddard Elliot discusses the public dimension of early martyr legends in *Roads to Paradise: Reading the Lives of the Early Saints* (Hanover, N.H.: University Press of New England: 1987), 18–23.
11. Sherry L. Reames discusses Jacobus's "tendency to equate sanctity with isolation, joylessness, virtual sterility, and contempt for the values of lesser men" in *The* Legenda aurea: *A Reexamination of Its Paradoxical History* (Madison: University of Wisconsin Press, 1985), 195. In addition, see her comments in "Saint Martin of Tours in the 'Legenda aurea' and Before," *Viator* 12 (1981): 146–64.
12. *La Légende dorée: Le système narratif de Jacques de Voragine* (Paris: Cerf, 1984), 140–41.
13. For a general discussion of how English hagiography came into conflict with

lay values and practices, see Susan Crane, *Insular Romance: Politics, Faith, and Culture in Anglo-Norman and Middle English Literature* (Berkeley and Los Angeles: University of California Press, 1986), 92–104, 128–33. The most widely discussed virgin-martyr legend is, of course, the *Second Nun's Tale*, and both Sherry Reames and Janemaric Luecke have commented upon the denigration of human experience in Chaucer's Cecilia legend. See Reames, "The Cecilia Legend as Chaucer Inherited It and Retold It: The Disappearance of an Augustinian Ideal," *Speculum* 55 (1980): 38–57; and Luecke, "Three Faces of Cecilia: Chaucer's *Second Nun's Tale*," *American Benedictine Review* 33 (1982): 347. I have maintained that the devaluation of human nature which Reames and Luecke have observed in Chaucer's legend is typical of virgin-martyr legends composed in Middle English during the late thirteenth and fourteenth centuries in "Changing Ideals of Sainthood in Late Medieval Virgin Martyr Legends," (Ph.D. diss., Indiana University, 1989), 37–70.

14. Heffernan notes that the saint's renunciation of society tends to be especially pronounced in legends of female saints (*Sacred Biography*, 185–299).

15. Geoffrey Chaucer, *The Second Nun's Tale*, line 323 in *The Riverside Chaucer*, ed. Larry D. Benson [based on N. F. Robinson, ed., *The Works of Geoffrey Chaucer*, 2d ed.] (Boston: Houghton Mifflin, 1987).

16. For example, when, in the *South English Legendary*, Christine's companions express fear that they will die for her disobedience, the saint dismisses them as "luþer conseilers." Likewise, Margaret calls sympathizers "wikkede conseillers," while Cecilia orders mourners to "beþ stille." See, respectively, *South English Legendary*, ed. Charlotte D'Evelyn and Anna J. Mill, EETS.OS 235 (London: Oxford University Press, 1956), p. 317, line 53, p. 296, line 135; and *Early South English Legendary*, ed. Carl Horstmann, EETS.OS 87 (1887; reprint, Millwood, N.Y.: Kraus, 1987), p. 495, line 225.

17. In a typically abrupt fashion, Jacobus immediately introduces the central conflict: "Catherina Costi regis filia omnibus liberalium artium studiis erudita fuit. Cum autem Maxentius imperator omnes tam divites quam pauperes ad Alexandriam convocaret. . . ." *Legenda aurea*, ed. Th. Graesse (1890; reprint, Osnabrück: Otto Zeller, 1969), 789–90. The edition of *Seinte Katerine* by S. R. T. O. d'Ardenne and E. J. Dobson includes the text of the full Vulgate *Passio Sancte Katerine* along with a discussion of the development of the Katherine legend. See EETS.SS 7 (London: Oxford University Press, 1981), xiii–xxxiv, 132–203.

18. *North English Legendary*, ed. C. Horstmann, *Altenglische Legenden: Neue Folge* (Heilbronn, 1881), p. 172, lines 683–84.

19. Auvo Kurvinen makes detailed comparisons between Capgrave's legend and its closest known Latin analogue, the "Staneborn Version" of the *Vita Sancte Katerine*, in "The Source of Capgrave's *Life of St. Katharine of Alexandria*," *Neuphilologische Mitteilungen* 61 (1960): 268–324.

20. Capgrave does not, of course, neglect these conventional hagiographical frameworks. See especially 1.100–133, 155–96, 288–301.

21. Although I can cite no English examples, a number of fourteenth- and fifteenth-century Italian women faced the same hostility toward female learning and the same stark choice between marriage and intellectual pursuits that Capgrave's Katherine encounters. See Margaret L. King, "Book-Lined Cells: Women and Humanism in the Early Italian Renaissance," *Beyond Their Sex:*

Learned Women of the European Past, ed. Patricia H. Labalme (New York: New York University Press, 1980), 66–90.

22. Anne Eggebroten makes this distinction in "Laughter in the *Second Nun's Tale:* A Redefinition of the Genre," *Chaucer Review* 19 (1984–85): 55–61.

23. For example, when in the Middle English prose life of St. Katherine the saint's mother accuses her of asking for the impossible, Katherine insists, "I wote wel by verray reson þat þer ys oon moche better þen I can deuise hym who so had grace to fynde hym." See *The Life and Martyrdom of St. Katherine,* ed. Henry Hucks Gibbs (London, 1884), 12. In the *Vita Sancte Katerine* she defends herself in similar terms. By contrast, Capgrave's Katherine offers no response to her subjects' *grutchynge,* but happily returns to her books (2.1457–90).

24. Note the similarity between Katherine's mystical marriage (3.1198–1309) and the heavenly wedding Margery Kempe envisions in *The Book of Margery Kempe,* ed. Sanford Brown Meech, EETS.OS 212 (Oxford: Oxford University Press, 1940), 86–87.

25. *Altenglische Legenden,* p. 169, lines 370–74.

26. *The Play Called Corpus Christi* (Stanford: Stanford University Press, 1966), 237–64.

27. Kolve, 240.

28. Kolve, 242.

29. See especially Stouck, Pearsall, and Kurvinen, cited in notes 4 and 19.

30. Gordon Whatley discusses the amplification of the Erkenwald legend in "A 'Symple Wrecche' at Work: The Life and Miracles of St. Erkenwald in the *Gilte Legende,* BL Add. 35298," *Legenda Aurea: Sept siècles de diffusion,* ed. Brenda Dunn-Lardeau (Montreal: Bellarmin, 1986), 333–43. Other legends of English saints have been substantially embellished in the 1438 *Gilte Legende,* including the legends of Edward the Confessor and of Alban and Amphibalus.

31. For Bokenham's apologies and explanations see lines 8359–65, 365–68, and 6347–64 in *Legendys of Hooly Wummen,* ed. Mary S. Serjeantson, EETS.OS 206 (1938; reprint, New York: Kraus, 1971). It is worth noting that even though Bokenham avoids lengthy historical, social, or geographical digressions in his narratives, he composed a substantial geographical treatise, the *Mappula Angliae,* so that his friends might better understand the lives of English saints that he had composed at their request. See "*Mappula Angliae* von Osbern Bokenham," ed. C. Horstmann, *Englische Studien* 10 (1887): 6.

32. For example, the first known legends describing the life as well as the martyrdom of Katherine appeared in the thirteenth or early fourteenth century. The same is true of the Alban and Amphibalus legend. See George F. Reinecke's comments in the introduction to his edition of Lydgate's *Saint Alban and Saint Amphibalus* (New York: Garland, 1985), xxvii–xxviii.

33. The evidence usually advanced is that one of the four manuscripts containing Capgrave's Katherine legend, Arundel 396, was among the possessions of the Augustinian nunnery at Campsey, Suffolk. See J. Fredeman, "The Life of John Capgrave, O.E.S.A. (1393–1464)," *Augustiniana* 29 (1979): 229; and Peter J. Lucas, introduction, *John Capgrave's Abbreuiacion of Cronicles,* EETS.OS 285 (New York: Oxford University Press, 1983), xxviii. Lucas also cites Derek Pearsall's tenuous conclusion that simply because another of the Katherine

manuscripts, Arundel 168, consists largely of female saints' lives it "presumably" also belonged to a nunnery. For this opinion, see Pearsall, 137, n. 76.

34. Pearsall, 130. See also Stouck, 281.

35. "Patrons of Letters in Norfolk and Suffolk, c. 1450," *PMLA* 27 (1912): 188–207; *PMLA* 28 (1913): 79–105. See also Gail McMurray Gibson, *The Theater of Devotion: East Anglian Drama and Society in the Late Middle Ages* (Chicago: University of Chicago Press, 1989).

36. Bokenham composed his legends of Katherine, Agatha, Margaret, Dorothy, Anne, Mary Magdalene, and Elizabeth for friends in the area. He also claims to have written some (presumably lost) lives of English saints "at the instaunce of my specialle frendis" ("Mappula Angliae" 6).

37. Among the many fifteenth-century women who encouraged the production of saints' lives are Elizabeth de Vere, Isabel Bourchier, Katherine Howard, Katherine Denston, Agatha Flegge, and Isabel Hunt—all patrons of Bokenham; Anne Mortimer, Lady March, at whose request Lydgate composed his legend of Margaret; Margaret, Duchess of Clarence, Symon Wynter's patron; and the anonymous "gentill woman" who asked Capgrave to write a life of St. Augustine. For a discussion of the growing importance of women as patrons and book owners, see Susan Groag Bell, "Medieval Women Book Owners: Arbiters of Lay Piety and Ambassadors of Culture," *Signs* 7 (1982): 742–68.

38. Eileen Power, *Medieval Women*, ed. M. M. Postan (London: Cambridge University Press, 1975), 42–46, 53–57; Ann S. Haskell, "The Paston Women on Marriage in Fifteenth-Century England," *Viator* 4 (1973): 459–71; and H. S. Bennett, *The Pastons and Their England* (Cambridge: Cambridge University Press, 1922), 62–66.

39. For example, the Anglo-Norman narrative preserved in British Library, Addit. 40143 deals with Katherine's conversion and mystical marriage instead of her conflict with Maxentius. Auvo Kurvinen discusses this text in "The Life of St. Catharine of Alexandria in Middle English Prose" (diss. Oxford, 1960). In addition, I have argued that Nicole Bozon adapted Jacobus a Voragine's virgin-martyr legends in ways which reduce the challenges to social values and secular authority which characterized the Latin texts ("Changing Ideals," 71–86), and William MacBain has pointed out that in her *Vie de sainte Catherine* Clemence of Barking attenuates the stark opposition between good and evil with "the *agréments* needed to gain the attention of her courtly audience." See "Five Old French Renderings of the Passio sancte Katerine virginis, *Medieval Translators and their Craft*, ed. Jeanette Beer (Kalamazoo, Mich.: Medieval Institute Publications, 1989), 63. There was no rigid class division between readers of French and readers of English in late-medieval England; studies have shown, however, that during the late thirteenth and fourteenth centuries middle-class readers, including members of the gentry, displayed an increasing preference for English, while French thrived among the aristocracy and among those who considered themselves to be members of a cultural elite. See Crane, *Insular Romance*, 4–10; and P. R. Coss, "Aspects of Cultural Diffusion in Medieval England: The Early Romances, Local Society, and Robin Hood," *Past and Present* 108 (1985): 35–79.

40. The profound conservatism of middle-class English people during the fifteenth century has been widely discussed. Among the many interpretations of this phenomenon are Janet Coleman, *Medieval Readers and Writers 1350–*

1400 (New York: Columbia University Press, 1981), 278–80; Paul Strohm, "Chaucer's Fifteenth-Century Audience and the Narrowing of the 'Chaucer Tradition,' " *SAC* 4 (1984): 18–32; Rodney Hilton, "Ideology and Social Order in Late Medieval England," *Class Conflict and the Crisis of Feudalism: Essays in Medieval Social History* (London: Hambledon Press, 1985), 246–52; and Sylvia L. Thrupp, "The Problem of Conservatism in Fifteenth-Century England," *Speculum* 18 (1943): 363–68.

41. For discussions of the changes in literary taste which occurred during the first decades of the fifteenth century, see Strohm; Hilton; and Coleman, 269–70, 278–80.

42. "Epistle on Mixed Life," *Yorkshire Writers*, ed. C. Horstmann (London, 1895), 1:264, 271.

43. Hilton, 271.

44. Hilton, 267.

45. On the medieval mystics' attitudes toward the active life, see Ray C. Petry, "Social Responsibility and the Late Medieval Mystics," *Church History* 21 (1952): 3–19; Richard Kieckhefer, "Mysticism and Social Consciousness in the Fourteenth Century," *Revue de l'université d'Ottawa* 48 (1978): 179–86; and Wolfgang Riehle, *The Middle English Mystics*, trans. Bernard Standring (London: Routledge & Kegan Paul, 1981), 15–19. Christine de Pisan also endorsed the mixed life as a means by which lay women might reconcile spiritual aspirations with their legitimate temporal concerns. See *The Treasure of the City of Ladies*, trans. Sarah Lawson (New York: Penguin, 1985), 45–46.

46. See especially Lawrence R. Poos, "Social History and the Book of Hours," in Roger S. Wieck's *Time Sanctified: The Book of Hours in Medieval Art and Life* (New York: George Braziller, 1988), 33–38; and John Harthan, *Books of Hours and Their Owners* (London: Thames & Hudson, 1977).

47. Kate Mertes, *The English Noble Household 1250–1600: Good Governance and Politic Rule* (New York: Basil Blackwell, 1988), 138–60.

48. Mertes, 147–48.

49. Nigel Saul, *Scenes from Provincial Life: Knightly Families in Sussex 1280–1400* (Oxford: Clarendon, 1986), 159.

From Aeneid to Eneados: Theory and Practice of Gavin Douglas's Translation

A. E. C. CANITZ

In the Pologues to the Books of his *Eneados,* Gavin Douglas specifies very precisely what he regards as the task of the translator. He rejects the medieval view of the translator as one who culls narrative materials from other writers' works in order to retell them in his own manner, and instead emphasizes the translator's obligation to treat the text with the strictest fidelity. While vividness and originality are still important to Douglas, his understanding of their proper application is new: it is not the task of the translator to produce an original rendering of well-known materials and to reshape them in such a way that the product becomes distinctly his own, but to be original in the use and even in the creation of resources which will enable him to reproduce the text as faithfully and as accurately as is possible in another language, recapturing the "freshness" of the original for a new audience with a different linguistic and cultural background. The translator's claim to fame thus does not rest on the extent to which he has created his own version of the story material, but on the degree to which he has re-created the original author's text in all its aspects, from isolated stylistic effects to the philosophy and the overall design underlying the entire work. In proposing a theory of translation based on the postulate of accuracy and fidelity, Douglas separates himself from Chaucer and other medieval adapters and adopts the humanist view of genuine translation, with its stress on the integrity and inviolability of the text.

This kind of translation, as Douglas implies in his criticism of William Caxton in Prologue I, ought not only to be accurate in specific details, but must also faithfully reproduce the balance and proportions of the work. The translator is not at liberty to abbreviate or even omit some parts while expanding others, depending on his own interest, but he must retain the design governing the sequence and proportions of the

Medievalia et Humanistica, New Series, Number 17 (Paul Maurice Clogan, ed.) Rowman & Littlefield Publishers, Inc.

individual parts in the original. In his flyting with Caxton (I, Prol., 137–282),[1] Douglas indignantly charges the earlier writer with having translated the *Aeneid* at second hand, from a French recension, rather than directly from the original Latin (I, Prol., 141); in consequence, there are serious distortions in the texture of the verse (I, Prol., 147–52) and confusions in the locations and characters stemming from misspellings of place names and proper names (I, Prol., 221–48), besides perversions of parts of the plot (I, Prol., 155–67). Important as they are, however, these are minor charges compared with the two major ones—namely that Caxton has, by means of undue abbreviations and considerable omissions, distorted the structural balance and proportions of Virgil's work (I, Prol., 154–56, 168–76, 249–59) and that he utterly fails to understand the significance of the pagan gods and of the underworld. Douglas also accuses Caxton of failing to perceive that "vnder the clowdis of dyrk poecy / Hyd lyis thar mony notabill history" (I, Prol., 194–95). In consequence of this deplorable lack of perception and sympathetic understanding, Caxton calls Book VI "fenȝeit and nocht forto beleif" (I, Prol., 179), being thus inconsistent, because other parts of his translation also contain the gods as agents. A translation that fails to show an understanding of central passages setting forth the framework of the original author's views, which in turn inform the entire rest of the work; a translation that omits one-quarter of the original, reduces another half to one-sixth its length and expands one-twelfth to become one-half; a translation that on top of all this is so inaccurate that it is "no mair lyke [the *Aeneid*] than the devill and Sanct Austyne" (I, Prol., 143)—such a translation cannot but incur Douglas's wrath.[2] But in censuring Caxton, Douglas also advances his own principles of translation—namely faithfulness to all aspects of the original, from accuracy in the spelling of names all the way to a sympathetic comprehension and interpretation of the original author's philosophic stance, which itself must be reflected in the translation.

In a second passage of criticism, Douglas directs his attention to Chaucer, the "principal poet but peir" (I, Prol., 339), who, however, "standis beneth Virgill in gre" (I, Prol., 407). While Douglas censures Caxton on the grounds of having distorted the scheme and balance of the *Aeneid*, he might have brought the same charge against Chaucer, who reworked the *Aeneid* material twice, in the *House of Fame* and in the *Legend of Good Women*, both times emphasizing Virgil's Book IV while relying for the rest on Ovid's version, which he condenses to the bare minimum of the plot line. In the *Legend of Good Women* Chaucer is, in accordance with Alceste's command to write "a gloryous legende / Of goode women, maydenes and wyves" (*LGW*, Prol. G, 473–74), interested in the *Aeneid* only insofar as it concerns Dido and thus retells only Books I to IV, devoting almost half the lines of the "Legend of Dido" to the adaptation of Book IV itself. In the description of Venus's temple in the *House of Fame*, Chaucer paraphrases the complete *Aeneid*, including Ovid's reference to Aeneas's wedding and his account of Aeneas's apotheosis, in 325 lines (*HF,* 143–467), out of which he takes 126 lines to render Virgil's Book IV alone while he compresses the contents of the succeeding books and of Ovid's continuation into thirty-five lines (*HF,* 433–67). While Chaucer reproduces Virgil's opening lines verbatim, he does not pretend, as Douglas claims, to be actually translating; indeed, he even inserts an explicit disclaimer into the inscription which the dreamer–narrator finds in Venus' temple:

> "I wol now synge, *yif I kan,*
> The armes and also the man
> That first cam, thurgh his destinee,
> Fugityf of Troy contree,
> In Itayle, with ful moche pyne
> Unto the strondes of Lavyne."
> (*HF,* 143–48)

Although Chaucer changes the proportions of the *Aeneid*—he will not translate "word for word, Virgile" because that "wolde lasten al to longe while" (*LGW,* 1002–3)—he is at least not guilty of Caxton's other offense of having translated entirely at second hand rather than having gone *ad fontem,* as Douglas in the spirit of humanism demands that a translator do.

Douglas also uses the charge he brings against Chaucer's treatment of the Dido and Aeneas story as a means of launching his discussion of the impossibility—and indeed, the undesirability—of word-for-word translation. When he gently criticizes Chaucer for claiming that "he couth follow word by word Virgill" (I, Prol., 345), he is again not quite just to the elder poet. At the opening of the Dido legend, Chaucer writes,

> Glorye and honour, Virgil Mantoan,
> Be to thy name! and I shal, *as I can,*
> Folwe thy lanterne, as thow gost byforn,
> . . . .
> *In thyn Eneyde and Naso* wol I take
> *The tenor, . . .*
> (*LGW,* 924–29)

Far from claiming to write a literal translation, Chaucer explicitly disclaims such an ability and is content with following "the tenor" not of Virgil's work only, but also of both Virgil's and Ovid's handling of the story of Dido. Nonetheless, the point serves Douglas well to begin his argument against literal translation, in which he provides examples to support his thesis that different languages often have no exact equivalents, and that even if words with the same denotations may be found, the connotations of such words will not be the same, so that it is often necessary to use circumlocutions or other collocations in order at least to approximate the import of the original word or phrase. In addition, there are the prosodic problems of having to find pairs of rhyming words to end the "Scottis" couplets and of writing in a language with far fewer inflectional endings than Latin has. And, of course, there are those of

> our tungis penuryte,
> I meyn into compar of fair Latyn
> That knawyn is maste perfite langage fyne.
> (I, Prol., 380–82)

Apart from his observations on the lack of exact equivalents in the two languages, Douglas also seems to be conscious, at least in part, of the problems connected with the transference of a literary work from one culture into another. When he writes,

> Sum tyme the text mon haue ane expositioun,
> Sum tyme the collour will causs a litill additioun,
> (I, Prol., 347–48)

he appears to be alluding to the difficulty which the translator faces in trying to make graphic and even to make thinkable what is originally outside the audience's range of cultural experience and perception. On the basis of his own observation and on the additional authority of St. Gregory and Horace (I, Prol., 395–402), Douglas therefore rejects slavish adherence to the letter of the original in favor of capturing what he perceives to be the spirit, the tone, the atmosphere, the idea—in short, the "sentence" of the work.

Douglas finds Chaucer guilty of a further, more serious transgression, however. In depicting Aeneas as being false to Dido and as having broken his oath to her, Chaucer has, as Douglas says, "gretly Virgil offendit" (I, Prol., 410); in other words, Chaucer does violence to Virgil's systematic and consistent portrayal of the hero as one who is without "spot of cryme, reproch or ony offens" (I, Prol., 420). Virgil's Aeneas, being reminded by Mercury of his mission to found Rome, sacrifices all human desires, including his own; in obeying the commands of fate, he becomes the innocent cause of Dido's death as the gods use him as their tool. But while retaining the individual narrative elements of the departure scene, Chaucer altogether changes Aeneas's character in letting Aeneas himself, rather than the objective narrator, report Mercury's visit; as a result, the god's visit appears as a mere pretext for a departure which is not motivated by *pietas* but by self-interest. In addition, Chaucer's Aeneas swears an un-Virgilian oath of eternal faithfulness to Dido (*LGW*, 1234) and leaves Carthage, even though Dido is with child (*LGW*, 1323) and even though he has caused her to be in danger of imminent attack by the neighboring lords. In Chaucer's adaptation Aeneas has thus become a most callous perjurer who is ready to sacrifice Dido for the momentary satisfaction of his own pleasure. What Douglas criticizes in Chaucer's retelling is that in isolating the Dido and Aeneas story and seeing it from Dido's point of view, Chaucer may have given it more spice but has altered the character of "pius" Aeneas so much that Aeneas can no longer emerge as the model man and model prince whom the Renaissance came to see in Virgil's hero as he is gradually further and further refined by the trials which his destiny has in store for him; in Chaucer's adaptation Aeneas loses his larger-than-life stature as a hero and becomes all too human. Seen from the perspective of the *Aeneid* as a whole, Chaucer's changes in Aeneas's behavior and motivation amount to a distortion of Aeneas's character and, in consequence, to a subversion of Virgil's design for Aeneas's development and growth as a hero and as the progenitor of the Roman imperial line. Since Chaucer is not concerned with the whole of the *Aeneid*, however, but only with one small part, Douglas graciously and in tongue-in-cheek fashion will "excuss Chauser fra all maner re-pruffis" (I, Prol., 446) on the grounds that Chaucer "was evir (God wait) all womanis frend" (I, Prol., 449).

Douglas's practice generally matches his theoretical precepts, and he is satisfied that he has been faithful to the text, yet the work is subtly changed. A mass of minor, line-filling additions increases the length of the work and slows the pace of the narrative. Other additions, the frequent explanatory expansions, emphasize the presence of a scholarly translator–narrator and thus distance the audience from the narrative; at the same time, explanatory substitutions reduce the cultural distance between the work and its new audience. Apart from thus "modernizing" Virgil, Douglas also tends to create a greater immediacy by concretizing and actualizing images which Virgil leaves ambiguous or vague. It is the accumulation of such small changes which gives the *Eneados* a texture and flavor distinctly different from those of the *Aeneid*.

While accusing others of having distorted the proportions of the original work, Douglas is not entirely innocent in this respect, either. In translating Virgil's hexameter lines into decasyllabic couplets he greatly increases the number of lines; on the average the ratio is approximately one Latin line to just over one "Scottis" couplet, but the ratio in the individual books varies: in Book I Douglas renders Virgil's 756 lines in only 661 couplets, but in Book X, for instance, he expands the original

908 lines to 1,108 couplets; Book X is thus proportionately more than one-third longer than Book I. Many of Douglas's expansions and additions are caused by the demands of his different meter; as he charmingly admits, he occasionally needs some padding "to lykly my ryme" (I, Prol., 124).[3] Often, these small additions simply consist of line-filling tags such as "I gess," "but dowt," "but dreid," "but less," "I wiss," "al and sum," "sans faill," and "schortlie to conclude." At other times, Douglas completes lines by using doublets—for instance, "to fle and to depart," "declynys and goys doun," "fame and gude renown," "trewth and verite," "eneuch and sufficient," and "habitatioun and residens"—whose chiefly metrical function becomes all too obvious when they are linked with "or" instead of "and," as in "depart or ga / Furth," "grund or erth," "helmstok or gubernakil of tre," and "bowellis or entralis."[4] In addition to being useful for metrical purposes, such pairs of synonyms seem to accommodate Douglas's desire for "the fowth [plenitude] of langage" (I, Prol., 120), although they also tend to sound somewhat pedantic and schoolmasterly; in this respect Douglas seems at times more dedicated to satisfying the needs of the "masteris of grammar sculys" who "wald Virgill to childryn expone" (Direction, 47, 43) than to approximating Virgil's densely packed style as closely as possible.

Douglas does not, however, depend on the Virgilian commentators alone when it comes to finding the right word or phrase. On the contrary, he also creates words; he makes colloquial expressions literary; and as he emphasizes, he uses loan words from other languages:

> Nor ȝit sa cleyn all sudron I refuss,
> Bot sum word I pronunce as nyghtbouris doys:
> Lyke as in Latyn beyn Grew termys sum,
> So me behufyt quhilum or than be dum
> Sum bastard Latyn, French or Inglys oyss
> Quhar scant was Scottis—I had nane other choys.
> Nocht for our tong is in the selwyn skant
> Bot for that I the fowth of langage want.
>   (I, Prol., 113–20)

Apart from announcing his intention of borrowing words or pronunciations, which he sometimes needs "to lykly my ryme" (I, Prol., 124), Douglas here also raises the issue of linguistic accuracy in his translation. What he strives for is the "fowth" of language, and the more varied his resources are, the more likely is this fund of possibilities to provide him with exactly the right word or phrase for the particular context. Douglas borrows freely from other languages—not only French, Latin, and Greek, but also Dutch and Flemish. In addition, his vocabulary includes words drawn from Scandinavian stock, native colloquialisms made literary by their use in the *Eneados,* alliterative collocations, and aureate neologisms coined for the occasion. Some of the onomatopoeic words, such as verbs mimicking birdcalls or nouns imitating the sound of water or the noise of clashing weapons, are likely to have already existed in colloquial usage and to have now for the first time been used in literature.[5] But the same is less probable for Douglas's aureate terms; words such as "coniugall," "contegwyte," "etheryall," "malivolous," and "redymyte" seem to be Douglas's creations. According to *M.E.D., O.E.D.,* and *D.O.S.T.,* none of these terms is recorded before use by Douglas. In creating such neologisms Douglas shows himself to be entirely attuned to the "idea of the poet as the refiner and enricher of his native and national language [, which] is central to Renaissance thought about poetry."[6] Having praised Virgil's "flude of eloquens" and Chaucer's "Mylky fontane" (I, Prol., 4 & 342), Douglas tries to emulate both his models so that the perceived poverty of the "Scottis" language might be turned into "fowth," not only through increased copiousness of vocabulary but also by means of added variety in the levels of diction, which range from the extremely colloquial to the most aureate.

The use of the colloquial element becomes particularly pronounced in the short un-Virgilian utterances which Douglas frequently puts into the mouths of his characters. In the translation of Book V, for example, Douglas increases the excitement of the various races of the funeral games by making the spectators and the participants call to one another where Virgil indicates only that there is much shouting. Virgil's general expressions, such as

> tum vero ingeminat clamor, cunctique sequentem
> instigant studiis, resonatque fragoribus aether.
> (V, 227–28)

become far more specific in Douglas's translation and addition:

> The noyss and brute tho dowblys lowd on hycht,
> For, on the costis syde, fast euery wight
> Spurris the persewaris to roll bissely:
> "Set on hym now! Haue at hym thar," thai cry,
> That huge clamour fordynnyt al the ayr.
> (V, iv, 123–27)

By particularizing the characters' utterances in direct speech, Douglas makes the action appear to be unfiltered by the narrator's consciousness,[7] thus increasing the immediacy and vigor of the narrative and "actualizing" the happenings.[8] The result is often a change in tone and mood, intensifying the noise and bustle in the scene reported.

Douglas also tends toward a similar concretization regarding the characters' emotions. Where Virgil has a character sigh, Douglas not only reports the sigh but also specifies its kind and cause; where Virgil leaves it to the reader to imagine the precise mixture of emotions expressed by the character, Douglas often removes any vagueness or ambiguity, thus forcing his own interpretation and his own emotional response on his audience and preventing his readers from effecting their independent imaginative apprehension of the character's state of mind. When Dido at the beginning of Book IV reproaches herself for betraying the memory of her first husband, Virgil's Dido alludes most delicately to the possibility of an alliance with Aeneas:

> si non pertaesum thalami taedaeque fuisset,
> huic uni forsan potui succumbere culpae.
>   (IV, 18–19)

Using the relatively broad term "culpa," whose meaning in classical Latin can be as weak as "error" or "weakness," Dido vainly tries to gloss over the perceived impropriety of her feelings. Douglas's Dido, in contrast, is far less tender in her word choice and spells out precisely what is on her mind:

> War not alsso to me is displesant
> Genyvs chalmyr or matrymone to hant;
> Perchans I mycht be venquist in this rage,
> Throu this a *cryme of secund mariage.*
>   (IV, i, 37–40)

Similarly, in the scene of Dido and Aeneas's meeting in the under-world, Douglas's particularization helps to bring about a slight change, especially as regards the portrayal of Aeneas. Whereas Virgil appears to have equal sympathy for Dido and Aeneas, Douglas, while being more sympathetic toward both, seems to have special compassion for Aeneas, who in consequence appears to be warmer and more tender than he is in the *Aeneid.* The individual changes are slight, but their cumulative effect is considerable. Near the beginning of his speech Aeneas asks, "funeris heu! tibi causa fui?" (VI, 458), but Douglas, as he often does elsewhere,[9] treats the question as a statement—"Allace, I was the causar of thy ded!" (VI, vii, 69)—and thus as a remorseful self-accusation. In Aeneas's appeal to Dido not to turn away, Douglas inserts "so sone" and changes the possessive pronoun from plural to singular.

>   . . . teque aspectu ne subtrahe nostro. (VI, 465)

Withdraw the not *sa sone* furth of *my* sight! (VI, vii, 86)

Thus he makes the scene much more intimate and allows Aeneas to ask for a much smaller favor: Aeneas knows that Dido *will* leave, and he asks only that she not leave just yet. An insertion in the preceding line also serves to increase the impression of Aeneas's tenderness and compassion toward Dido: Douglas changes the neutral imperative "siste gradum" (VI, 465) into the loving plea "Abide, *thou gentil wight*" (VI, vii, 85). Finally, in the last line of Aeneas's speech, Douglas translates "quod te *ad*loquor" (VI, 466) as "that *with* the speke I may" (VI, vii, 88); the substitution of "with" for "ad-" transforms Aeneas's one-sided demand that he be heard into a plea for renewed mutual communication. Even when Dido turns away—not "inimica" (VI, 472), but "aggrevit" (VI, vii, 100)—Aeneas is not "casu concussus iniquo" (VI, 475), but "perplexit of *hir* sory cace" (VI, vii, 105). By inserting the pronoun Douglas has again removed Virgil's ambiguity, making Aeneas feel only compassion for Dido and her pain, and excluding the possibility of Aeneas's feeling hurt by the apparent haughtiness with which Dido tries to protect her deeply injured feelings. Whether or not one agrees with John Speirs's judgment that "Douglas' rendering [of this meeting] disappoints,"[10] it is certain that Douglas's version is sufficiently different from Virgil's to create a changed image of the two characters.

While such changes in the characterization are rare, two factors seem to influence the translation of the preceding passage in Aeneas's favor. First, throughout the *Eneados,* particularly in Prologues I and IV, Douglas is at pains to exonerate Aeneas from the standard medieval charge of having been a traitor to Dido by breaking an oath which Virgil, however, never makes him give. The portrayal of Aeneas as "maynsworn fowlely" (I, Prol., 422) is precisely the point on which Douglas criticizes Chaucer as having "gretly Virgill offendit" (I, Prol., 410); in his advocacy of Aeneas Douglas here tends toward the opposite pole. A second influence seems to stem from the larger cultural environment, here especially the Christian concept of contrition preceding the plea for forgiveness. Such Christian overtones are occasionally present elsewhere in the translation, although Douglas appears consciously to avoid a Christianization of the translation itself and to confine the expression of Christian views to the Prologues. Nonetheless, when Aeneas explains to Dido in Book IV that he leaves not by his own choice but at the command of the gods, Douglas twice translates "sponte" as "fre will" (IV, vi, 121, 160). Dido here appears a little less restrainedly dignified and a little more emotional than in Virgil, mainly because of frequent interpolations of the line-filling "allace!" into her speeches; she also seems a little more bitter, for after Dido has addressed Aeneas as her "gest," no longer her "spowss," Douglas gives her the un-Virgilian line

My gest, ha God! quhou al thyng now invane is,
(IV, vi, 85)

making her echo the sentiment of the vanity of the world familiar from medieval religious lyrics. Otherwise, however, the translation of scenes involving Dido and Aeneas is extremely close to the original.[11] Having based his censure of Chaucer and Caxton chiefly on their handling of Book IV, Douglas is likely to have taken particular care to ensure that his translation of the same passage would be above criticism.[12]

Book IV, however, also provides typical examples of the cultural transference which Douglas, according to his pronouncements in Prologue I, considers to be part of the translator's task; as he says, "Sum tyme the text mon haue ane expositioun" (I, Prol., 347). Given that Douglas's primary audience consisted of courtly readers—who could not be assumed to be acquainted with the customs and the geography and mythology of the ancient world, beyond what is regularly mentioned in English, Scottish, and French vernacular literature—Douglas incorporates explanatory notes into the text of the translation. He uses familiar terms to explain geographical and cultural references:

> *that* horribill *mont,* Cawcasus *hait* (IV, vii, 9)

> Avernus *the well,*
> *Quhilk lowch is situate at the mouth of hell*
> (IV, ix, 81–82)

He provides proper names for Virgil's kennings or other periphrastic expressions:

> Saturnys son, *hie Iupiter* (IV, vii, 21)

> to *An,* hir deir systir, (IV, viii, 102)

He replaces the less standard names of gods, peoples, and places with their more usual ones:

patrique Lyaeo (IV, 58)	:	and to Bachus part also (IV, ii, 13)
Libycae gentes (IV, 320)	:	the pepill of Affrik (IV, vi, 77)
Pergama (IV, 344)	:	Priamus palyce (IV, vi, 126)

And he almost always avoids the various names—such as Achivi, Argivi, Argolici, Danai, and Pelasgi; and Dardanides, Phryges, and Teucri—which Virgil uses for the Greeks and the Trojans, respectively.

Such explanatory expansions and substitutions reduce the distance between the world of Virgil and that of the sixteenth-century Scottish reader. However, when Douglas uses phrases such as "quhik hait . . ." or "quhilk clepyng we . . .", he defeats his own purpose, for such overtly introduced explanations only distance the *Aeneid* further from his audience. Having summarized the metamorphosis of king Picus into a woodpecker, the narrator adds,

clepit a Speicht with ws,
Quhilk in Latyn hait Pycus Marcyus,
(VII, iii, 91–92)

and Virgil's "virago," used in reference to Juturna, is laboriously explained,

(Quhilk term to expone, to myne avyss,
Is a woman exersand a mannys offyss)
(XII, viii, 57–58)

instead of being translated as, for instance, "stowt wench," the term with which Douglas describes Camilla in Book XI.[13] Such explanations particularly draw attention to themselves when they occur in the speeches of Virgilian characters; then, the absurd situation arises in which pre-Roman characters explain to each other what certain things are called in Middle Scots. Anchises, addressing Aeneas, hopes that Jupiter

with his fyry levin me omberauch,
That we intill our langage clepe fyreflauch,
(II, x, 155–56)

and Evander tells Aeneas about the "nymphis and fawnys" in the surrounding woods:

Quhilk fairfolkis, or than elvys, clepyng we.
(VIII, vi, 7)

Although the purpose of such explanatory interpolations is to help nonexpert readers bridge the gap between Virgil's and their own cultural environment and experience, these explanations often have exactly the opposite effect. Even if it could be assumed that the reader was expected to regard such passages as authorial glosses to be read in a different tone of voice, the running commentary only emphasizes the presence of these cultural differences. Too much attention to details in such cases spoils the possibly less accurate, but certainly more unified and more spontaneously conceived, impression in the reader's mind.

While such explanatory notes are woven into the text chiefly to assist the nonscholarly reader, the translator's remarks on Trojan, Carthaginian, and Ausonian rites appear to serve a different purpose. Here the translator seems to be at least as much the theologian who is eager to preserve his congregation of readers from heretical usages as he is the humanist whose main objective is to render an accurate translation of a work from classical antiquity. It has been argued that Douglas "diminishes" the sacred rites which Virgil depicts in the work.[14] At times he does, as when he downplays the religious significance of the "pueri . . . innuptaeque puellae" who "sacra canunt" (II, 238–39) as they surround the Trojan horse, which has been newly brought into the city. Douglas's image of "childer and madis 3yng / Syngand karrellis and dansand in a ryng" (II, iv, 69–70) removes the "possible Vestal virginity" of the girls and "compromises somewhat the effect of Virgil's awe-inspiring myster-ies,"[15] but these lines are preceded by a passage in which Douglas's expansion of Virgil's lines, now expressed in Christian terminology, gives the activities increased holiness. Virgil's general "ducendum ad sedes simulacrum orandaque divae / numina conclamant" (II, 232–33) gains further religious seriousness in Douglas's translation because Douglas characteristically specifies the individual actions, and thus indicates the duration and intensity, of the supplication:

> Onto the hallowit sted bryng in," thai cry,
> "The gret fygur! And lat wss sacryfy
> The haly goddes, and magnyfy hyr mycht
> With orysonys and offerandis day and nycht!"
>
> (II, iv, 57–60)

Instead of substituting Christian terms of divine service as he does here, however, Douglas more commonly tends to take a slightly patronizing attitude toward the sacred rites of the Trojans and other characters. When Virgil describes characters involved in religious rituals, Douglas almost always adds a comment such as "on thar gyss" (IV, viii, 107) or even "on thar payane gyss" (IV, vi, 43). The effect of these intrusions by the narrator is again a distancing of the narrative from the audience and an abrupt interruption of the narrative flow, for the reader is each time reminded that the characters belong to a different time and culture, and to an inferior culture at that. For all their purported objectivity these remarks sound condescending, implying a certain degree of pity for those who have not yet seen the light of Christianity but are still caught in their pagan error without having reached the high degree of con-sciousness which Douglas in Prologue VI conventionally attributes to Virgil himself. The narrator, however, outdoes himself when he has Dido invoke Proserpina "by our gentile lawys" (IV, xi, 50) just before uttering her curse. Dido is here anachronistically cognizant of her own pre-Christian paganism. On the other hand, Dido's libation preceding the first banquet for Aeneas is completely Christianized in Douglas's transla-tion of "in mensam libavit honorem" (I, 736) as "the cowpe with the rich wyne / Apon the burd scho blyssit" (I, xi, 85–86).

Such anachronisms generally do not cause Douglas any concern. On the contrary, Douglas tends to conjecture the purposes of unfamiliar customs and cultural symbols and usually tries to find cultural equivalents for Roman usages which would otherwise have no immediately obvious meaning for a late-medieval Scottish audience. His practice of cross-cultural translation, including additions and explanatory substitutions, accords exactly with his theoretical statements in Prologue I, especially that

> Weill at a blenk sle poetry nocht tayn is,
> And ȝit forsuyth I set my bissy pane
> As that I couth to mak it braid and plane.
>   (I, Prol., 108–10)

For the "thalami taedaeque" (the "bridal bed and bridal torches"; IV, 18) of which Dido used to think herself weary, Douglas substitutes "Genyvs chalmyr" (IV, i, 38) and later for "taedas" alone (IV, 339) "the band of mariage" (IV, vi, 117);[16] and when Anna wipes the blood from Dido's wound, Douglas imaginatively pictures the situation and lets her use the part of her garment which is both softest and nearest to hand as she bends over her sister, changing Virgil's general "veste" (IV, 687) to specifically "hir wympil" (IV, xii, 88), thereby giving the action even greater tenderness. In both these cases, what he sees with his mind's eye are not a Carthaginian queen and her sister, but two courtly ladies of late-medieval Scotland, fully conversant with courtly vernacular literature such as the *Roman de la rose* or Gower's *Confessio Amantis*. Again, when Douglas comes to translate Turnus's siege of the Trojan camp during Aeneas's absence, he adds enough concrete detail to Virgil's description to evoke a vivid image of a fortified city assaulted and defended by medieval armies. In Douglas's translation the Trojan camp gains "fowcy dichis" (IX, ii, 24) and "boss turettis" (IX, ii, 30), and the assaulting forces under Turnus approach "with browdyn baneris gay" (IX, ii, 45) not mentioned by Virgil. While these added details are essentially anachronisms, their presence increases the vividness and intensity of Douglas's translation and makes his images far more dynamic and vibrant than the original ones. Douglas actually *sees* the characters and situations with his mind's eye, and not surprisingly he pictures them in the only manner available to his concrete experience. In John Speirs's words, "the civilized Roman world presents no challenge to Douglas' medieval Christian world; he simply does not recognize it as different and alien."[17] He still lacks the historical sense of the past and the new Renaissance "sense of the historical distance and difference inherent in classical texts,"[18] with the result that he can freely "modernize" Virgil while still remaining faithful if not to the *letter* of Virgil's text, then to what he understands the "sentence" of the text to be. In the process, the Trojans, Carthaginians, and Ausonians, whom Virgil had brought forward into imperial Rome, now make a second leap in space and time to adapt to a late-medieval Scottish milieu.[19]

Just as Douglas *sees* characters and situations before he translates any

particular passage, he also *hears* the accompanying sounds. In this respect, too, his translation is far more concrete and specific than Virgil's
original. The first lines of the description of Aeolus's cave provide a
typical example. The force of the winds is already indicated in Virgil's
repeated voiced and unvoiced sibilants and labio-dental fricatives.

>   hic vasto rex Aeolus antro
>   luctantis ventos tempestatesque sonoras
>   imperio premit.
>   (I, 52–54)

But Douglas increases the noise by replacing Virgil's relatively abstract
and colorless adjectives and verbs with more specific and descriptive ones,
expressing vast forces barely held in check:

>   quhar Eolus the king
>   In gowsty cavys the wyndis lowde quhissilling
>   And braithly tempestis by his power refrenys
>   In bandis hard schet in presoun constrenys.
>   (I, ii, 5–8)

In the description of the subsequent storm at sea, in which part of
Aeneas's company is shipwrecked, Douglas again increases the fearsome
tumult of the storm, adding concrete, expressive details as he relies on
Virgil's text as well as on his own imaginative faculty and on descriptions
of tempests in alliterative poetry in creating the image of a ship in a
storm. Virgil's lines

>   incubuere mari totumque a sedibus imis
>   una Eurusque Notusque ruunt creberque procellis
>   Africus et vastos volvunt ad litora fluctus;
>   insequitur clamorque virum stridorque rudentum
>   (I, 84–87)

express much less force, uproar, and danger than Douglas's

>   Thai ombeset the seys bustuusly,
>   Quhil fra the deip til euery cost fast by
>   The huge wallis weltris apon hie,
>   Rollit at anys with storm of wyndis thre,
>
>   . . . .
>   Sone efter this, of men the clamour rayss,
>   The takillis graslis, cabillis can fret and frays.
>   (I, ii, 53–60)

By substituting specific, technical terms ("takillis" and "cabillis") for a
generic one ("rudentes") and by specifying the exact sound in detail
("graslis" and "fret") as well as picturing the result ("frays") indicated by

those sounds, Douglas brings the *Aeneid* down to the level of everyday life, making it more human and less heroic by removing Virgil's "blurred images,"[20] which give epic grandeur and dignity to the characters and their actions. Later, Douglas concretizes Virgil's general indications of Aeneas's commands on how to act during his absence. While Aeneas merely warns the Trojans "si qua interea fortuna fuisset, / neu struere auderent aciem neu credere campo" (IX, 41–42), in Douglas's translation these abstract instructions become concrete and specific. Here Eneas

> Gaif thame command, *gif thai assalȝeit wer*
> *Or hys returnyng*, be hard fortoun of weir,
> That thai ne suld in batale thame array,
> Nor in the plane *thar ennemys assay.*
>
> (IX, ii, 17–20)

Douglas's particularization is, of course, logically correct, but there should be no need for Aeneas to give his Trojans such specific commands: the larger-than-life heroes in his forces know without being told, but Douglas reduces them to a company of pressed men who do not know what to do unless they have been given precise instructions.

On the other hand, Douglas's battle descriptions are on the verge of gaining additional force and vigor from the influence of alliterative heroic poetry, which modifies his word choice and his rhythms. In this respect Douglas's sigh "Quha is attachit ontill a staik, we se, / May go na ferthir bot wreil about that tre" (I, Prol., 297–98) rings more true than in any other. When Douglas expands battle scenes rather than translating them "al maste word by word" (Direction, 46), the alliterative idiom asserts itself even in the pentameter lines and infuses the narrative with so much energy that "the very words whack and dodge and echo,"[21] as in the translation of Virgil's passage

> abduxere retro longe capita ardua ab ictu
> immiscentque manus manibus pugnamque lacessunt,
> ille pedum melior motu fretusque iuventa,
>
> (V, 428–30)

where Douglas expands the middle line into eight of his own:

> And from the straik thar nek drew far abak.
> Now, hand to hand, the dynt lychtis with a swak;
> Now bendis he vp hys burdon with a mynt,
> On syde he bradis fortil eschew the dynt;
> He etlys ȝondir hys avantage to tak,
> He metis hym thar, and charris hym with a chak;
> He watis to spy, and smytis in al hys mycht,
> The tother keppys hym on hys burdon wycht;

Thai foyn at othir, and eggis to bargane.
Lychtar on fute and agil was the tane
And in hys lusty 30uth sum deil ensuris.

(V, viii, 9–19)

Such major expansions, however, are extremely rare; having to conform
as closely as possible to Virgil's structure and wording, Douglas cannot
fully exploit the latent resource of alliterative phrasing. Virgil's epic
similes, especially, leave the impression of being wholly inorganic parts
when they reappear in Douglas's translation, for in translation they break
the arc of the narrative and hamper its flight, becoming undesirable
elements which interrupt rather than extend the particular image because they are alien to their new, almost alliterative surroundings. In the
scenes describing storms at sea, however, Douglas uses alliteration freely
and exploits its characteristic potential for onomatopoeia. Onomatopoeic
alliteration, together with his habit of specifying and concretizing, makes
Douglas's sea far more real than Virgil's. "Aeneas's boat becomes a
'ballingare' (originally a whaling ship) and the booms, masts, and riggin
are rearranged to make sense, rather than left in disarray in order to
terrify."[22] But in consequence, the perspective changes. Virgil's tempest
is seen from the point of view of one of the horrified mariners, who hears
the sound of the breaking oars and has just enough time to take in the
general view of the disaster before he is engulfed by the water:

stridens Aquilone procella
velum adversa ferit, fluctusque ad sidera tollit;
franguntur remi; tum prora avertit et undis
dat latus; insequitur cumulo praeruptus aquae mons.
hi summo in fluctu pendent; his unda dehiscens
terram inter fluctus aperit; furit aestus harenis.

(I, 102–7)

Douglas's storm, in contrast, is narrated by an objective, disinterested
outsider who has time to observe and record every stage of this fascinating shipwreck and who enjoys making the most of its description:

A blastrand bub out from the north brayng
Gan our the forschip in the baksaill dyng,
And to the sternys vp the flude gan cast.
The aris, hechis and the takillis brast,
The schippis stevin frawart hyr went gan wryth,
And turnyt hir braid syde to the wallis swyth.
Heich as a hill the iaw of watir brak
And in ane hepe cam on thame with a swak.
Sum hesit hoverand on the wallis hycht,
And sum the swowchand sey so law gart lycht
Thame semyt the erd oppynnyt amyd the flude—
The stour vp bullyrrit sand as it war wode.

(I, iii, 15–26)

Douglas has tidied the wreckage even while describing the disaster, but the result of his visual and acoustic precision is that the impression created in this scene is radically changed.

Douglas would have justified all his various ways of subtly changing the texture of Virgil's work by reference to his desire "to mak it braid and plane" (I, Prol., 110), for "Sum tyme the text mon haue ane expositioun" (I, Prol., 347); and he would have pointed out that "Scottis" is after all a "bad, harsk spech and lewit barbour tong" and "rurall wlgar gross" (I, Prol., 21, 43) incapable of the subtleties of Virgil's elegant and polished Latin. Indeed, given the sovereign ease with which Douglas makes his changes, he probably would not even have regarded many of them as such.[23] However, it does not follow that Douglas is incapable of literal translation; on the contrary, he often, though only briefly, imitates Virgil's sentence structure and, if possible, even his word order. But rarely is Douglas's version as close to Virgil's original as in the translation of the scene with which the epic closes: the death of Turnus. While Douglas's habits of double translation and of explanatory substitution assert themselves even here, the passage is essentially left as it is. Turnus's death scene is not touched up with specific, concrete details; Douglas, for once, refrains. And by refraining from adding anything, he retains the starkness of this slaying. However, whereas Virgil's text ends just at the point where the Trojans' struggle to fulfil their destiny has reached completion, Douglas adds Maphaeus's thirteenth book, with the result that the reader is taken from the final, oppressive scene of unrelieved slaughter into the festive atmosphere of Aeneas's wedding and eventually to his apotheosis. Despite his fidelity to Virgil's text in the final lines of Book XII, Douglas betrays Virgil after the end. Having censured Caxton for interpolating extraneous material from Baccaccio and other sources, Douglas cannot resist incorporating Maphaeus's supplement.

Notes

1. Text quotations are taken from *Virgil's Aeneid Translated into Scottish Verse by Gavin Douglas, Bishop of Dunkeld*, ed. David F. C. Coldwell, 4 vols., STS 25, 27, 28, 30 (Edinburgh and London: Blackwell, 1957–64); *Virgil: Eclogues, Georgics, Aeneid, The Minor Poems*, ed. and trans. H. Rushton Fairclough, 2 vols., Loeb Classical Library, rev. ed. (Cambridge, Mass.: Harvard University Press, 1978); *The Riverside Chaucer*, ed. Larry D. Benson, 3d ed. (Boston: Houghton Mifflin, 1987). All italics in the quotations are mine.
2. Douglas's criticism of Caxton is entirely correct; in fact, Douglas might have added the further point that Caxton's version introduces extraneous material from Boccaccio's *De casibus* and other sources (e.g., a second motivation for Dido's suicide and a list of the kings and consuls of Rome).

3. Priscilla Bawcutt, "Douglas and Surrey: Translators of Virgil," *Essays and Studies*, n.s. 27 (1974): 52–67, shows that Surrey in his only slightly later translation of *Aeneid* II and IV manages to retain Virgil's tautness and economy by avoiding the various line-filling devices, particularly the doublets, which Douglas uses freely. Surrey's use of blank verse, however, frees him from the need to find rhyme words—a need which for Douglas occasionally poses great problems, as when he has Juno cry " 'Ho!' " (III, vi, 52) because he has to find a word which rhymes with "Iuno" in the preceding line. This particular instance, together with several others, is discussed by Hans Käsmann, "Gavin Douglas' *Aeneis*-Übersetzung," in *Festschrift für Walter Hübner*, eds. Dieter Riesner and Helmut Gneuss (Berlin: Erich Schmidt Verlag, 1964), 175.

4. Käsmann lists further examples of such pairs of synonyms in "Gavin Douglas' *Aeneis*-Übersetzung," 175–76. Such doublets are often suggested by the Latin commentaries which by the sixteenth century usually accompanied Virgil's text; thus, Ascensius's gloss "numero: idest multitudine ingruentum" is silently incorporated into the text: "By *multitude and nowmyr* apon wss set" (II, vii, 109–10). Similarly, synonym pairs linked with "or" often derive from discrepancies among the Latin commentators or even from indecisions in a single commentary, where alternative glosses are given in an "aut . . . aut" construction. See Bawcutt, "Douglas and Surrey," 64, and her *Gavin Douglas: A Critical Study*, (Edinburgh: Edinburgh University Press, 1976), 124.

5. Bawcutt, *Gavin Douglas*, 158, 162.

6. A. C. Spearing, *Medieval to Renaissance in English Poetry* (Cambridge: Cambridge University Press, 1985), 61.

7. Similar instances also occur in other books—e.g., III, vi, 192–93 (III, 454) and IV, vi, 38 (IV, 299).

8. E. M. W. Tillyard, *The English Epic and its Background,* (London: Chatto and Windus, 1954), 340–41, provides a detailed analysis of the small additions and changes with which Douglas increases the immediacy of the action in VIII, ix, 113–24 (the departure of the Arcadian cavalry from Evander's settlement; VIII, 592–96).

9. Douglas also lets characters answer their own rhetorical questions, e.g. IV, vii, 18. In the quoted case, however, Douglas's edition of Virgil may well have been differently punctuated; Virgil's sentence can be taken as either question or exclamation. Priscilla J. Bawcutt discusses textual problems in her article "Gavin Douglas and the Text of Virgil," *Edinburgh Bibliographical Society Transactions*, vol. IV (1955–71); 211–31. Bawcutt concludes that many of Douglas's seeming inaccuracies and mistranslations are actually faithful and accurate translations of errors in Ascensius's 1501 edition of Virgil, which Douglas must have used as his working text.

10. John Speirs, "The Scots 'Aeneid' of Gavin Douglas," in his *The Scots Literary Tradition: An Essay in Criticism,* 2d ed. (London: Faber & Faber, 1962), 177.

11. Speirs, "The Scots 'Aeneid',," 178, argues that Douglas "views [the Dido and Aeneas story] as a medieval Christian moralist, for whom human love must always be subordinate to obedience to the divine will. This may not be exactly what Virgil meant by *pietas*, [. . .] but it is the medieval Christian equivalent or development from it."

12. Nonetheless, Douglas's phrasing is strongly influenced by Chaucer's in *LGW*;

for a discussion of these resemblances, see Priscilla Bawcutt, "Gavin Douglas and Chaucer," *Review of English Studies,* n.s. 21 (1970): 413–15.

13. Bawcutt explains Douglas's phrase "be myne avyss": both Servius and Ascensius gloss "virago" as "mulier, quae virile implet officium" (*Gavin Douglas,* 121).

14. Alan Hager, "British Virgil: Four Renaissance Disguises of the Laocoon Passage of Book 2 of the *Aeneid,*" *Studies in English Literature* 22 (1982): 27.

15. Ibid.

16. In "Gavin Douglas's Latin Vocabulary," *Phoenix,* 24 (1970); 55–56, 62–63, Colin D. Gordon cites further instances of such explanatory substitutions—e.g., "fasces" (VI, 818) as "ensenʒeis [i.e., emblems] . . . Befor hym born throu all Romys tovne" (VI, xiv, 27–31). On the other hand, Douglas's translation of the boxing match and the chariot race during the funeral games seems to betray his inability to visualize these Roman sports; thus, the boxing match, transferred into Douglas's own environment, becomes a quarterstaff contest.

17. Speirs, "The Scots 'Aeneid'," 169.

18. Spearing, *Medieval to Renaissance,* 13.

19. Käsmann, "Gavin Douglas' *Aeneis*-Übersetzung," 170, however, argues that "Belege für die Mediaevalisierung der *Aeneis* halten einer genaueren Überprüfung nicht stand," and maintains that the text itself remains unaffected by the medieval concepts which Douglas introduces in the Prologues and that translations such as 'nun' for 'sacerdos' are caused by gaps in the ME vocabulary rather than by any "spezifisch mittelalterliche Blindheit" on Douglas's part.

20. The expression is taken from W. R. Johnson, *Darkness Visible: A Study of Vergil's Aeneid* (Berkeley: University of California Press, 1976), 75. Johnson, however, uses the expression particularly to distinguish the "deliberate blurring" in Virgil's epic similes from the "clarity of picture" in Homer's (55).

21. Robin Fulton, "Douglas and Virgil," *Studies in Scottish Literature* 2 (1964): 125.

22. Hager, "British Virgil," 24.

23. In "Gavin Douglas' *Eneados:* A Reinterpretation," *PMLA* 67 (1952): 856–58, Bruce Dearing argues that Douglas expands certain passages in order to give them stronger political overtones. Most of these expansions, however, are in fact a result of Douglas's tendency to use pairs of synonyms, to add line-filling tags, and to supply explanatory comments; the ratio of Latin to "Scottis" lines in the passages quoted by Dearing does not significantly vary from the average of 1:2.2. The only passage which actually supports Dearing's argument is VI, ix, 190–92 (VI, 620), where Phlegyas admonishes "all wightis, prynce and kyng," rather than more generally "omnis," to observe justice.

Church Reform and Social Structure in Western Europe

GILES CONSTABLE

Uta-Renate Blumenthal, *The Investiture Controversy: Church and Monarchy from the Ninth to the Twelfth Century*. Philadelphia: University of Pennsylvania Press, 1988. Pp. xxi, 191.

R. I. Moore, *The Formation of a Persecuting Society: Power and Deviance in Western Europe, 950–1250*. Oxford and New York: Basil Blackwell, 1987. Pp. vii, 159.

In spite of their different titles and approaches, these two books deal with the same period and, broadly speaking, the same subject: the changes in western Europe in the eleventh and twelfth centuries and in particular the results of the reform movement commonly referred to as the investiture controversy. Blumenthal reaches back into the Carolingian age and ends in the first half of the twelfth century. Moore goes from the eleventh century to the first half of the thirteenth. To some extent he picks up where Blumenthal leaves off, showing how a new alliance between church and state, dominated by a sense of hierarchy, replaced the older type of alliance, of which Blumenthal studies the origins and demise. Both writers (like some recent historians of the French Revolution) show some sympathy for the old régime and recognize that what is usually considered a movement of progress and reform involved losses as well as gains for society.

Blumenthal's book is a revised translation, made by herself of her work on *Der Investiturstreit*, which appeared in German in 1982.[1] It is the most comprehensive, up-to-date, and accessible account of the investiture controversy in English and will be useful to students and teachers as well as researchers, for whom its value is somewhat diminished, however, by the lack of notes. On the whole it reads well, but it is marred by a number of small misprints, errors, inconsistencies, and infelicities of style,[2] including an unusual system of writing dates by which Philip I of France and William Rufus are dated 1060–108 and 1087–100 (142). "Regular secular clergy" (7) is a confusing term for canons, to whom it presumably refers. (The text in German refers both to the secular clergy and to houses of canons and canonesses.) "Condominate" is used, as a noun, for joint rule or condominium, and "observation" (of a rule) for the more usual

101

observance. These are small matters, but they disturb the flow in reading an otherwise distinguished book.

The subtitle "Church and Monarchy from the Ninth to the Twelfth Century" is a more accurate description of the book's subject than the main title, "The Investiture Controversy." Blumenthal does not in fact believe that investiture, though important, was the main issue between the kings and popes in the eleventh century. "The investiture prohibition . . . ," she says (121), "emerges as a result of the dispute between pope and king and not as its underlying cause." The real problem, for her, grew out of the tradition of sacral kingship which took root in the Carolingian period and was associated, as Robert Deschman has recently shown for Anglo-Saxon England, with monastic christological piety. Blumenthal's first chapter is concerned with monastic reform and piety in the tenth and early eleventh centuries and sets the stage for the second chapter, on the German emperors and the legacy of Rome in the eleventh century, when the kings created a "state church" that became "the leading central institution of the empire" (36, citing Kempf and Mitteis). Henry II "paved the way for a stable and unchallenged theocratic regime" (46) which was fostered by his successors Conrad II and Henry III, who especially emphasized "the quasi-priestly aspects of the imperial dignity" (53).

The central task of the reforming popes in the second half of the eleventh century, who are the subject of chapter 3, was to deprive the monarchy of the sacrality "with which it had entered a seemingly indissoluble bond in the Carolingian period in the west" (124). Blumenthal takes a broad and on the whole cautious approach, stressing the slow evolution, many sources, and various interpretations of the reform movement. The monastic reforms which fostered the concept of theocratic rule also "prepared the way for the reform of the church at large" and were linked, through the regular canons, to "the renewal of Christian life in general" (65, 68). "An inquiry into the wellsprings of the reform is in effect an inquiry into the origin of the movement to exclude lay influence from the church" (87). Yet she also stresses the contribution of important individuals and events. The papacy under Leo IX, for instance, "almost overnight . . . became a living and ever-present reality for all Christians" (73). Leo set the course which was followed by his successors, including Gregory VII, to whose relations with Henry IV chapter 4 is devoted, and under whom the relationship between *regnum* and *sacerdotium* was transformed by "the new-found spiritual and moral strength of the reformed papacy" (94). Gregory's dealings with Henry were inspired by a sense of responsibility as well as of right; and Canossa, for Blumenthal, was a primarily pastoral rather than political event (123). "Convinced of his divine mission," Gregory "claimed the right to depose not only bishops but also secular rulers" (118). He deprived the kings of their sacrality, leaving them purely secular figures, and struck at the roots of the state church system.

In its place the reformers promoted a concept of a hierarchical society run by clerical bureaucrats who sought to divide and conquer. This is the central theme of Moore's book on *The Formation of a Persecuting Society*,[3] in which he studies the reappearance in the eleventh century of the persecution, which since the fifth century had virtually disappeared in the West, of minorities and marginal groups. He studies in particular the parallels in the treatment of heretics, Jews, and lepers, whom most previous scholars have studied separately. Heresy became "the policy of the church" in the second half of the eleventh century, when the reformers derived much of their program from earlier heretics, but it reappeared, Moore says, "as the Gregorian revolution lost its zeal and began to come to terms with the world again." Some heretics still sought to achieve the radical reform program of apostolic poverty and separation of spiritual and secular authority, but others reacted against the Gregorian "ideal of a hierarchically organized church which claimed the right to intervene in every area of life and thought" (19).

The success of the reformers and the concentration of power in the hands of the clergy thus helped to create the circumstances with which Moore is concerned. The response to the cases of Arnold of Brescia and Eon of l'Etoile in the middle of the twelfth century "marks a very clear watershed in the history of the Church" (24) and the beginnings of a new type of cooperation between church and state against all minorities and dissidents. In the course of the century Jews were increasingly limited to specific activities and areas and were juridically defined as serfs, the possessions of the king (34, 40). The same period, especially the second half of the century, saw "a transition from a relatively compassionate to a relatively stern attitude to the lepers and a greater degree of coercion in their confinement" (58). Lepers were no longer regarded simply as ill but also as a distinctive, sometimes almost quasi-religious, order, parallel to hermits and monks, and subject to special and increasingly repressive treatment.

The most original feature of Moore's book lies in the explanation he proposes for the similarity in the treatment of these groups, who presented, he argues, no real threat to society. He rejects out of hand the view "that three entirely different groups of people, characterized respectively by religious conviction, physical condition, and race and culture, should all have begun at the same time and by the same stages to pose the same threats, which must be dealt with in the same ways" (67). He does not deny that they were perceived as presenting a threat. The language of contamination that was—and still often is—applied not only to these groups, but also to homosexuals, prostitutes, the poor and unfortunate generally, certainly expressed fear. Leprosy in particular may have really threatened the growing and increasingly urbanized population of the twelfth and thirteenth centuries. But he denies that this was the cause for the special treatment of these groups and attributes it to what Leach called a changed " 'internalised version of the environment' which defined them more exactly than before and classified them as enemies of society" (99). Persecution was the cause of their distinctiveness (67, 84) and the result of the assertion of control by the increasingly hierarchical and centralized society which developed after the Gregorian revolution in the eleventh century (144, 146). "As always, the establishment of the high culture demanded the ruthless elimination of its actual and potential rivals. And of these the greatest was Judaism" (151).

This is a stimulating and original thesis, which will doubtless be debated by medievalists, and historians of Europe generally, for years to come. Are high cultures and hierarchical societies necessarily persecuting societies? Was late-medieval society, which in some respects was pluralistic and corporative, really shaped in a hierarchical mold by the Gregorian reform? Was the distinctiveness of heretics, Jews, and lepers the result of their persecution, and was their treatment as similar as Moore argues? In the late Middle Ages, as in the eleventh century, much heresy became the policy of the church, and lepers were not always treated without compassion and concern, as the behavior of many saints shows. The Jews are undoubtedly Moore's best example, but in the sentence quoted at the end of the previous paragraph he seems to concede, surprisingly and not altogether convincingly, that Judaism really was a rival to the high culture of the late Middle Ages, rather than its partner. It was certainly seen as an enemy, however, and was perhaps made into and treated as one by the conceptually hierarchical and centralized society which emerged in the twelfth and thirteenth centuries.

To these questions Blumenthal offers no answers, since she is looking backward rather than forward, but she would agree, I think, with Moore in stressing the importance of the eleventh and twelfth centuries, which saw, he says, "the most profound and most permanent change that overtook Western Europe between the invention of agriculture and the industrial revolution" and in attributing "the transformation of European society" at that time in large part to the reform of the church (102). Moore is openly doubtful about the benefit of these developments and at the end of his introduction raises the question of whether "the epoch since 1100" should be seen as "one of progress or decline" (5). Reversing the formula of Paul Hyams, he views the church as an "engine of radical change"[4] and stresses how the papacy, "captured for reform in the revolution of the eleventh century"—the terminology is striking—forced on the church innovations, such as regular attendance at mass and confession to priests, which consolidated its control over the laity (71). Literate clerics replaced laymen as "the agents of government and the confidants of princes" and served as "the agents as well as the theorists of persecution," representing "a new stage in the specialization and professionalization of government" (136).

This anticlerical tone is entirely lacking in Blumenthal, but she too clearly feels that the more decentralized society of the pre-Gregorian age, when sacral kings worked with and through regional churches, had virtues which were hidden to the reformers, who in turn introduced changes which were not entirely beneficial. Moore waxes eloquent about the consequences of subjecting the self-regulating communities of the early Middle Ages to centralized control, and attributes "the growth of the mentalities and mechanisms of persecution" to the increasing commitment to social and political hierarchy (144). He even defends the ordeal, in which communities acted as "a source of justice and order," and attributes its abolition to the assertion of combined clerical and royal power (131; see note 4). "Just as trial by ordeal expressed the authority of the community its judicial role, popular heresy represented . . . the assertion of collective values and communal independence against the subordination of religion first to seignurial and later to bureaucratic power" (133). The picture this suggests of a just, orderly, tolerant, localized society in the early Middle Ages is doubtless overdrawn but not necessarily untrue, and it represents an important antidote to the black colors with which the past was painted by the reformers in the eleventh century and of which the broad import has been accepted by almost all later scholars.

Notes

1. The valuable bibliographies have been brought up to date; and chapter 5, dealing with the investiture controversies in England, France, and Germany after the death of Gregory VII, has been extensively revised.
2. "Eduard," for instance, appears for "Edward," and Hugh Candidus is referred to, without explanation, both that way and as Hugh the White. In the quotation on p. 109 (not in the German edition) "propriety" looks like a mistake for "property."
3. Aside from a number of small misprints, I noticed very few errors in this book. The "abbot" of Remiremont (48) should, I think, be "abbess," and *"pauperes"* (102) may simply mean poor rather than "servile."
4. See p. 128, n. 8, where he also argues against Hyams and Peter Brown that the

ordeal "did not 'wither away' through any general erosion of confidence in its operation" and agrees with Robert Bartlett that "ordeal was brought to an end by deliberate clerical opposition"; and p. 138, where he attributes to the influence of clerical *literati* "the displacement of ordeal by inquest" and other developments usually seen as the result of "the victory of reason over superstition and of truth over custom."

Habitats and Habitudes

DAVID HERLIHY

Wendy Davies, *Small Worlds: The Village Community in Early Medieval Brittany.* Berkeley and Los Angeles: University of California Press, 1988. Pp. xi, 227. 33 illustrations, 13 tables.

Stephen D. White, *Custom, Kinship and Gifts to Saints: The* Laudatio Parentum *in Western France, 1050–1150.* Studies in Legal History. Chapel Hill and London: The University of North Carolina Press, 1988. Pp. xx, 313. 10 figures, 13 tables.

The monastic cartulary—compilations of formal acts usually involving private individuals—is a crucial source in the study of early-medieval social history. To be sure, the acts seem at first brush banal and boring. They are in the overwhelming majority conveyances of land—donations, sales, exchanges, leases, and the like. The recipient of the land is in most cases the monastery that redacted the cartulary, but in receiving the land the monastery sometimes acquired an archive of earlier records, involving only laymen and establishing the donor's right to make the gift. Not all entries, in other words, are directly linked to religious institutions. The transactions were first recorded on separate charters, and these were copied into chartularies only at some later date. In this form most such transactions have reached us. While the cartularies rarely refer to the great events of the day, they illuminate numerous corners of medieval private life. These two books are brilliant examples of their uses.

The principal source of Davis's book is the cartulary of a single monastery—that of the Holy Savior of Redon in southeast Brittany about sixty-five kilometers from Rennes, the provincial capital. Founded in 832, the monastery grew rapidly to become the dominant religious establishment of the region. Its cartulary and related charters number almost 350, more than 30 percent of which are concentrated in the 860s. The numbers thereafter decline rapidly, though the early tenth century is still sparsely represented. Davis, a British historian who has done much distinguished work in the history of Celtic Europe, has put the cartulary into a data base. Although she does not explain the structure of the data base, it has obviously enabled her to accomplish the most tedious task in this kind of research: the linking of the names of people and of places across hundreds of entries.

Davis's approach is systematic and consciously intended to attract readers from beyond the narrow ranks of Carolingian specialists. She accordingly begins with a sketch of the Carolingian empire and its principal institutions in the ninth century. She then describes the geography of eastern Brittany, the main focus of the documents. Plow agriculture was the chief support of the rural economy, though vine raising was important in the southern zones and pasturage everywhere. Markets and trade existed, but it is hard to estimate their importance. Coined money was essential to the Breton peasants but chiefly for special uses, such as the payment of taxes; this could not be considered a monetized economy. Settlement was based on the tenure known as the ran, seemingly a family farm and probably the Breton equivalent of the west-Frankish *mansus*.

The chief surprise that emerges from her examination of agriculture and settlement is the absence of the classical manor—the great estate with an extensive demesne cultivated through labor services imposed upon serfs. There were unfree cultivators in Brittany—Davis estimates their number at about 25 percent of the population—but they seem to have been obligated only to rents and not to labor.

The family certainly exercised constraints over what its members could do with their properties (the focus of White's book), but noble women at least could donate or bequeath land as they chose, and they figure importantly among the monastery's donors. Davis tries to measure the status of the free peasants on the basis of the numbers and distributions of the properties they owned. The richest stratum was very small (about 2 percent of the total population), and most free peasants (63 percent) were in the category of simple owners.

Davis also considers population mobility: the network of communications on land and water, and who traveled and why. The life of most peasants was confined to their district of origin, called the *plebs,* but some among them could appear in various capacities (chiefly as witnesses) in more than one *plebs.*

Several levels of government exerted varying pressures upon the peasants of eastern Brittany. *Machtierns,* apparently present in every *plebs,* presided over the settling of disputes but seem not to have had fiscal or military functions. Their origins are unclear, but they do not seem to have been agents of outside authority. *Maiores* may have been stewards of great landowners, but perhaps they were simply village elders. *Missi* represented the "prince" *(princeps)* of Brittany, the highest regional authority and, more distantly and rarely, the Carolingian king or emperor. Feudal terms, such as *fidelis,* are there, and the monastery succeeded in constructing by the late ninth century a territorial *seigneurie,* an enclave of authority precocious for its age. But a feudal system existed only in embryo. On the whole, the large territorial powers impinged little upon the lives of the peasants, who seem to have ruled themselves chiefly through their own institutions and customs. This is perhaps the reason why Davis entitles her book "small worlds."

I have two reservations about her otherwise excellent work. Most of the rents given in the leases she cites are very small, verging on token. The granting of easy leases for token rents to favored tenants was a common practice—and a common bane—of ecclesiastical great properties all over Europe. It does not seem possible that leases of this kind could have fed a large monastic community with heavy responsibilities to both church and state. There had to be some other source of food and revenue that the cartulary does not explicitly describe. Davis does not really confront this problem and seems unaware of its existence.

Several of her principal arguments—the definition of status, the reconstruction of social networks—rest on the assumption that the same name identifies the same person. The large stock of personal names shores up confidence that this is so, but other practices—frequent reliance on only a single name to identify the person, variations in spelling, perhaps the use of different names by the same person—give reason for doubting that names appearing in different areas or over a decade or more really do identify the same person. The basis of her confidence in her nominal linkages needed further discussion, and this also would require some information about the data base she constructed.

In spite of these shortcomings, Davis has provided a full and fascinating picture of Carolingian communities, much different from those deriving from the manorial surveys. Her work confirms that the Carolingian universe contained more, and more varied, worlds than we had reckoned.

Stephen White, an American historian with much experience in legal history, also utilizes cartularies, but for purposes much different from Davis's. His interest is the *"laudatio parentum,"* or the "approval of relatives," the conventional name given to a practice widely encountered in charters of the eleventh and twelfth centuries. When a donor alienated land, he or she was often joined by relatives who approved the conveyance. Many historians have seen in the practice evidence of the solidarity of the early-medieval kindred, but never before has it attracted an independent study.

White examines the *laudatio* as it appears in the cartularies of five Benedictine monasteries in western France: Saint Aubin of Angers, Marmoutier, Saint Mary of Noyers, La Trinité of Vendôme, and Saint Vincent of Le Mans. Most entries are dated between 1050 and 1150, which corresponds to the period when the *laudatio* was most common. The limitation of his inquiry to one region and five monasteries has allowed him to proceed with considerable rigor; the book contains, along with many tables, twenty pages of statistics in its appendix.

White also reviews at length old and more recent interpretations of the *laudatio* and finds them helpful but not ultimately satisfying. Did a legal rule require that the consent of relatives be secured in alienating land? There is no compelling evidence that this was so, and more profoundly, the question itself is misapplied in an early-medieval context. Legal norms were not yet clearly differentiated from other kinds of ethical norms or maxims influencing society; they were not clearly defined and effectively enforced by courts staffed by professionals.

Did the norms identify precisely who among the donor's relatives should give consent? Here, White proceeds pragmatically, carefully reconstructing the various kin groups that appear in the charters. Some of the consenting kindreds may indeed represent a descent group from common grandparents that has been subject to natural vicissitudes of marriages and deaths. But rigorous consistency in the composition of the groups is not visible. Moreover, maternal kin are present, but there remains a strong patrilineal bias; in sum, why particular relatives were or were not asked to consent cannot be determined.

White here again emphasizes his chief argument: legal norms cannot explain the *laudatio*. In his view, the contemporary religious view of the universe played a crucial role. Gifts in early-medieval society, as in many primitive communities, were not isolated acts. Rather, they established permanent ties between donor and recipient and imposed upon the latter obligations of reciprocity. In the medieval expression of this principle, the donor hoped to exchange an earthly inheritance for a heavenly one. His gift created a lasting relationship among the donor, the monks, and the saints that they served. But for various reasons, the gift involved the donor's relatives as well. In a negative way, relatives, and even descendants as yet unborn, had to be dissuaded from contesting the donation. In a positive way, relatives and future descendants were invited to participate in the lasting spiritual benefits that the gift engendered. Moreover, relatives and descendants could ensure that the monks fulfilled their obligations of perpetual intercession with their saint and with God. The *laudatio parentum* embodied a strategy of spiritual survival that the landed elite of western France pursued in the eleventh and twelfth centuries.

White goes on to consider why the *laudatio* fell out of favor in the thirteenth century. As his own monasteries do not yield much material for this period, he must rely on the work of French medievalists, chiefly Georges Duby and Robert Fossier, for his data. The factors that outmoded the *laudatio* are again complex. They include the new legal culture, the separation of legal norms from other norms, and their enforcement by courts and trained jurists; the emergence of the patrilineage, which excluded from the principal descent group matrilineal relatives; and the decline of Benedictine monasticism and the religious system it had once sustained. The history of the *laudatio* thus becomes a commentary on many legal, social, and religious changes across the central Middle Ages.

I have two small criticisms to make of this book. The data from his five cartularies do not address the last theme he considers: the decline of the *laudatio*. In considering the decline, he essentially comments only on the work of others. The character of the book changes ever so slightly between its body and its conclusion. Moreover, I rather missed any discussion of why the *laudatio* initially comes into view from about the year 1000. For as the work of these other historians also establishes, the practice is not encountered in the earliest medieval donations (and not found, at least not in a formal way, in the charters of Redon). White quite properly emphasizes the cultural and religious factors, rather than the economic, in his interpretation of the *laudatio*, but had these factors changed in the course of the eleventh century? What does explain its appearance? The question remains open, but any effort to resolve it will have to take White's stimulating book as its point of departure.

Medieval cartularies seem to the unperceptive to be aggregations of trivial transactions. It is a pleasure to watch how these two energetic and skilled historians find within seemingly formless records order and, for a dark period of medieval history, illumination.

Saints, Scholars, and a Royal Councilor

JAMES W. ALEXANDER

The Book of St. Gilbert. Trans. with introduction and notes by Raymonde Foreville and
Gillian Keir. Oxford: Clarendon Press, 1987.
Rodney M. Thomson, *William of Malmesbury.* Woodbridge (Sf): Boydell, 1987.
Sally Vaughn, *Anselm of Bec and Robert of Meulan: The Innocence of the Dove and the Wisdom
of the Serpent.* Berkeley and Los Angeles: University of California, 1987.

British, American, and French scholars have recently produced thoughtful books, important to their fellow historians, on saints, scholars, and
prelates of the twelfth-century English church. Superseded are the interpretations of early modern and Victorian historians, based largely on
chronicle sources and on religious partisanship. The books here reviewed
typify contemporary concern with record as well as with narrative evidence, with the social context of religious affairs, and with a thorough
attempt to view great saints and scholars as historical rather than hagiographical figures. Among the more important recent works which provide a context for the books here discussed are Frank Barlow, *The English
Church, 1066–1154* (1979); *idem, William Rufus* (1983); Margaret Gibson,
Lanfranc of Bec (1978); Helen Clover and Margaret Gibson, eds. and
trans., *The Letters of Lanfranc Archbishop of Canterbury* (1979); Martin Brett,
The English Church Under Henry I (1975); and Antonia Gransden, *Historical
Writing in England, c. 550–c. 1307* (1974).

The Book of St. Gilbert, *William of Malmesbury,* and *Anselm and Robert* are
very different books. *Gilbert* joins its predecessors in the Medieval Texts
series in exemplifying thorough, careful editing of documents, introduced with learning and with grace, accompanied by felicitous translation. *William* is a literary and intellectual biography. *Anselm and Robert* is a
political and religious study of relations between the Anglo-Norman
church and state during the reigns of William II and Henry I; unlike the
authors of the other two works, Vaughn seeks controversy with high
spirits and with iconoclastic argument. Who, after all, is a more exalted
icon in matters Anselmian than Sir Richard Southern?

The Book of St. Gilbert is a specialist's work, one worthy of its companions
in the Nelson's and Oxford Medieval Texts series. Foreville, among the

most authoritative French historians of early Angevin England for more than four decades, brings immense learning, clear prose, and impeccable scholarship to her readers; Keir provides a graceful translation of the texts. The *Book* includes a biography of the founder of the Order of Sempringham, letters relating to the 1160s rebellion of the lay brothers over alleged maladministration and moral improprieties, documents and letters bearing upon the canonization of Gilbert, and narratives of his miracles. The canonization documents also present invaluable source material for this history of the order. Almost a quarter of the volume consists of an excellent introduction to the texts of the letters and documents. It provides a biography of Gilbert and places him in the context of the founding and history of his order; Foreville then discusses the growth and decline of the order as well as its nature and internal crises. As is customary with books in this series, her introduction concludes with a discussion of the history and transmission of the manuscripts and a mention of earlier editions of her materials. She shows Sempringham's uniqueness as a double order in which the predominance of the nuns was maintained by canonical statute; Foreville alludes (too briefly; liii–liv) to comparison with Fontevraud, the mixed community founded by Robert of Arbrissel in the early twelfth century. I did miss, in this superb study with its texts, a reference (p. 2, n. 1) to Charles Young's *Hurbert Walter, Lord of Canterbury and Lord of England* (1968).

Rodney Thomson's *William of Malmesbury* is the first book-length study to concentrate solely on the life and works of William, alleged by the dust jacket to be "England's greatest historian after Bede"; what probably is meant here is "nonacademic historian." Thomson has spent nearly two decades of research and thought on this historian; his effort and concern were well-spent. Surely, pending the unlikely discovery of major unprinted evidence, there will be no need for a further book-length study of Malmesbury's greatest historian and scholar. This admirable work is divided into two parts: the first a study of William as monk and as historian, the second an examination of William's intellectual background in the context of Carolingian and post-Carolingian writers. The first section is more likely to be of interest to medieval historians who lack compelling interest in the somewhat rarefied pursuit of what Thomson has called "Studies of the Writer at Work."

Chapter 1, "William of Malmesbury and his Environment," is a life-and-times narrative, securely placing the monk–scholar in his political, monastic, and social milieu. Thomson speaks of William's probable educational background; he stresses the Benedictine influence on the formation of William's thought processes and on the suppositions from which he approached the world of the historian and of the scholar.

Thomson discusses William's use and evaluation of his sources as well. He makes telling comparisons with the work of the Venerable Bede and of John of Salisbury. The second chapter expands on the first, examining William "as historian and man of letters," beginning with a discussion of William's reputation in the writings of modern historians, then proceeding to consider the man of letters in his relation to the historian, demonstrating William's wide and deep reading in classical, patristic, and later writers. I do question Thomson's acceptance of William's guilt for "love for the pagan classics" (pp. 12, 27); this is a convention going back (at least) to St. Jerome. The author makes an excellent presentation of William's work as a historical critic of his sources, both secular and religious, and speculates about William's travels in search of archival materials. Thomson assesses the historian as a stylist and as a judge of others' style, and William as a judge of historical sources in relation to both content and historical context.

The first part concludes with an analysis of William's reading—what he did read, not merely what was available to him. Thomson addresses theology and patristics, earlier English writers, writings from the classical and post-Augustinian periods, Greek and Arabic sources (through Latin transmission), law, and Roman and later histories. Thomson devotes chapters to the Malmesbury library, and proceeds to the section concerned with "Studies of the Writer at Work," a part of which reveals more than the first did that this book originated in a series of articles. He addresses the genesis and sources of the *Liber Pontificalis* and William as a critical historian, devoting particular attention to the Carolingian sources of the *Gesta Regum*. The chapter entitled "William and Some Other Western Writers on Islam" is rather slight; I do not think it could have been otherwise, given the paucity of the sources. Thomson's *William of Malmesbury* is a thoughtful, judicious book; its author has illuminated William and his world more thoroughly than has any previous writer on this greatest of twelfth-century English historians. The book's chief flaw—shared with the other books here reviewed—is the lack of a bibliography; bibliographies are dull to prepare and expensive to set up in type, but necessary in a scholarly work.

Neither *The Book of St. Gilbert* nor *William of Malmesbury* should be the occasion of controversy. This had already proved not to be the case with Sally Vaughn's *Anselm of Bec and Robert of Meulan*.[1] Vaughn's interest in Anselm as an ecclesiastical statesman has been manifest for fourteen years. She here pursues, as in her previous work, a refutation of what she presents as the customary view of Anselm as, while doubtless a saint and scholar, an otherworldly monk with neither talent for, nor interest in, secular politics. *Anselm and Robert* is a satisfying and unique attempt to compare and contrast the careers of Anselm and Robert of Meulan, courtier and councilor to William II and Henry I; she finds both men skillful and wise in service to their chosen masters, Robert to his kings, Anselm to his king. The approach works well.

Vaughn argues her Anselm-as-successful-politician thesis with less assertiveness, with more subtlety and skill than in her previous published works. Her book is also more convincing than were her earlier studies. At the end of this essay, I shall return to the differences between the approaches and conclusions of Vaughn and of Sir Richard Southern. Before so doing, I will summarize her important scholarly study, although limitations of space forbid me to convey the richness of her work. Not that—as we shall see—this book is either without flaws or definitive; rather, it is provocative.

Conventional biography of modern figures is impossible for those of the Middle Ages, and Vaughn wisely does not attempt to go where her sources do not lead her. Essentially, Vaughn looks at Robert[2] and Anselm at the royal court; she examines the relations of these men, each with his own claims to greatness, as they focus upon the English investiture controversy and allied issues. Vaughn's prologue analyzes the history and historiography of her protagonists and sets the context for her subsequent narrative. Vaughn's narratives of Anselm's and Robert's lives before they became adversaries at the court of the Anglo-Norman kings is necessarily uneven; there is much more source material on the saint than on the councilor. She presents the fullest assessment of which I am aware of Robert, both before and during his tenure as royal adviser. When presenting the early career of Anselm at Bec, she properly stresses the important role of Benedictine abbots in the secular world and argues that Anselm was experienced in politics before he became archbishop of Canterbury. Vaughn relates and examines the contacts (usually hostile) between Anselm and Count Robert before the abbot of Bec became the archbishop of Canterbury; she believes that their conflicts in Normandy prefigured those in England. Vaughn never loses sight of the fact that no matter how successful he was in his contentions with worldly powers, Anselm's ambience was monastic, and she shows convincingly that his monastic background contributed greatly to his triumphs in secular politics. She does not hang enough pennons on the fact that both the Benedictine and Cluniac traditions (if not constitutions) called for engagement with the world as well as seeming withdrawal from it; even the Cistercians, an order founded in the lifetimes of Robert and Anselm, were never really withdrawn, despite the intentions of their founder. After all, St. Bernard was engaged actively as a councilor to kings and magnates, even if his advice was ignored more often than not. And of course, many monks became bishops and archbishops, posts which inevitably placed them in the feudal structures of England and of Normandy.

Vaughn's presentation of the archbishop's confrontations with William Rufus and Robert is carefully considered in the context of *Regnum* and *Sacerdotium*, what would now be described anachronistically as church–state relations—a distinction which medieval people would not have recognized. She shows Anselm as a superb and cunning ecclesiastical statesman in his see's argument with the archbishop of York concerning the primacy of the British church; she proves that Anselm was even more triumphant in this dispute than was Lanfranc, his mentor and predecessor both at Bec and at Canterbury. She also demonstrates Anselm's success, in the period 1093–1100, in distancing himself from papal meddling; he intended, although in a different context, to join the king in maintaining the autonomy of his jurisdiction from outside authority. Both prelate and monarch apparently preferred to solve their own problems. While Vaughn ably discusses the theoretical bases of Anselm's politics, she is less satisfactory when dealing with Robert's (perhaps owing to the comparative silence of her sources), but she should have elaborated Rufus's perception of theocratic kingship.

Vaughn's discussion of relations between Henry I and the archbishop—and, of course, Count Robert—is more nuanced than that pertaining to the reign of Rufus, probably because the sources are more full. In her analyses of relations between *Regnum* and *Sacerdotium* in both reigns, Vaughn should have referred to comparisons and contrasts with the Becket controversy, both when she speaks of the relations of Anselm and Rufus and when she addresses the more clearly defined problems which embroiled Henry I and his archbishop; there are meaningful parallels to be drawn.[3] The author has missed this opportunity to enrich her work. Not that I wish to suggest a comparison between the learned, saintly Anselm and the truculent Thomas of London, rightly removed by the Roman church from the calendar of saints in 1960. As Vaughn shows, Anselm realized the importance of strong kingship for the welfare of the church. Thomas did not, although the English church fared well after his own unnecessary martyrdom. Surely she could not have applied her analysis of the Anselm–Henry dispute to the Becket controversy: "the rivalry of these two men was conducted with remarkable subtlety and political sophistication" (p. 312).

C. Warren Hollister, commenting on Vaughn's study, states that "this book settles and closes the issue (of the politics and polemics of the English Investiture Controversy)"; it does neither, as is demonstrated by the exchange of articles by Vaughn and Southern in a recent issue of *Albion*.[4] I think this makes her book the more valuable, since it has obviously stimulated interest and controversy about her topic. Southern criticizes Vaughn's *Anselm and Robert* on several counts, after making graceful acknowledgment of her contributions to the scholarly debate. He thinks Vaughn's interpretation of Anselm's motives unconvincing; Vaughn finds the archbishop's conduct in political affairs somewhat disingenuous, although motivated by high-minded goals (pp. 183–87). Southern does not agree with Vaughn's argument that Anselm welcomed his appointment as archbishop; he argues that Anselm's protestations against his appointment were genuine, not merely formality. I do not oversimplify in saying that Southern thinks Anselm meant exactly what he said; Vaughn does not agree. Nor does Southern agree that Anselm tinkered with the collection of his letters in order to suppress those which might have tarnished his reputation. Southern does not find Anselm a man of the world comparable to Robert of Meulan; he argues, rather, that Anselm was, owing to three decades of monastic ways, precisely *not* a man of the secular world, although he operated successfully enough within it (p. 203).

In her response to Southern, Vaughn rivals her critic in generous obeisance to his scholarship and thoughtfulness. Yet she firmly begins her rebuttal with the bald statement that her views and Southern's concerning the archbishop's role in secular politics "seem almost mutually exclusive" (p. 205). She charges—gently—that Southern misrepresents her view of Anselm the politician, interpreting her data in such a way as to make the archbishop seem devious and insincere. She rightly points out that she did not argue that the saint was opportunistic; rather, he was obedient to God's perceived will that he assume the burdens of being the shepherd of the church in England (p. 209). I think Vaughn is right on target when she states that she less disagrees with Southern than emphasizes a different aspect of Anselm's monastic and intellectual background—his obligation to be a faithful steward of the church's possessions and rights.

Vaughn's book, as well as Southern's *St. Anselm and His Biographer* (Cambridge, 1963) and their present (and ongoing) debate on Anselm as statesman, are stimulating and thought-provoking. Have we a right to expect anything more from serious historians?

Notes

1. Richard W. Southern, "Sally Vaughn's Anselm," *Albion* 20 (1988): 181–204; Sally Vaughn, "Anselm: Saint and Statesman," *ibid.*, 205–20; Southern, *ibid.*, 695–96.
2. Vaughn, *Anselm and Robert,* refers to a forthcoming study of Robert's twin sons.

It has since been published: David Crouch, *The Beaumont Twins* (Cambridge, 1986).
3. See James W. Alexander, "The Becket Dispute in Recent Historiography," *Journal of British Studies* 9 (1970): 25–26.
4. See note 1; page references hereafter are to these two articles.

Celtic Fringe or Celtic Center? Rethinking Medieval Welsh and Irish History

MICHAEL ALTSCHUL

R. R. Davies, *Conquest, Coexistence, and Change: Wales, 1063–1415* (History of Wales, vol. II). Oxford: Clarendon Press and University of Wales Press, 1987. Pp. xvi, 530; 13 maps, 6 diagrams.

Christopher N. L. Brooke, *The Church and the Welsh Border in the Central Middle Ages* (Studies in Celtic History, 8). Woodbridge, Suffolk, and Wolfeboro, N.H.: Boydell Press, 1986. Pp. xiv, 127.

Katherine Simms, *From Kings to Warlords: the Changing Political Structure of Gaelic Ireland in the Later Middle Ages* (Studies in Celtic History, 7). Woodbridge, Suffolk, and Wolfeboro, N.H.: Boydell Press, 1987. Pp. ix, 191.

The histories of medieval Wales and Ireland cannot be written in isolation from England. There is, however, a tendency, when viewing Britain or the British Isles as a whole, to put England so much into the foreground that Wales and Ireland become relegated to secondary or afterthought status—a status encapsulated in the phrase "Celtic fringe," so frequently encountered in surveys and textbooks. There are drawbacks as well as merits to viewing things from a perspective based in London or centered on the English Channel. Taking a stance on the Anglo-Welsh border or the Anglo-Irish border can yield some very different, equally interesting, and perhaps in ways more fundamentally illuminating historical truths, even about England itself. This is the great and unifying virtue of the books under consideration here.

To hail Davies's book as definitive is in fact to understate both its quality and its historiographical importance. No previous work of its scope or kind had ever been attempted. The nearest approximation, published in 1911, was the second volume of Sir John Lloyd's *History of Wales from the Earliest Times to the Edwardian Conquest*.[1] Comparisons between the two are both inevitable and instructive. Lloyd's book was exclusively a political narrative in character and basically concerned itself only with native (or "Welsh") Wales. It ended with the wars of King Edward I because it saw as its theme the story of a valiant but ultimately futile native resistance, led and symbolized by the princes of Gwynedd, to the encroachment of a foreign (English) power. Davies's book also ends with a study of political resistance, the Glyn Dŵr revolt; but this very choice of culminating or watershed episode suggests, and in turn is informed by, a far richer and deeper context than that envisioned by Lloyd. The medieval Welsh experience, per se and in its relations with England, is not only the story of the native rulers of Gwynedd and the similar polities of Powys and Deheubarth, but also the story of the great Anglo-Norman marcher families such as the Clares and the Bohuns and of the Anglo-Welsh marcher lordships such as Glamorgan and Brecon. Further, it is also the story of cultural assimilation and mutual adjustment, English as well as Welsh, both on the March and in the Edwardian Principality after its establishment in 1284. The book is based on Davies's pioneering *Lordship and Society in the March of Wales 1282–1400*[2] and his sure grasp of the sources and of the specialized scholarship, both English-language and Welsh-language. Davies pays a full measure of attention to politics and government institutions; but he firmly embeds these in stimulating analyses of shifts in social status and structure, rural change and urban growth, and patterns of Welsh "national" consciousness exemplified or expressed in law, the language of myth, and religion. The achievement is nothing less than a superb and comprehensive assessment of power and culture in both native Welsh and Anglo-Welsh society. Lloyd's work emphasized conflict and was designed to culminate in the fact of final political conquest; Davies, by contrast, emphasizes contact as well as conquest. Of equal importance, he sees conquest both as process and as experience and shows that in its political, social, and cultural ramifications, its ultimate realization and significance were fully achieved only in the days of Glyn Dŵr. Above all, he demonstrates that the March, pre-Edwardian native Wales, and the Principality were integral and integrated components of Welsh history in the Middle Ages. That history has now, at last, been viewed and treated as a proper whole.

Considered from this perspective, the English (or Anglo-Normans) were not simply "foreigners" in the midst of the Welsh, nor were the Welsh merely a local or marginalized people on the "fringe" of English power and interests. Within their more circumscribed and text-criticism orientation, the essays comprising Brooke's volume are also informed by this largeness of concept. Brooke has collected and revised essays previously published in collaborative volumes or journals not now readily accessible. His concerns are ostensibly narrow and rather technical: to examine the authenticity, purposes, and significance of certain eleventh- and twelfth-century texts central to an understanding of the structure and development of the church in the age of the initial Anglo-Norman contacts and conquests. The source criticism is painstaking and expertly done and always controlled by the larger interpretive framework. The texts are major, ranging from the Book of Llandaff,[3] through the chronicle of St. Peter's Abbey (Gloucester) and the *Vitae* of St. Cadog by Lifris and Caradog, to no less a work than Geoffrey of Monmouth's *History of the Kings of Britain*. The theme is even larger. The texts reveal a complex triangular struggle involving the efforts of Canterbury to assert primacy over the entire Welsh church, the counterclaims by St. David's to independence from Canterbury for the sake of its own assertions of primacy in Wales, and the resistance to St. David's by other Welsh bishops. The latter helped prompt—not always easily—the victory of English ecclesiastical policy. The upshot was the collapse of the older Celtic tradition in southern Wales and the remodeling of dioceses along English (and thus continental) lines. The texts concern themselves with issues of jurisdiction and organization; they tell us little about the attitudes or behavior of ordinary people. But such small, regional, and incremental changes impelled and made possible the larger patterns of social and cultural-spiritual change of the sort addressed by Davies's book. The conquest of the Welsh church was earlier and more complete than the conquest of the land and people of Wales. Brooke's essays provide important insights into this process and its wider lessons and implications.

The bifurcation between "native" and "English" has characterized the study of medieval Ireland even more than that of Wales. G. H. Orpen's *Ireland under the Normans* stands as the counterpart of Lloyd's *History of Wales* in its wealth of political detail and even in its date of original publication. It is also its ideological counterpoise.[4] To Orpen, all virtue and progress were on the English side, and he ended his account by the mid-fourteenth century because he saw the later Middle Ages as the triumph of a retrogade Celticism—an outcome (and a judgment) exactly the opposite of the Welsh pattern as Lloyd conceived it. While present-day historians have repudiated Orpen's anti-Gaelicism, they have never-theless also tended to confine themselves to the study of Anglo-Irish society, leaving native Ireland almost wholly to philologists and literary scholars.[5] Simms's fascinating study is doubly welcome, therefore, because it provides for the first time both a substantial monograph on post-invasion medieval Gaelic Irish society and an analysis of its most charac-teristic yet little-understood political symbol, the king *(rí)*. The thesis is exactly conveyed by the title of the book, and it is one of signal impor-tance for our understanding of medieval Ireland as a whole. Simms traces the evolution from the theocratic and ceremonial kingship of pre-Norman times[6] to a territorial and professionalized system of lordship reminiscent of and analogous to that devised by the Anglo-Irish (and indeed English and Welsh) aristocratic elites themselves. Positions such as those of *ollamh* and *brehon (breitheamh)*, masters of oral tradition in poetry or history and law, yielded functional precedence to bureaucrats. Chieftains transformed their subjects' customary renders into tenurial rents and came above all to base and to validate their power on the use of professional mercenaries, the famed Scottish "gallowglasses" *(gallóglaich)*. The title *rí* itself yielded to the more common, and more accurate, secularized term *tighearna* (lord). Simms's book does not make for easy reading, but it deserves and will richly repay careful study and reflection. If the native Irish rulers were not explicitly Anglicized, it is now clear that they responded to the same sorts of pressures and opportunities, and devised over time many of the same institutions, as their Anglo-Irish counterparts. The book should encourage historians to view both native Ireland and Anglo-Ireland as parts of a larger, single entity, along with due attention to the still wider context demanded by the continuing contact with England itself. Both that perspective and the historical task it poses are ambitious; but as Davies has shown for Wales, they are by no means impossible of ultimate realization. Medieval Ireland, no less than medieval Wales, deserves that the effort be made.

Notes

1. Sir John Edward Lloyd, *A History of Wales from the Earliest Times to the Edwardian Conquest,* 2 vols. (London, 1911; 3d ed., 1939). On vol. 1, see note 3.
2. R. R. Davies, *Lordship and Society in the March of Wales 1282–1400* (Oxford, 1978). Cf. my review, "Conquests and Cultures, Norman and non-Norman," *Medievalia et Humanistica* X (1981), 217–22.
3. The construction and reliability of the *Liber Landavensis* for political and social as well as ecclesiastical history are topics of major current interest, to a large extent inspired by Brooke's articles. The most authoritative studies are those by Wendy Davies, *An Early Welsh Microcosm: Studies in the Llandaff Charters* (London, 1978) and *The Llandaff Charters* (Aberystwyth, 1979). These works, along with her *Wales in the Early Middle Ages* (Leicester, 1982), do not in and of themselves replace vol. 1 of Lloyd's *History of Wales,* but map out the directions and dimensions that an authoritative one-volume survey would entail.
4. Goddard Henry Orpen, *Ireland under the Normans 1169–1333,* 4 vols. (Oxford, 1911–20).
5. The standard accounts that have superseded Orpen are A. J. Otway-Ruthven, *A History of Medieval Ireland* (London, 1968), and J. F. Lydon, *The Lordship of Ireland in the Middle Ages* (Dublin, 1972). Of monographic works on the Anglo-Irish community, special mention should be made of the important study by Robin Frame, *English Lordship in Ireland 1318–1361* (Oxford, 1982). Apart from Eoin MacNeill's *Celtic Ireland* (Dublin, 1921), written as a refutation of Orpen, the only general history of native Ireland is the brief and exploratory

survey by Kenneth W. Nicholls, *Gaelic and Gaelicised Ireland in the Middle Ages* (Dublin, 1972).

6. The authoritative works on the earlier tradition are Francis John Byrne, *Irish Kings and High-Kings* (London, 1973) and, in briefer compass, D. A. Binchy, *Celtic and Anglo-Saxon Kingship* (Oxford, 1970).

The Nobility of Later Medieval England

JAMES GIVEN

Chris Given-Wilson, *The English Nobility in the Late Middle Ages: The Fourteenth-Century Political Community*. London and New York: Routledge & Kegan Paul, 1987. Pp. xxii, 222. $39.95.

Juliet R. V. Barker, *The Tournament in England, 1100–1400*. Woodbridge and Wolfeboro: The Boydell Press, 1986. Pp. 206. $40.00.

Constance Bullock-Davies, *Register of Royal and Baronial Domestic Minstrels, 1272–1327*. Woodbridge and Dover: The Boydell Press, 1986. Pp. xvi, 227. $45.00.

In recent years there has been renewed interest among historians in the nobility of later medieval England. Each of the works under review here can be understood as a contribution to this growing body of scholarship. Of these three works, the one that is most general and will be of the greatest interest to readers is Given-Wilson's *The English Nobility in the Late Middle Ages*. In this work, Given-Wilson has sought to synthesize much of the recent scholarship on the fourteenth-century English nobility—scholarship which has shifted its attention from the study of the peerage to the examination of the lesser ranks of the nobility; to the study of local, rather than national, politics; and to a consideration of the interaction between national and local politics.

The first part of Given-Wilson's work is devoted to an examination of the different ranks of the English nobility. In general, in the fourteenth century aristocratic society in England was becoming more rigidly stratified. At the top of the aristocratic social pyramid was a small group of titled aristocrats—earls, dukes, and marquises. These were men who commanded sufficient resources to make them a political threat to the king if for any reason their sympathies were alienated. Given-Wilson argues that in the fourteenth century, promotions to these titled ranks of the nobility took on a more blatantly political overtone than at any time since the twelfth-century civil war of King Stephen's reign. Successful kings, such as Edward I and Edward III, were able to cement their control of the kingdom by promoting loyal and trustworthy men to these ranks. Edward II and Richard II, however, in their efforts to provide their nominees with the landed resources necessary to support their

127

titles, engaged in unscrupulous manipulations of property rights that did much to antagonize the rest of the greater nobility.

Having dealt with the political importance of the titled nobility, Given-Wilson discusses the process by which the peerage took shape. By 1400 this consisted of some sixty to seventy families distinguished from the rest of the nobility by the fact that their members had acquired hereditary right to an individual summons to Parliament. They were also distinguished from lesser members of the nobility by their frequent and direct access to the king and by the greater size of their estates, which seem to have produced annual incomes ranging from £300 to £1200.

Beneath this group came the gentry, which Given-Wilson basically sorts into two categories. The first group was the "county" gentry, consisting of belted knights and esquires and numbering perhaps 2,300 to 2,500 families, which formed the real political commmunity of the shires, its members serving as sheriffs, justices of the peace, and members of Parliament, as well as making up the retinues of the great barons of the realm. The other group was the "parish" gentry, some 6,000 to 7,000 families, composed of poorer esquires, gentlemen, lawyers, merchants, and some of the richer yeomen. According to Given-Wilson, one of the key themes of fourteenth-century politics was the enhanced political role of the gentry. Although their political horizon was largely local, they were, as a group, possessed of a significant portion of the landed wealth of the kingdom; it was also they who controlled local Crown office. Their rise in importance in the fourteenth century is shown by the eagerness of the greater nobles to recruit them into their followings and by the growing influence of knights of the shire in Parliament.

With this description of the different strata of the fourteenth-century nobility out of the way, Given-Wilson turns to a discussion of the economic and political fortunes of this group. In doing so, he presents two fairly novel but persuasive arguments. First, he claims that despite the decline in rents caused by the demographic collapse of the mid- and late fourteenth century, the income of the peers was rising during this period. Some improved their situation by shifting production from arable to pasture. Most, however, increased their revenue by acquiring more land, occasionally by purchase, more commonly by marriage or royal grant. Members of this group also endeavored to group their estates in more concentrated blocks so as to facilitate their administration. Finally, changes in the land law, such as the spread of entails, jointures, and enfeoffments to use, made it possible for peers to protect the integrity of their estates more effectively and to evade many feudal obligations to their overlords. Peers also benefitted from access to new forms of revenue, the most important of which was cash transfers from the Crown. Given-

Wilson argues that the fourteenth-century kings created a virtual "budget of noble assistance." In the reign of Henry IV, for example, perhaps one-third of royal revenue was expended on annuities for members of the nobility. The greater magnates, who received the lion's share of royal largess, in turn spent large sums rewarding the members of their affinities.

The other argument that some scholars may find controversial is Given-Wilson's assertion that the growing consolidation of the regional power of great lords, who concentrated their estates and built up powerful local affinities among the gentry, was not necessarily a threat to the political stability of the kingdom. For Given-Wilson, the negative consequences of "bastard feudalism" have definitely been exaggerated. According to his interpretation, the fourteenth-century kings, far from being disturbed by the growing regional power of the greater magnates, probably saw it as advantageous. As kings such as Edward I and Edward III demonstrated, great magnates could be made to function as a species of reliable royal deputies in the shires. It was only a king who tried to interfere too drastically with local patterns of landholding and power or who allowed a great magnate to turn his power into a weapon, to the detriment of his fellow landowners, who encountered significant political trouble.

I have here summarized only some of the major points made in this interesting and illuminating work. Given-Wilson has managed to pack a great deal of information and insight into a relatively brief book. In doing so, he has produced the best available introduction to the nobility of late-medieval England, a work that should be consulted by anyone who is interested in the social, economic, or political history of that kingdom.

A significant aspect of aristocratic life in the late Middle Ages was the tournament—surely the most popular of aristocratic sports. It is to this important, but relatively little explored, topic that Juliet R. V. Barker has devoted her *The Tournament in England, 1100–1400*. In this careful work Barker traces the evolution of the tournament, a twelfth-century import into England from France, from the early days of the great *mêlée* tournament, which differed little from actual warfare, through its evolution in the late Middle Ages into a whole series of different military exercises and games, ranging from the relatively benign tournaments *à plaisance*, featuring individual jousts and stressing pageantry and spectacle, to the deadly feats of arms, fought with real weapons against enemies of the kingdom, such as the Scots and the French. Barker divides her work into a series of topical chapters dealing with such things as the relationship of the tournament to war, the tournament and politics, the tournament as spectacle, the different types of combat, and armor and weapons.

Against those who maintain that late-medieval tournaments, which had largely turned into jousts fought with special armor and weapons, had little benefit as military training, Barker argues that there was a close link between the tournament and war throughout the period. Although jousts may have had limited potential as a form of military training, other hastiludes (to use the generic term for all military sports), such as the feats of arms, which involved passages of arms with sword, lance, axe and dagger, had very real relevance to actual military practices. Barker also claims that those Englishmen who were most active in war were also usually those who were most active in tourneying. Finally, tournament ideology helped shape the nature of real warfare, as in the development of rules about the ways in which ransoms were negotiated and collected, rules which were modeled on the practices followed at tournaments.

In her chapter on tournaments and politics, Barker notes that tournaments often presented problems for English monarchs, as they provided opportunities for malcontents to assemble with their armed followers and plot mischief against the Crown. They were at times used as a cover for the prosecution of private feuds. Finally, the tendency for disturbances to spill out of the tournament grounds could present a problem of public order. These factors led English kings such as Richard I and Edward I to try to regulate hastiludes by setting up a licensing system and by attempting to regulate the size and equipment of the retinues that attended tourneyers. Tournaments, however, were not simply a source of unease for English kings. They could also be used by monarchs such as Edward I and Edward III, both active patrons of aristocratic military sports, as very successful vehicles of royal propaganda.

Barker also draws attention to the importance of the tournament for aristocratic culture. The tournaments *à plaisance* of the late Middle Ages—which were heavily influenced by chivalric romances, which saw participants self-consciously imitating the behavior of the fictional heroes of chivalry, and which emphasized spectacle and ritual—provided not only opportunities to impress peers and inferiors with a display of wealth and pride, but also served as occasions for the exchange of cultural values. They thus played an important role in the spread of chivalric customs through upper-class society.

Finally, Barker notes that tourneying became progressively more exclusive during the Middle Ages. The growing popularity of individual jousts, as opposed to the mass *mêlée* of the twelfth century, limited the numbers who could take part. More important, the rapid escalation in costs of equipment and the growing emphasis on pageantry which required tourneyers to bring with them large and impressively equipped retinues, meant that increasingly, only the very wealthy, or those with access to the patronage of the wealthy, could take part. By 1400 the "tourneying society" was a relatively small and tight-knit one, composed of very wealthy men, members of families that had often been involved in tournaments for generations, and in which the most important patron was the king.

Barker has brought together a great deal of information on a great variety of topics relating to the tournament. She has succeeded very well in her goal of producing the first major serious study of the tournament in medieval England. Anyone who is interested in tournaments should begin his investigation of the subject with her monograph.

The least significant, and perhaps the least satisfying, of these three works is Constance Bullock-Davies's *Register of Royal and Baronial Minstrels.* In this work Bullock-Davies has put together a catalog of minstrels and other entertainers. The material in this catalog derives largely, but not exclusively, from royal wardrobe and exchequer accounts. "Minstrel" was a generic term used to designate minor court servants. Many of these servants were amateur musicians who, although their primary tasks involved other activities, could be called on to perform on certain occasions. Others were highly trained professional "string men." The register that the author has compiled contains, by my count, 563 different entries, with information not only on named minstrels but also on anonymous individuals and groups who performed at one time or another for the king or a great baron. The author has provided a brief introduction to the register, which unfortunately does not provide much information on minstrels or their functions. The researcher coming to the register with little background in the subject would do well to consult her much fuller and more enlightening remarks in *Menestrellorum multitudo: Minstrels at a Royal Feast* (Cardiff: University of Wales Press, 1978).

Although one can only admire the prodigious diligence of Bullock-Davies, who has amassed a vast amount of data, one cannot help having some doubts about the usefulness of the material she has gathered. As she makes clear in her introduction, the material in the register is not the result of systematic research; the entries were collected incidentally, in the process of other research. Although the self-imposed limits of the register are 1272 and 1327, she has nevertheless included some material, chanced across in casual reading, from well outside this period. We are thus confronted with a register which is neither an exhaustive catalog of all known minstrels from a given period nor a properly constructed random sample of minstrels active at a particular time. One therefore is left uncertain as to whether any valid generalizations about the nature of medieval minstrels can be based on the material contained in this register.

If one is interested in pursuing the career of a particular late-thirteenth or early-fourteenth-century minstrel, however, Bullock-Davies's register is certainly the place to begin one's search.

To conclude, all these studies can be read as contributing to an understanding of the process by which the English nobility in the late Middle Ages transformed itself from a "class-in-itself" into a "class-for-itself." Given-Wilson draws attention to how the fourteenth-century English nobility became a more self-conscious and internally stratified ruling elite; how it protected its position of economic and social dominance; and how it increasingly organized itself politically into a system of ramifying patronage networks that, although based on local concentrations of wealth and power, were nevertheless united around the institutions of the monarchy. Barker's treatment of the tournament illustrates the process by which a specifically noble social and cultural institution was created, and casts light on how that institution shaped aristocratic behavior in the late Middle Ages. Barker's research also makes clear that spectacle, pageantry, ritual, ceremony, and chivalric romance were coming to play an ever more important role in the cultural life of the English nobility in the late Middle Ages. Bullock-Davies's register provides material with which one can begin to explore other aspects of the way in which an aristocratic, court-centered culture was being fashioned in this period. Perhaps none of the three authors whose works have been discussed in this review would feel comfortable with seeing his or her book grouped under the organizing principle I have suggested in this paragraph, but all three works help illustrate how the nobility of later medieval England managed to preserve its position of dominance and control in the face of the great challenges it confronted in this period.

Burckhardtian Legacies

ANTHONY MOLHO

L' Époque de la Renaissance 1400–1600, Premier Volume: *L'Avènement de l' Esprit Nouveau (1400–1480),* publié sous la direction de Tibor Klaniczay, Eva Kushner, André Stegmann (Budapest: Akadémiai Kiadò, 1988). Pp. 593.
Lauro Martines, *Power and Imagination—City-States in Renaissance Italy* (Baltimore: The Johns Hopkins University Press, 1988). Pp. xiii, 370.

For well over a century, a resilient metaphor, first coined by Jacob Burckhardt, has been at the heart of Renaissance studies. This metaphor has been the conceptual grid almost invariably applied to the cluster of events gathered, by specialists and nonexperts, under the rubric of the Renaissance. This is a genetic or, if one prefers, a filiational metaphor. It asserts the view that a biological link binds us to the Renaissance, especially to the Renaissance in Italy. This link was bluntly asserted by Burckhardt at the very beginning of Part II of his famous work. "The Italian," he wrote, "is . . . the firstborn among the sons of modern Europe." For the past century, Burckhardt's insight and our own convictions have shaped historical interpretations of the Renaissance. If the Renaissance in Italy ushered in the great era of modernity, we, as products of the modern age, are able to recognize and understand our ancestors, the men and women of the Renaissance. We remain confident that we inhabit the same spiritual universe they did; that our world and that of the Renaissance are bound in a common moral and epistemological universe; that in matters of consequence we share comparable values; that we are their sons and daughters and they are our fathers and mothers. An enormous amount of historical work has been rooted in the assumption of the confident familiarity which historians bring to bear when examining the history of late-medieval Italian history.

In the past few years, this metaphor has come under question, and increasingly, a tension has been evident in the collective work currently being done by scholars who study the Renaissance.

On the one hand, as one might expect, the Burckhardtian paradigm has continued to exert its magnetic force. If anything, there appears to have been an accentuation of the trend to spot every sort of trace of modernity in fourteenth- and fifteenth-century Italian society. Burckhardt and his immediate followers focused their attention on a small

number of selected fields: the state, the economy, psychological perception. But now, the list of these attributes of modernity is more comprehensive: family structures, the history of childhood, the relations between
the genders, the consciousness of spatial relationships, and so on. On the
other hand, for the past several years there have been traces of a new
penchant—it might be too soon to call it a tradition—of an increasingly
acute skepticism among some scholars about the efficacy of the filiational
metaphor, about the notion that we, in the waning years of our century,
could be thought to share the moral idiom of individuals such as Petrarch
and Cosimo de' Medici, Filelfo and Francesco Foscari, Isabella d'Este, and
Vittoria Colonna. Without singling out research projects which have
contributed to this sense of skepticism, one should credit historians on
three continents—Europe, North America, and Australia—with opening
up for us scholarly vistas which, until recently, were almost completely
unimagined.

The cumulative impact of much of this new work has been to raise
important questions regarding historical teleology. In our work as students of late-medieval and early-modern European society, do we focus
our attention on the influence which ideas and institutions have exerted
on our own world, tracing links between present and past, seeing the past
from the perspective of our own accomplishments and failures? Or do we
ascribe a kind of integrity to the culture and society of the late-medieval
era, historicizing ideas, political movements, and institutions? In reality,
of course, the dichotomy is not nearly that stark, for it is misleading to
imagine that one can separate oneself from contemporary society and
see whole, as it were, the integrity of the past. Yet it is also true that until
very recently, much of the historiography in our field privileged the
notion of continuity. Relying on a filiational metaphor coined in the
nineteenth century, it had fashioned a teleology which underscored the
organic links that bind us to our ancestors of half a millenium ago.

*   *   *

Considerations such as these come to mind when examining the two
books under review here. Conceived and written under different circumstances, bringing to bear the erudition and reflection of very different
groups of scholars, and in all likelihood addressed to different audiences,
these two works nonetheless bring into useful focus some key divergences
and tensions regarding method and approach that are evident today in
the field of Renaissance studies.

Before examining these, some comments are in order about the
contents of these two works and about their authors. Lauro Martines, one
of the most imaginative historians of late-medieval Italy, noted for his

books on the sociology of Florence's humanists and of the city's jurists, has written an admirably elegant and urbane synthesis, one that draws on a lifetime's work in Italian libraries and archives but also points to new research which he is currently conducting. Let it be said at the outset that of all such synthetic works available in English and known to this reviewer, this is by far the most accomplished, surely the one that is most likely to entice its readers (most of whom, one suspects, will be North American undergraduate students) to continue their explorations in this subject.

Power and Imagination was first published in 1979. Now it is reissued in a second edition, identical to the first save for a short new preface and for a bibliographical supplement. The merits of the work have been pointed to by past reviewers, and there is no need to rehearse them in detail here. Suffice it to say that since the publication of the first edition, to this author (and, it should be added, also to his students who over the past decade were asked to read this book) the virtues of Martines's treatment appear to be threefold: thorough familiarity with the extensive literature of the field and an admirable command of many published and unpublished sources; a chronological treatment which enables the reader to trace the political and cultural history of the Italian city-states from their first developments in the eleventh century to the end of the sixteenth; and last but certainly not least, elegance of exposition, Martines's ability to organize and present his material in an engagingly urbane style. A recent comparison with the second work under review here also points to the merits of a single voice fashioning a synthetic narrative of this sort, endowing it with a cohesion and consistency which, often and quite understandably, collective works lack.

Over the past several years, the Akadémiai Kiadó of Budapest has published a series of volumes, sponsored by the International Comparative Literature Association, under the rubric *A Comparative History of Literatures*. Volume 7 of this series, eventually to comprise four tomes, is dedicated to *L'Époque de la Renaissance 1400–1600*. The first tome of this volume, entitled *L' Avènement de l' esprit nouveau (1400–1480)*, edited by Klaniczay of Budapest, Kushner of Montreal, and Stegman of Tours, is under review here. Two characteristics of the work shape its character: its collaborative nature and the approach chosen by the volume's editors in their study of literary texts. The first of these is evident immediately from a glance at the book's table of contents. The work consists of nine sections, each of which comprises a minimum of four to a maximum of seven chapters. Each chapter was assigned to a different scholar (Stegman, Péter Kulcsár, Hana Jechovà, and Samuel Y. Edgerton, Jr., were each responsible for two). Thus, scholars with very different scholarly backgrounds have been drawn together by this enterprise, and one discovers with considerable pleasure that national origins notwithstanding (it should be noted that among the contributors one finds not only several North Americans and Western Europeans, but also six Hungarians and one scholar from the DDR), communication among them is easy, as nearly all of them share basic assumptions about the period under study.

In their thoughtful and carefully crafted introduction, the three editors explain their approach. While their principal preoccupation remained the history of literature (9): *il ne fallait pas . . . perdre de vue l'histoire des formes, responsabilité de cette série littéraire*), they were obviously intent upon framing their study of literary texts within a much broader context: *L' histoire littéraire que nous préconisons est, avant tout, une histoire attentive aux textes et aux relations qui s'engendrent entre eux, sans que soient oubliées les conditions exactes de leur production et de leur réception* (7). An internalist approach, therefore, would be coupled to an effort to provide a historical and sociological framework. But instead of urging individual authors to analyze texts both in relationship to other texts and to the contexts of their production and reception, the decision was made to assign individual aspects of this enterprise to experts and to strive for the fashioning of a comprehensive view based on the cumulative picture which would emerge from individual contributions. The format of the volume followed this decision. One starts with a section devoted to *Les mutations politiques,* slowly moves through *L'univers de la nouvelle civilisation* to *Les supports de la nouvelle culture,* and then passes to topics closer to the center of literary studies, *Le nouvel esprit humaniste; Le renouveau spirituel; La révolution artistique; Diffusion et refraction du savoir.* Only the last two sections address properly literary issues: *L' héritage littéraire médiéval: persistances et mutations* and *Essor de la littérature savante.* The contexts presented here, for all their richness and complexity, do not lack surprises. It is surprising that politics (but then, as we shall see, only politics of a certain kind) is assigned such primacy over economics; that questions of social relations and of social classes are almost entirely neglected; that given the laudable interest of the editors in studying questions of popular piety, the state of the European countryside and of the peasantry are passed over in silence; that almost no references are found to the endemic nature of epidemics; and that given the very intense preoccupation of many recent historians to "marginal" groups in late-medieval society, the entry "juifs," and the names of Carlo Ginzburg, Keith Thomas, and Richard Trexler do not even appear in the book's very thorough index.

The self-appointed hope of the three editors was that the *convergence des questions posées* (10) would facilitate the emergence of a picture of the fifteenth-century Renaissance. It should come as no surprise that the very questions posed by the editors have shaped the *convergence* reached in this volume. There are, obviously, the very chronological boundaries within which this enterprise has been conceived. A definition of the Renaissance which examines only the period beginning in 1400 (or thereabouts) runs the risk of looking at a series of phenomena which at least (but not only) in the Italian situation had been set into motion a long time before. As we already noted, not the least merit of Martines's treatment was that, echoing suggestions made in the past by Armando Sapori and Robert Lopez, he set out to describe the long sweep of Italian history from the eleventh through the sixteenth century. Following the synthetic work of Martines and a number of more specialized studies (one thinks, for example, of Peter Herde's work on the history of political theory, of Quentin Skinner's contributions to the history of Ciceronianism, of Ronald Witt's on rhetorical traditions, and of many others), it should be clear by now that this chronological choice is especially helpful to one studying the broad sweep of late-medieval European ideas and describing, with a greater degree of precision, the cadences of change which took place in the realm of thought starting at the time of the great economic revolutions at around the year 1000. But then, the chronological boundaries chosen by the editors are themselves signs of a particular view of the Renaissance.

Here we return to considerations presented at the opening of this essay. The fact of the matter is that the rhetoric which animates nearly this entire enterprise (which, significantly, is shared by the overwhelming majority of the volume's international cast of contributors) is solidly grounded in the range of Burckhardtian images of the Renaissance which have so dominated our studies. This volume aims to study the *avènement de l'esprit nouveau,* an expression whose meaning is clear not only in the volume's introduction, but also in most of the individual contributions, particularly those concerned with tracing the institutional and political contexts of Renaissance literature. The Renaissance, we are told by the editors, is intimately related to the *surgissement des nations, au développement de la bourgeoisie sur les ruines du système féodal ou du moins de l'emprise nobiliaire* (10). Here, then, is the framework within which the Renaissance took place, for the Renaissance, in Burckhardtian terms, witnessed the emergence precisely of those institutions which define our modern world. And continuing to follow the great Swiss historian's vision, these phenomena were accompanied by a *bouillonement culturel* (12). The conviction that the study of the Renaissance implies the study of the origins of our contemporary world is evident in nearly all the contributions to this volume. René Pilorget writes about the *renforcement de l' État* (41) and the late György Bónis about the *États souverains* (43); De Lamar Jensen refers to a *système complexe de diplomatie internationale qui . . . a persisté presque jusqu'à nos jours* (51); Péter Kulcsár concludes that during the period in question *l'Europe prend le tournant décisif vers la formation des nations modernes* (63). The underlying and sustaining assumption which informs the work of these scholars is precisely the nineteenth-century teleological vision, the familial metaphor according to which the advent of modernity could be located at the very moment of the changes which took place in the course of the Renaissance.

To make the above observation is to say nothing at all about the contents of the volume's individual contributions. There are some very fine essays here, most of which do not necessarily present the results of new research, but which rather summarize the state of the question on a whole range of topics. Specialists will have to evaluate for themselves the qualities of these essays. A student of late-medieval Italian society such as this reviewer could not help but learn a very great deal from them, particularly those which were written by East European scholars who, quite understandably, focused on historical developments in their region. Yet as is evident, the aim of these observations is not to evaluate individual contributions, but to present a brief analysis of the overall conceptual structure of this volume. From that perspective, the book's striking quality is the teleological vision which animates its editors and most of its contributors.

Of all the book's contributors, the one to have expressed himself with greatest caution when addressing the alleged modernity of the Renaissance was the author of the very first essay, the late Myron P. Gilmore, who wrote on *L' Europe en 1400*. It is then perhaps no accident that Martines, himself a student of Gilmore's, embraced a very different view of the modern world's relationship to the Renaissance. One will look in vain in his treatment for references to the Burckhardtian vision. Martines's Renaissance Italy is a historical period which has its genesis sometime early in the eleventh century, progresses through two stages of economic and cultural development, and in the sixteenth century comes to an end. The institutional and intellectual links to past cultures are examined here in some detail. Yet save for some allusive statements to individualism (81–82), to the emergence of a secular view of the state (126–28), and to some others there is no discussion here on the aftermath of the Renaissance. In short, there is no readily available conceptual structure in Martines's analysis which will make possible an easy linkage between the Renaissance and the modernity of more recent times.

Some readers, particularly those who wish to view the past from a clearly defined contemporary perspective, might find serious disadvantages in such an approach. To this reviewer, on the other hand, this is one of this work's key qualities. Martines, freed from the rhetorical baggage bequeathed to us by Burckhardt, can now try to examine the culture of late-medieval Italy by seeking to reconstruct the very meaning which Italians themselves bequeathed to words which they used. Thus, the expression "state" does not lead him to assume that the states of the late-medieval period led necessarily to the creation of modern states; the discussion of late-medieval entrepreneurship does not inevitably flower into some kind of modern capitalism; the analysis of humanism and art is not seen in terms of the discovery of some ineffable truths which, since the Renaissance, have conditioned the sensibilities of "modern" people. The task which Martines has set for himself is to remove from our eyes as many veils as a sensitive and linguistically sophisticated modern historian can, and to try to see as clearly as is possible a world which existed a very long time ago and which was very different from our own. The fact that he—or we, in our own inquiries—can never really recover the past, that under the very best of circumstances we shall be able to perceive things only in a "dim light" (x), offers us no alternative but to bring to bear as critically and cautiously as we can all our philological acumen upon the texts (sources) which the past has bequeathed upon us. And Martines, now as in his previous work, has shown that in this realm he is a master second to none.

Having said this, there remains a question. What is the rhetorical function of the term "Renaissance" on the book's subtitle? What resonances did Martines wish to elicit in his readers' minds by appropriating a term which, in the normal course of events, is used to underscore altogether a different kind of intellectual enterprise than the one which he has undertaken here? It would have been useful for him to have explained more carefully—in fact, he does not do so at all—the meaning he imputes to a term which over the past many generations has come to represent a view of the relationship of present and past which, with a good deal of aplomb, Martines has very effectively undermined in this book.

The Florentine Renaissance: Before, During, and After

MICHAEL ALTSCHUL AND EDWARD J. OLSZEWSKI

Hans Baron, *In Search of Florentine Civic Humanism: Essays on the Transition from Medieval to Modern Thought*. Princeton: Princeton University Press, 1988. 2 vols. Vol. 1: pp. xiv, 297; Vol. 2: pp. 218. $29.50 each volume.

Arthur Field, *The Origins of the Platonic Academy in Florence*. Princeton: Princeton University Press, 1988. Pp. xvi, 302. $47.50.

Edward L. Goldberg, *After Vasari: History, Art, and Patronage in Late Medici Florence*. Princeton: Princeton University Press, 1988. Pp. xviii, 309, 35 illustrations. $49.50.

Of the making of books on Renaissance Florence there is, happily, no end. While for many years Renaissance scholars have consciously broadened their focus beyond a traditional Florentine emphasis, that emphasis retains both its allure and its merit. The works under discussion here explore Florence's own consciousness of its originality and of its heritage or legacy. They frame three centuries of Florentine history and cultural creativity, from the age of Petrarch and Bruni through Ficino to Vasari and his Baroque epigone Baldinucci; and explore the many dimensions of Florentine achievement, including classical humanism, political thought, philosophy, art history, and, not least, the nature and function of elite patronage. Collectively, these books provide a valuable window on recent scholarship on the origins, flowering, and aftermath of the Florentine Renaissance.

Hans Baron died shortly after the publication of *In Search of Florentine Civic Humanism*, making this work a memorial to a scholar of wide and significant influence in modern Renaissance studies. These volumes are, in fact, a convenient collection of Baron's seminal articles preparatory or supplementary to his major books: *The Crisis of the Early Italian Renaissance* (Princeton, 1955; 2d ed., 1966); *Humanistic and Political Literature in Florence and Venice at the Beginning of the Quattrocento* (Cambridge, Mass., 1955); *From Petrarch to Leonardo Bruni* (Chicago, 1968); and *Petrarch's "Secretum"* (Cambridge, Mass., 1985).

Baron devoted himself to the study of the intellectual foundations and early development of Florentine humanism, especially in the age from the mid-trecento to the mid-quattrocento. His works have come to be grouped under the general rubric of the "Baron thesis." In its broad formulation, his interpretation has found wide acceptance. The Florentine Renaissance represented the rejection of "medieval" religious–monastic ideals of holy poverty *(paupertas)* and the *vita contemplativa,* and the development in their place of a secular, civic-based and republican-oriented ideology founded on the principles of the legitimation of wealth *(divitiae)* and the *vita activa et politica.* There thus emerged a serious and meaningful cultural–political ethic, termed "civic humanism," praising (and vaunting) Florentine society and history and the city's devotion to republican *libertas.* Its major spokesmen were Leonardo Bruni (in particular, his *Laudatio Florentinae Urbis* and *Historiae Florentini Populi*),[1] and, less extensively, Coluccio Salutati (in his letters) and Matteo Palmieri (the *Vita Civile*). This new and full-fledged "modern" typology of the citizen and of the republican polity was only in part inspired by a fresh approach to classical authorities, above all Cicero and Aristotle (the *Politics* and the *Ethics*). According to Baron—and here his thesis has had a far more skeptical or critical reception by scholars—it was also rooted in, and reflected, the realities of Florentine society in the age of the Albizzi and the early Medici, and first burst forth as a response to the threat posed by Gian Galeazzo Visconti, duke of Milan, to Florentine independence in the years 1400–02. The skepticism is based not on the validity of his dating or redating of certain key literary texts, but rather on the causal pattern and inferences he drew on this basis. Baron underestimated more gradual shifts of taste and interests and alternate sources for their inspiration, as well as the rhetorical structure and objectives of the Quattrocento dialogue and history as literary genres.[2] Nonetheless, his achievement has enduring value. He showed that there *was* such a thing as Florentine civic humanism, and further that it was an original and significant installment in the history of republicanism as well as in the history of humanism taken as a whole. No less important, he reminded scholars that the social and political contexts of the Italian city-state often provided specific and crucial impetus to the evolution of Renaissance culture.

This two-volume collection of essays enables us to see, in single compass, the genesis and the final statements of Baron's approach and argumentation. The essays span half a century of detailed and dedicated scholarship and show a remarkable consistency that rarely, if ever, lapses into mere repetition. Volume 1 contains three original and five reprinted articles, one of which has been expanded and divided into three separate pieces. The reprinted essays all first appeared in the 1930s, laying out forcefully Baron's insistence on the unique and decisive role of Florence in the development of a secular civic ethic as the hallmark and essence of Renaissance ideology. Two of the essays have been translated into English for this publication. All five have titles slightly altered from their original (and familiar) forms, along with modifications or amplifications of the texts. The article that first appeared in *Speculum* XIII (1938) under the title "Franciscan Poverty and Civic Wealth as Factors in the Rise of Humanistic Thought" has been considerably revised and expanded, especially on Petrarch and the Trecento, to nearly double its original length (present chapters 7–9, pp. 158–257). Major additions or changes in the other are largely contained in a number of footnotes concerned with some of the basic scholarship on the Florentine trecento and quat-trocento that has appeared since the publication of *The Crisis* . . . in 1955. Those essays (giving original titles and journals of publication to facilitate references) are "Das Erwachen des historischen Denkens im Humanis-mus des Quattrocento," *Historische Zeitschrift*, CVLII (1932); "La Rinascità dell'etica statale romana nell'umanesimo fiorentino dal quattrocento," *Civiltà Moderna*, VII (1935); "The Historical Background of the Floren-tine Renaissance," *History*, n.s. XXII (1937); and "Cicero and the Roman Civic Spirit in the Middle Ages and the Early Renaissance," *Bulletin of the John Rylands Library*, XXII (1938).

Volume 1 also contains three new essays. Two (present chapters 3–4, 43–93) are devoted to a close reading of Bruni's *Historiae*, stressing the nature and significance of his contrastive treatment of Rome (ancient and contemporary) and Florence and his handling of events of the late fourteenth century. The final essay (present chapter 10, 258–88) exam-ines the social treatises of Leon Battista Alberti. Baron argues that the civic spirit of the *Della Famiglia* (1434) derived more from stoic tradition and Xenophon than from Cicero and Aristotle, and that his *De Iciarchia* (1469) represented, and contributed to, the retreat from civic humanism in the later quattrocento into private and more patrician or aristocratic values. Missing from the discussion is that emphasis on private and public decorum that links these works with Alberti's better-known and far more influential artistic treatises, the *Della Pittura* and the *De Re Aedificatoria*. Baron has, however, firmly established the civic humanist credentials of the *Della Famiglia* and has rescued the *De Iciarchia* from what has hereto-fore been almost total, but undeserved, neglect.

The second volume does not have the fully integrated character of the first. Its eight essays fall into two groups of three articles each, along with two singular pieces. The first set deals with the Italian Renaissance in broad pan-European perspective; the second set is essentially autobio-graphical. The initial group includes Baron's finest work of large-scale synthesis, "Fifteenth Century Civilization and the Renaissance," originally published in volume 1 (1957) of the *New Cambridge Modern History* (present chapter 11); and two bibliographically oriented pieces from the *Journal of the History of Ideas*, XX and XXI (1959, 1960), "The *Querelle* of the Ancients and the Moderns as a Problem for Modern Renaissance Scholarship," and an extended review of Eugene Rice's 1958 book, *The Renaissance Idea of Wisdom* (present chapters 13–14). The other set of three is comprised of an expanded version of a sympathetic evaluation of Burckhardt first published in *Renaissance News*, XIII (1960), a charming brief memoir presented as a speech in 1965 and hitherto unavailable in its original English-language form, and a defense of *The Crisis* . . . which first appeared as a preface to the Italian language edition of that book in 1970 (present chapters 16–18).

The two singular works are a condensed version of the article "A Sociological Interpretation of the Early Renaissance in Florence," which was first published in the *South Atlantic Quarterly*, XXXVIII (1939) and which, in spirit as well as in date of composition, essentially belongs to volume 1 of this collection (present chapter 12); and Baron's most extensive and important foray into later Florentine history, "Machiavelli the Republican Citizen and Author of *The Prince*," (present chapter 15). Baron establishes that Machiavelli had not yet begun *The Discourses* when he composed *The Prince* in 1513 and that any allusions to the former in the latter are inconsequential asides added around the time of the second (1516) dedication to Lorenzo. Baron's larger concern is to emphasize the civic and republican nature and intent of *The Discourses*—in other words, to demonstrate that Machiavelli was a sincere and legitimate heir to the earlier civic humanist tradition. This laudable and important insight is, however, to some degree marred by his insistence on an absolute dichotomy between *The Prince* and *The Discourses*. He overlooks or underappreciates themes and characteristics common to both works (and indeed *The Art of War* and even *The History of Florence*): the preference for classical models, largely mythological of fictitious; the obsession with avoiding faction; the need for legitimate as well as secure institutions *(ordini)*; the scorn for halfway or halfhearted measures; and above all the desire for decisive leadership, founded on popular consent and participation, to preserve or restore the *libertà* of the city and of the civic community.[3] Baron emphasizes that the circumstances of Machiavelli's world were far different from those of the insular and self-congratulatory days of Leonardo Bruni's Florence; but by placing Machiavelli in the context of a tradition stemming from the early quattrocento, he has shown him to be a disciple or representative of that culture of civic humanism, to the study of which Baron dedicated his life's work and for the history of which he still remains our most powerful and important authority.

The argument that from the mid-quattrocento Florentines retreated from the public ethic of civic republicanism to an apolitical and aristocratic ethos dominated by Neoplatonic metaphysics is crucial to Baron's schema. This proposition receives careful and serious scrutiny in Arthur Field's *The Origins of the Platonic Academy in Florence* (also the result of decades of study and publication). Field's description of the birth of a philosophical culture in Florence focuses on the crucial decade from the Peace of Lodi in 1454 to Cosimo de' Medici's founding of the Platonic Academy c. 1462–63. The Tuscan interest in Greek language and letters has been generally dated to the fall of Constantinople and the consequent arrival in Florence of the Byzantine humanist John Agyropoulos (1410–87), who took a university appointment there in 1457.[4] Field does not accept Eugenio Garin's theses that Agyropoulos was a dedicated Platonist and that the emergence of Neoplatonism in the latter half of the century was to be credited to his influence rather than to Marsilio Ficino or the Medici Academy. He offers evidence that would seem initially to support Garin's stand by demonstrating an interest in Florence in the writings of Plato some thirty years before Ficino's Latin translation of Plato's dialogues appeared in the early 1480s. Too, Ficino's reputation was well established and his ideas were well developed when Cosimo de' Medici first took him into his court. Although Agyropoulos's university position was a lectureship on Aristotle, he is a pivotal figure in Field's study. Field has examined the content of Agyropoulos's lectures from the notebooks of one of his most devoted followers, Donato Acciaiuoli, and finds no evidence for Agyropoulos as a Platonist. Garin would seem to have verified this point in his statement that Acciaiuoli had "suppressed" the Neoplatonic elements in his notes on Agyropoulos's lectures. If so, this would be unusual, as Field observes a predilection for Platonic metaphysics in Acciaiouli's commentaries on Aristotle.

Acciaiuoli is also a major figure in Field's study for providing access through his voluminous notes to Agyropoulos's lectures. He was the grandson of the anti-Medicean Palla Strozzi, who during his exile to Padua in 1441–44, had housed Agyropoulos. The Medici took political power in Florence in 1458, but with the participation in the government of more independent minded citizenry, Medici influence began to wane. This led to the del Poggio putsch of 1466, which both put the Medici out of power and prepared conditions for their return. Field notes how these political events were important in the development of philosophical thought as Acciaiuoli observed the failures of the Florentine government. As an "organic humanist" (that is, one of independent means) threatened by the ensuing economic and social decline, his sympathies now leaned toward the Medici, and his ideas favored pursuit of the contemplative life, even arguing that this was Aristotle's true message. Also, the Medici cause was capable of tolerating divergent views. Field explains that this was possible because the Medici camp was a true party, with a vision that transcended the narrow interests of family, class, or faction. Too, Cosimo's success lay in his ability to appropriate issues or change stands and in his patience as he allowed his opponents the opportunity to fail and fall out of favor.

Acciaiuoli differs with Agyropoulos in the interpretation of the nature of friendship. Acciaiuoli also departs from Aristotle in the *Nicomachean Ethics*, yet he does not agree with Ficino either. Finally, Acciaiuoli in his commentary of 1463 on the *Nicomachean Ethics*, which he had dedicated to Cosimo de' Medici, differs with his own notations of 1450 concerning the path to individual perfection. His later emphasis is on the contemplative life rather than good works. Leone Battista Alberti's *De Iciarchia* of 1469 offered a parallel in its emphasis on patrician values. Acciaiuoli observed that the government of Florence encountered difficulties when individuals began to seek political status; he argued that society ultimately depended on true friendship, which was promoted only by the contemplative life. In the 1470s Niccolò Tignosi da Foligno, who lectured on Aristotle, had complained of the Platonic nature of Acciaiuoli's theory of ideas. Because Acciaiuoli's Platonism came out of Aristotle, it was initially more appealing to Florentines and prepared them for eventual acceptance of Ficino. The patrician Acciaiuoli, in debating the merits of the political life against the search for truth, preferred the latter.

Field cites another of the Platonic Academy's origins in the humanists' ties with scholastics with whom many of them had studied, who were friends, or who moved in the same social circles. As a result, humanist thought took on moral and speculative characteristics. For example, the physician Tignosi (1402–74) was the teacher of Ficino. Tignosi's belief in the central role of the intellect in moral conduct was one of the ideas he imparted to Ficino. Tignosi was also lavish in his praise of Cosimo, whom he had set up as a perfect model, even straining the bounds of courtly rhetoric as he maintained that all desires, minds of men, and classes of men "came together in the reason of his [Cosimo's] mind." Here Tignosi's language is revealing. He synthesizes the dignity of learning, the nobility of the soul, and human diversity in the contemplative life. Tignosi showed Ficino how philosophical thinking differed from humanistic thinking.

Another influence for Ficino was Lorenzo Pisano (c. 1391–1465), whose theological symposia offered a prototype for the Platonic Academy. Ficino had learned intellectual vigor from Tignosi, but he was indebted to Pisano for poetry and a belief in "the reality and comprehensibility of the world of ideas." By the end of the century, Ficino had become isolated from the interests of the ruling class. He would write to the son of Giovanni Canigiani, as the latter prepared for a takeover of the government, that the cares of the world were of little importance. Ficino's true life was a contemplative one in which the mind was not to be absorbed by the world but was, instead, to give order to it. Externals could be controlled once their interrelationships were understood. Ficino's systematic thinking was indebted to his academic training. From his contacts in the religious world he was pushed to explain the function of philosophy in uniting God and man. The world of humanism introduced him to secular conceptions of the contemplative life and the dignity of man.

Field's study will frustrate the reader who is interested in a clear development of philosophical thought from the civic humanism of Leonardo Bruni, Carlo Marsuppini, and Poggio Bracciolini to the contemplative ideas of Ficino's patrician circle; but Field makes clear that his study is not of the evolution of Neoplatonism, but rather an examination of its origins based on mutual influences, patronage, and political affiliations. In any case, documents do not exist to provide an uninterrupted thread from Bruni to Ficino. Although it may not be possible to relate various ideas in every case, Field establishes overlaps of thought where they occur. This may not be satisfying to those who wish to observe the emergence of a coherent philosophical system, but gradual changes of thought can be noted, and the reader is satisfied both by Field's ability to link ideas and by the picture of development that emerges.

Field reports that a major interest in philosophical studies had taken place c. 1455–58, when the Medici were out of power. He uses Acciaiuoli and Rinuccini as "organic intellectuals" to illustrate the position of Florentine humanists from c. 1455 through the 1460s. It was at the beginning of that period that they took up Greek language and literature to expand their culture. They are contrasted with the "traditional humanists" such as Cristoforo Landino and Marsilio Ficino, who were not of independent means and who worked as teachers, clerks, or clerics.

Culture had assumed a role of great importance in the aggrandizement of Medici rule through the decades. Given the weakening of Tuscany's position as an industrial state, as a military power, and in the area of politics, Cardinal Prince Leopoldo de' Medici (1617–75) sought to sponsor various projects in the arts both as the traditional duty of Florentine rulers and for their propagandistic merits. He patronized the important academies of the Crusca dedicated to the maintenance of linguistic purity and of the Cimento for pursuit of the sciences. He even convened a meeting of the Accademia Platonica in 1638. Edward Goldberg's *After Vasari* is a study of the failure of patronage in the attempt of

Filippo Baldinucci (1625–96) in the 1670s to create an up-to-date account of Giorgio Vasari's collection of artists' biographies.

The emphasis in Goldberg's study is on Baldinucci's projects for Prince Leopoldo. His major value to the prince lay in his skills of connoisseurship and art historiography in building a royal collection of more than 11,000 drawings and of artists' self-portraits. The prince wanted a comprehensive cabinet of drawings to represent the major schools of art, careers of individual artists, and stylistic continuity of the schools. As a parallel, he also planned to bring up to date Vasari's *Lives of the Artists,* which, by establishing the myth of the Florentine origins of the arts in modernity, had underscored a major dynastic achievement of the Medici house.

Two individuals, Lionardo Dati and Giovanni Battista Brocchi, had begun to assemble notes for such an enterprise before Baldinucci entered Leopoldo's service. The project required archival searches and solicitation of information from experts in other regions of Italy. Other duties had prevented Dati from accomplishing much before his death in 1652, and Brachi's assembled information was unsorted and incomplete at his death in 1683. It then became Baldinucci's responsibility, but was a demanding undertaking that failed to come to full fruition in Baldinucci's lifetime due to the death of Leopoldo and the reluctance of his successor, Grand Duke Cosimo III, to pursue the project with similar enthusiasm.

In separate chapters, Goldberg characterizes the career of Leopoldo as a cultural patron and discusses the qualifications of Baldinucci. The latter was of humble birth, not a practicing artist, lacking in formal education, and of negligible literary credentials. Baldinucci's success was threatened by C. C. Malvasia, whose history of art in Bologna anticipated Baldinucci's corpus, appearing in print in 1678. It challenged the premise of Florentine origins for the arts and contradicted Vasari by claiming that the arts were alive in Bologna before Giotto appeared on the scene in Florence. Additionally, Baldinucci's efforts to shore up Vasari's position were frustrated by two of his fellow Florentines, Ferdinando Leopoldo del Migliore and Giovanni Cinelli, who in response to Malvasia argued for a flowering of the arts in Florence as early as 1130.

Goldberg illustrates the petty nature of these debates and indicates how unnecessary they were. The venality and paranoia of the participants are demonstrated at length from letters, pamphlets, and published arguments. Baldinucci's engagement with Leopoldo del Migliore originated from a printing error in the phrase "co' Migliori," where the uppercase *M* was misinterpreted by Leopoldo as a pun on his name. Baldinucci had attempted to praise the antiquarian Giovanni Renzi as deserving of a position with the best, "coi migliori," but Lorenzo read this phrase as an attempt to embarrass him in a field in which he claimed no expertise.

Goldberg explores the issue of Giotto and the mythical origins of modern art in Florence as argued by these principals, but he is less informative about the usefulness and reliability of Baldinucci's *Notizie*. Baldinucci titled his biographies *"notizie"* rather than *"vite"* because he wanted to emphasize factual material and avoid the anecdotal. The reader is not clear of the extent to which Baldinucci's corpus presents new facts or cites new documents to correct and supplement Vasari's biographies, or the degree to which Baldinucci succeeds in avoiding gossip and apocrypha. Is his contribution to be found primarily in the biographies of artists who came to maturity after the publication of Vasari's second edition of artists' lives in 1568, or are the most reliable biographies those of artists active during Baldinucci's lifetime?

Baldinucci was able to publish only three of the six volumes of the *Notizie* before his death.[5] Goldberg's account of his difficulties is new and informative but less helpful in evaluating the usefulness and reliability of his biographies.

Field's study is supported by a generous complement of footnotes with extensive quotation of primary source material and reference to the secondary literature. His essay is tightly structured, well organized, critical, and argumentative. Goldberg's essay also contains exhaustive documentation in lengthy endnotes; he is fluent in the controversies surrounding the literary issues related to Baldinucci's publications and with the subtleties of the arguments. In the end, if the issues of the *Notizie* seem less important for the Florentines of the seventeenth and eighteenth centuries than those of the humanists for quattrocento Florence, it is not because they are politically unimportant, but because Florence had become politically unimportant and Ficino's contemplative life had been replaced by Baldinucci's aestheticism.

Notes

1. Baron's lifelong concentration on Bruni began with his edition of some of the shorter works: *Leonardo Bruni Aretino, Humanistisch-Philosophische Schriften,* ed. Hans Baron (Leipzig, 1928). Various editions and translations of Bruni's many treatises are conveniently listed in Russell Dees, "Bruni, Aristotle, and the Mixed Regime in 'On the Constitution of the Florentines'," *Medievalia et Humanistica,* n.s. XV (1987), 1–23.
2. For extended critiques see Gennaro Sasso, " 'Florentina Libertas' e Rinascimento Italiano nell'Opera di Hans Baron," *Rivista Storica Italiana* LXIX (1957): 250–76, and Jerrold Seigel, " 'Civic Humanism' or Ciceronian Rhetoric?," *Past & Present* XXXIV (1966): 3–48. George Holmes, *The Florentine Enlightenment 1400–1450* (London, 1969), views Florence's connections and relations with Rome as formative.

3. This is not to make *The Discourses* less republican, but rather to make *The Prince* something other than a cold-blooded "prescription for absolutism" or "handbook for tyrants." See especially J. H. Whitfield, *Machiavelli* (London, 1947) and *Discourses on Machiavelli* (Cambridge, 1969).

4. In a separate chapter, Field deals with the "Studio controversy" of 1455 involving the selection of a replacement to Carlo Marsuppini's chair at the university. Four Florentine candidates stepped forward, one of whom was supported by Poggio Bracciolini. Field contends that Francesco Filelfo (1398–1481), in exile in Milan, was never a serious candidate although favored by Acciaiuoli, who also championed Agyropoulos. The Signoria simplified the decision by splitting Marsuppini's former position and approving two lecturers. Francesco da Castiglione was to teach Greek, and Landino was given a minor position which led in 1458 to a chair in rhetoric and poetry. It was at this point that Agyropoulos was given his appointment to teach Aristotle. Field disputes Eugenio Garin's contention that Agyropoulos had competed with Landino and maintains that there is no evidence of any opposition to Agyropoulos.

5. The *Notizie* were published as vols. 1 (1681), 2 (1686), 4 (1688), and, posthumously, 5 (1702), 3, and 6 (both 1728). Baldinucci published a prospectus for his *Notizie* in 1681, with twenty-two of its sixty-eight pages comprising an attack on Malvasia. A sixteen-page pamphlet that same year, *Lettera a Capponi*, raised questions in an elegant and gracefully learned fashion concerning who can judge art and the merits of original works against copies. His Tuscan dictionary, the 188-page *Vocabulario toscano dell'arte del disegno*, was followed in 1684 by a 28-page pamphlet, *La Veglia*, which, Goldberg informs us, is both a comic exercise and a cultivated piece of writing. He had also published his life of Bernini for Queen Christina of Sweden in 1682.

Italian Renaissance Medals

STEPHEN K. SCHER

Graham Pollard, ed., *Studies in the History of Art: Italian Medals*. Vol. 21. Hanover: University Press of New England, 1987. Pp. 299. $35.00.

In March 1984 the Center for Advanced Study in the Visual Arts at the National Gallery of Art in Washington, D.C., in consultation with Douglas Lewis, curator of sculpture at the museum, presented a symposium on the subject "Italian Medals," the first in a series devoted to Italian sculpture and related works. The three-day event was well attended by distinguished scholars, collectors, and experts from this country and abroad. Most of the papers were interesting and often exciting, and the discussions that took place around the sessions were equally valuable.

Awaited with eager anticipation after a delay of more than three years, the symposium papers finally appeared as volume 21 in the National Gallery's Studies in the History of Art. Publication of the lectures completes an event that can serve as a model for future presentations.

Study of the Renaissance medal, not only Italian, but also German, French, English, and Dutch, covering a period from around 1400 to 1600, is still in a relatively early stage of art-historical investigation. Despite the great corpora and pioneering studies of such giants as George Francis Hill[1] and Georg Habich,[2] entire areas of medallic production, in particular the Italian sixteenth century, remain uncataloged in a similarly consistent and comprehensive fashion.[3] In the past two decades some of these vast gaps have been filled by catalogs of individual public and private collections such as that of the National Gallery's own Kress Collection,[4] Graham Pollard's volumes on the medals in the Bargello, Florence,[5] the catalog of fifteenth-century medals in Milan,[6] or Mark Jones's two initial studies of the French medals in the British Museum.[7]

Not only are certain basic general catalogs still needed, but also individual studies of artists, detailed and careful stylistic attributions, the unraveling of the complex meanings of medallic reverses, questions of connoisseurship, historical and archival research, and the scientific investigation of the fabric of medals from various sources and periods remain virtually untouched areas. This is due in part to the fact that both in scholarship and in the art market medals have often in the past, and to some extent still in the present, remained in a numismatic context rather than being treated as sculpture.

For the most part the papers in *Italian Medals* make useful contributions in all of these areas, although it would have made much more sense to have organized the volume chronologically rather than alphabetically, at the same time grouping the technical papers together.

After a brief introduction by Graham Pollard, who has contributed so much to medallic research by editing and reissuing the work of G. F. Hill and by his basic cataloging efforts, the first paper, by Charles Avery, deals with several wax models from the hand of Massimilano Soldani (1656–1740), one of the most important Tuscan Baroque medallists. Avery first reviews several of the earlier wax models that have survived, including the well-known examples of Jacopo Negroboni and Barbara Romana. In the captions for the illustrations of these two pieces Avery still lists the Negroboni as "formerly Henry Oppenheimer" and the Barbara Romana as "formerly Maurice Rosenheim"—the same description given by Pollard in his edition of Hill's *Medals of the Renaissance*.[8] Both of these important models have been in the possession of the Metropolitan Museum of Art, New York, since 1936, a fact that no one seems to have noticed.[9]

Avery follows Soldani's career in some detail and discusses the development of his work. At one point, however, it was difficult to reconcile the statement "Soldani concentrated on casting large medals *for which he is justly famous*"[10] with the rather modest quality of the examples one encounters. In fact, a review of the entire range of Tuscan Baroque medals, a task made simple now by the appearance of Vannel and Toderi's massive and valuable study, leaves one feeling profoundly disappointed by this work.[11] The casts are usually very rough, the portraits dull, and the reverse images often awkward.

The great value of Avery's article lies in the new light it casts on this work by presenting five of Soldani's wax models, four of which are illustrated. The remarkable beauty and excellent workmanship of the wax models reveals the true ability of Soldani at the same time that a comparison of the model with a cast example—in this case, the reverse of the medal of Ludovico Caprara or the medal of Louis XIV with the Hercules reverse—shows how much of the delicacy and refinement of Soldani's work was lost in the casting process. It can be assumed that the same is true for the work of some of the other Tuscan medalists of the seventeenth century, but such a situation is puzzling, since already by the sixteenth century the ability to reproduce in bronze the most minute and profuse detail of the wax model had reached a very high degree of sophistication, while in France in the early seventeenth century Guillaume Dupré was casting with great success large medals containing an equally remarkable degree of detail.

Casting techniques, metallic composition, and some of the surface characteristics of Renaissance medals as understood in the conservation laboratory are covered in three valuable articles: Arthur Beale's "Surface Characteristics of Renaissance Medals and Their Interpretation," Eugene Farrell's "Non-Destructive Instrumental Analysis of Medals," and Patricia Tuttle's "An Investigation of the Renaissance Casting Techniques of Incuse-Reverse and Double-Sided Medals." The study and connoisseurship of medals must include thorough comprehension of these complex subjects. When examining any single specimen the questions that need to be answered are whether it was cast or struck, when it was produced, whether its surface was tooled, the nature of the patina, the importance of its size and clarity in relation to other examples, and the nature of the particular alloy. The inclusion in the symposium of papers dealing with some of these points was of immense value.

Arthur Beale's contribution is more of a brief introduction to the subject and is useful in this respect. It is regrettable that Beale, who is one of the most experienced people involved in the scientific study of medals, could not have given us more information. On one point in particular an additional comment is required. The presence of a seam on the edge of a cast medal does not always denote an electrotype. It is not uncommon to find medals, particularly in French and Dutch seventeenth-century examples, that are made of two hollow repoussé shells or incuse-reverse casts that have been soldered together, showing a seam, but that are perfectly authentic.

Eugene Farrell's task is also, of necessity, introductory; it presents the various methods now in use to determine the physical composition of medals. In an increasing number of cases such analyses are being performed, and it is hoped that all such data can be gathered into a central repository to be codified and studied to reveal any patterns that would aid us in dating individual specimens, in perceiving workshop practices, and in following the movements of a particular artist. Farrell explains concisely and clearly all the nondestructive methods currently used to determine a wide range of characteristics of the Renaissance medal and includes many valuable references in his notes.

Finally, the exposition of casting techniques by Tuttle is of great value and is handled precisely and with clarity—not an easy thing to do with such a subject. Accompanied by diagrams, the article describes step by step the processes used to cast both uniface and two-sided medals. An especially interesting point is made regarding the greater precision and clarity of incuse-reverse in contrast to double-sided medals, although fine examples of the latter can certainly be compared favorably with the former. In addition, in collaboration with Eugene Farrell, a useful table of results from the X-ray fluorescence analysis of a group of incuse medals provides valuable data.[12]

A logical companion to the scientific papers is Graham Pollard's "The Italian Renaissance Medal: Collecting and Connoisseurship." Pollard begins by raising another of the questions often asked about medals: How many were produced of any given type? In the fifteenth century, very few, according to Pollard. Neither he, nor anyone else in the symposium, attempts to define in sufficient detail the various terms used to describe individual specimens of any given medal. Admittedly, such clarification would require an entire article, but the criteria established for the application of such terms as "original," "contemporary," "old," "later," and "aftercast," all of which are used in descriptions of medals, still require clarification and harmonization.

Pollard continues with a compact but useful survey of Medici medallic patronage and collecting in the fifteenth and sixteenth centuries, including the gathering of ancient coins—an important and fascinating subject that is also treated, as we shall see, by Martha McCrory in another of the symposium papers. Both of these authors, however, seem to have overlooked a very valuable source of information on this essential subject, which is so crucial to the understanding of Renaissance humanism, the origins of the medal, and the changing tastes of the fifteenth and sixteenth centuries, in the thesis by John Cunnally, *The Role of Greek and Roman Coins in the Art of the Renaissance*.[13]

Pollard concludes with a very brief and somewhat scattered review of the evolution of medal collecting, connoisseurship, and scholarship.[14] It is regrettable that so fascinating a subject could not have been expanded upon in the written version of Pollard's paper.

If we examine the papers in a roughly chronological sequence related to the history of the medal, we may begin with two that deal with aspects of the origins of medals and the sources of their imagery. Both subjects present intriguing problems and are worthy of extensive study, but unfortunately, their treatment by John Spencer and Cornelius Vermeule leaves much to be desired. These two studies are the most disappointing in what is otherwise an exciting collection. Both scholars commit the serious error of drawing conclusions based on evidence that is totally unsupported by careful research and sufficient deliberation. The analogies that are drawn are, therefore, almost completely untenable.

Spencer in "Speculations on the Origins of the Italian Renaissance Medal" tries to demonstrate some link between Roman terra-cotta lamps and Etruscan mirror backs and Renaissance medals. Basing his argument initially on the similarity in size and shape of these respective objects, but admitting the difficulty of proving their availability and direct influence,

Spencer proceeds to find some further link in their imagery as well; but realizing his inability to substantiate his arguments, he finishes by being tentative, apologetic, and certainly unconvincing. The only analogy that carries the slightest weight is the reference to the standard composition of the Three Graces as it is found in antiquity—for example, on a classical mirror back in the North Carolina Museum of Art (Spencer's figure 12) and the same image on the reverse of the medal of Giovanna Albizzi (figure 10). Here the relation of general source to later copy is too obvious and familiar to be questioned.

Far greater follies are committed by Cornelius Vermeule in his paper "Graeco-Roman Asia Minor to Renaissance Italy: Medallic and Related Arts." In spirit and form the Renaissance medal was built in large part upon the foundations of classical coinage, both Greek and Roman. On the obverse the association of the prince with ancient rulers and heroes was deliberate and pointed, while on the reverse forms drawn from a vast store of images from the antique world told in allegory, emblem, and myth the virtues and achievements of the medal's subject. All this is well known but has not been adequately studied. The anticipation, therefore, is very high for a valuable contribution to this subject from someone seemingly so well qualified as Cornelius Vermeule, who has worked with both ancient coins and Renaissance medals. Unfortunately, the reality is an embarrassment to such an extent that one wonders how, in the midst of so many interesting, scholarly, and carefully prepared papers, this totally inadequate, superficial, pretentious travesty found its way into print.

Vermeule's contention is that the Greek coins of Asia Minor under Roman rule were frequently used as sources for the imagery on Renaissance medals—not an impossible hypothesis, but one requiring some rather solid substantiation. Vermeule, with almost total abandon, attempts to prove his point through a series of completely unconvincing comparisons based on little or no hard evidence except the careless juxtaposition of objects that, with a considerable stretch of the imagination, could have some vague similarities.

Vermeule begins with a prologue that already contains a number of inaccuracies and meaningless phrases such as "iconographic obverses" and that is salted with irrelevant bits of erudition. The prologue leads to an introduction, which in turn passes on to a series of specific comparisons, the superficiality of which has already been mentioned. In most cases examples of Greek imperial coins, seemingly chosen at random by riffling through the pages of standard coin catalogs, are set forth categorically as sources for the medals illustrated, often with only the vaguest correspondence of figures and compositions and always without any sort of convincing solid evidence.

It is of little use to cite the individual examples offered by Vermeule, since one is as absurd as the next. Suffice it to say that if one's time is limited, this is the article to skip.

Returning to more solid stuff, a number of the papers are concerned with individual artists, beginning with Pier Giorgio Pasini's "Matteo de' Pasti: Problems of Style and Chronology." Pasini's paper is a curious mixture of vague ideas, generalities, and jumbled concepts with provocative theories, valuable considerations regarding the sequential dating of Matteo's medals based on style and historical events, and a refreshingly personal and emotional response that emerges even through a clumsy translation.

It is not entirely clear, for example, what Pasini means by his equation of Matteo's reverses with his work as a miniaturist in "a Gothic language" or the relation with Venetian Gothic sculpture. The same vagueness is present in the comparison between Gothic stylization and Renaissance naturalism. In some cases the concepts are valid and are expressed with sensitive and accurate observations, but in other instances statements do not make much sense or do not emerge clearly enough. Pasini's general discussion of the adoption of the elephant as a symbol by the Malatesta is quite interesting, but it loses force when he refers to the reverse of the medals of Isotta degli Atti.

Pasini attempts to describe Matteo's artistic personality in rather specific terms but without citing any hard evidence for his description, suggesting that he is doing so on pure conjecture and intuition. Yet in the end his involvement in his subject is contagious, resulting in an article that is flawed but quite provocative.

Christopher Lloyd's "Reconsidering Sperandio" deals with another of the most important quattrocento medalists, one whose reputation, as Lloyd points out in the beginning of his paper, has seen both good and bad days. On this point the paper begins well, discussing the elevation of Sperandio by Goethe to a position above that of Pisanello and the subsequent demolition of that position by G. F. Hill.

Soon, however, the paper runs into problems that the author himself remarks upon and attempts to excuse. He produces extremely farfetched comparisons between some of Sperandio's reverses and other examples of contemporary art which even a reference to "a shared heritage of images" does not entirely explain or excuse.

In assessing the quality of Sperandio's medals one is forced to choose a middle ground. Many of his portraits are masterful, among the finest in the Renaissance; others are clumsy and without character, which is also the case for most of Sperandio's reverses, which were copied, as they often were, from the work of other artists. When Lloyd describes the medallic double portrait of Ercole I d'Este and Eleanora of Aragon as "one of the artist's most winning conceptions," however, one tends to question the author's judgment, since this medal could be offered as an example of Sperandio's less attractive creations. It is awkward, stiff, poorly composed, and heavy, with little character or sensitivity.

The remainder of the article is devoted to the study of a medal whose subject is identified as Tito Vespasiano Strozzi, based upon comparison with a painting and a series of plaques with a portrait of the same man, a leading humanist poet. Lloyd's writing is sometimes convoluted, obscuring his arguments; and his analysis of the portrait plaques concentrates heavily on the changing physiognomy of the subject as a basis for dating but neglects the important question of the physical characteristics of the bronzes—that is, the quality of the casts, the degree of cold work present, patina, and so forth. The article raises many interesting questions but answers few of them and tends at times to float in some confusion.

One of the more enlightened aspects of the National Gallery symposium was the inclusion of scholars from related areas of art history. Such was the case of Julian Raby, whose paper "Pride and Prejudice: Mehmed the Conqueror and the Italian Portrait Medal" is excellent, being provocative, well researched, fully documented, and elegantly written.

Raby traces the medallic patronage of Mehmed II over three decades, preceded by contacts in the 1440s between the Ottoman court and European trading communities in the East that led to an interest on the part of Mehmed in Italian humanism, including ancient coins and contemporary medals. From the 1450s date two medals of a youthful Mehmed: one the silver "Tricaudet" medal; the other, known in two specimens, Oxford and Vienna, that shows the influence of Pisanello.

From the 1460s dates the fascinating contact by Mehmed with Sigismondo Malatesta and Matteo de' Pasti. Although no medals of the sultan exist from this period, Raby cites a fascinating letter from Sigismondo to Mehmed that reveals a great deal about both men and about the role played by medals in the Renaissance as a celebration of great men, associating those of the present, such as the lord of Rimini and his Ottoman correspondent, with Alexander the Great and other heroes of antiquity. The need to be glorified and remembered through portraits was not confined to the West, but cultivated with equal and surprising intensity by a Muslim ruler.

It was during the few years preceding Mehmed's death in 1481 that the most remarkable and well known of his medallic portraits were produced: the two extraordinary pieces by Costanzo da Ferrara and the work of Gentile Bellini and Bertoldo di Giovanni. Raby examines these medals with great thoroughness and insight, making a very important contribution not only to the study of medals but also to Renaissance sculpture in general and to the intriguing question of relations between the Islamic East and the Western world.

Several papers are devoted to major artists of the sixteenth century. Andrea Norris deals with Gian Cristoforo Romano; Douglas Lewis, with the work of "Moderno"; Giovanni Gorini directs our attention to Giovanni da Cavino; Martha McCrory studies Domenico Compagni; and Manfred Leithe-Jasper contributes a short piece on a medal of Vincenzo Danti.

In "Gian Cristoforo Romano: The Courtier as Medalist" Norris offers a thorough survey of the artist's career and medallic production at the court of Mantua, where his primary task, after his arrival there in 1497, was to satisfy the continual and enlightened demands of Isabella d'Este. Examining in some detail the three documented medals by Romano depicting Isabella, Pope Julius II, and Isabella of Aragon, duchess of Milan, Norris then considers other attributions to the artist, in particular two medals of Lucrezia Borgia, one of Jacopa Correggia, and another of Beatrice of Aragon—all of which she places convincingly in varying degrees of proximity to the style of Romano.

Nicely complementing the article on Romano and further enlarging our understanding of the Mantuan school is Douglas Lewis's study "The Medallic Oeuvre of 'Moderno': His Development at Mantua in the Circle of 'Antico'." Proceeding with deliberation and welcome sensitivity, Lewis first reminds us of the probable identification of the artist commonly known as "Moderno" with the Veronese artist Galeazzo Mondella (1467–1528) and his relationship with Pier Jacopo Alari Bonacolsi, called "Antico" (c. 1460–1528), in the Mantua of Francesco II Gonzaga (1466–1519) and, after 1490, his wife, Isabella d'Este (1474–1539). Fortunately, Antico signed a number of his medals, thus enabling us to identify his style without much effort, a style that is clearly established in the medals he did for Gianfrancesco Gonzaga of Rodigo (1443–96) and his wife, Antonia del Balzo (1441–1538).

Moderno, on the other hand, did not sign any medals, and Lewis's objective in his article is to convince us that a number of the medals from the Mantuan school are by this artist, medals that had previously been described as being "in the manner of Antico."[15] He begins by drawing an undeniable parallel between the figure of captive Mars on the reverse of Antico's medal of Gianfrancesco Gonzaga and the St. Sebastian on the glorious *Sacra Conversazione* relief by Moderno in Vienna. Having established this link between Antico and Moderno, Lewis develops further the evolution of Moderno's medallic production through a series of attributions based on stylistic analogies that are not always clearly perceptible. In fact, Lewis sometimes succumbs to the danger always present in the hazardous activity of stylistic attribution: the confusion of compositional motifs and iconographical conventions with true stylistic peculiarities. This is true, for example, in the comparison of the Mazzanti reverse with that of the Diva Faustina or of the central nude in Antico's Diva Julia with a figure in the Battle of Cannae relief, or Opportunity on the medal of Magdalena Mantuana, justly praised by Lewis, with the Maenad on the Orpheus plaquette. Collectively, the final attributions to Moderno may still be accepted, but the argument is weakened by being based on these comparisons.

Nonetheless, Lewis's determined and careful effort to construct a medallic oeuvre for Moderno is to be applauded. He undertakes a very difficult task with a certain measure of success, as can be seen in the helpful synopsis he includes at the end of his paper. Such monographic studies are exactly what are now needed in the field of medallic research.

Into this category falls the valuable article by Giovanni Gorini on one of the most fascinating and misunderstood of medallists, Giovanni da Cavino (1500–70). In this case the scene shifts from Mantua to Padua, arguably the birthplace of the Renaissance medal.[16] With Cavino we are confronted with several crucial questions involved in the study of Renaissance medals: the taste of Renaissance patrons, artists, and collectors; the collecting of coins and medals; the perception of style; the problem of forgeries; and the nature of the art market in the Renaissance.

Gorini does not really deal with these questions, and despite what appears to be a carefully organized text presents a selection of interesting thoughts and some useful documentary evidence regarding Cavino scattered throughout a confused and disjointed narrative. Describing Cavino's earliest development in Padua, which was a center of bronze casting, Gorini also emphasizes what he sees as the importance of the striking in 1508 by Camelio (Vettor di Antonio Gambello, 1455/60–1537) of a self-portrait medal. It is difficult to understand why Gorini considers this to have been "a true revolution in Veneto medal-making at the beginning of the sixteenth century." Camelio's pieces are small (29 and 37 mm.) and would have presented little difficulty for production by a local mint. In fact, in 1390 in this same city of Padua, Francesco II da Carrara struck medals of comparable size (32 and 36 mm.) imitating Roman sestertii and commemorating the recovery of the city from Giangaleazzo Visconti. These pieces can, with some justification, be recognized as proto-Renaissance medals; and because they imitate the form of Roman coins, they also have a particular relevance regarding Cavino, whose fame (or, more accurately, notoriety) rests upon the production of copies of Roman coins.

Gorini assigns this activity to Cavino's early years, when he also fulfills a number of commissions as a goldsmith. The author's examination of documents and his conclusions regarding the chronology of Cavino's work, along with his categorical assertion that the artist's copies of Roman coins were not intended to deceive, are not convincing. This is an extremely important question, and one that may never be answered. Many imitations of Roman coins were made during the sixteenth century, a large proportion no doubt intended to deceive the unwary collector.[17] Some of these pieces are quite crude and are classified generally as "Paduans," reflecting Cavino's stature and the association of his name with this sort of object. The quality of his work, on the contrary, is quite fine, both in the imitations of Roman sestertii and in the medals of contemporary people—a fact that is often overlooked.

Gorini proceeds with some confusion, referring unconvincingly to several sources for antique types and giving a haphazard review of the contemporary portraits. The work of Giovanni da Cavino is significant and worthy of further examination, especially in the identification of his style and in the chronology and significance of his work. Gorini makes a scattered, but useful, effort in this direction.

Of immediate relevance to the subject of coin collecting in the Renaissance with the related areas of the antiquities market and forgeries is the excellent article by Martha McCrory, "Domenico Compagni: Roman Medalist and Antiquities Dealer of the Cinquecento." In a tightly conceived, extremely interesting study McCrory goes far beyond her stated subject. She concentrates on the collecting activities of Francesco II de' Medici, Grand Duke of Tuscany (1541–87), who was building upon the already considerable holdings gathered by his forebears. The significance of Roman coins, particularly large bronzes, not only as representations of the entire series of emperors, good and bad, but also as sources for classical dress and iconographic types, is emphasized by McCrory. She describes how and where the coins were found, the awareness of forgeries, and the methods employed to identify them.

It was also common for copies to be made deliberately and without intent to deceive, and the number and fame of the artists engaged in this activity is surprising. In particular McCrory reviews the career of Domenico Compagni, also known as Domenico de' Cammei, and his association with the Medici court as a gem engraver, medalist, and, in particular, coin dealer. The latter pursuit undoubtedly led him to cut the dies for imitations of ancient coins, illustrated and catalogued by McCrory, that are now in the Bargello and that were already listed in 1587 in the inventory of the possessions of Cardinal Ferdinando de' Medici, who became grand duke in that same year. The dies are of both Greek and Roman coins and reflect a wide interest in classical coins. Compagni's work in this area immediately brings to mind the identical activity of Cavino, and McCrory does not neglect to discuss this point and some of its most interesting ramifications.[18]

Manfred Leithe-Jasper of the Kunsthistorisches Museum, Vienna, has contributed a very brief, but sensitive, article on "A Medal of Leone Baglioni by Vincenzo Danti," which is more a detailed catalog entry but a model of its sort. Leithe-Jasper describes the medal, which exists in only three examples; cites the former scholarship; gives historical information about the subject, Leone Baglioni; and offers an accurate and thoughtful critical analysis of the style and quality of the work. He does not, however, seem to take into consideration the quality of the actual cast, which is flawed and quite rough. All Leithe-Jasper's observations are accurate, indicating a fine critical eye, and they combine to provide the kind of stylistic evaluation that is much needed in medallic scholarship.

Leithe-Jasper equates the initials "V. D." on the truncation of the bust of Baglioni quite unequivocally with the Perugian artist Vincenzo Danti, using as a basis of comparison the reliefs on the borders of the mantle of the bronze figure of Pope Julius III in front of the cathedral of Perugia, as well as the artist's later works in Florence. It is unfortunate, however, that illustrations of one or two of these essential elements in his argument were not included with this excellent little study.

Richard J. Tuttle has contributed a very thorough paper on the subject *"Bononia Resurgens:* A Medallic History by Pier Donato Cesi." Admitting the poor quality of the medals he is discussing, Tuttle concentrates, rather, on the patron of the project, Pier Donato Cesi, bishop of Narni, and resident vice legate and papal governor of Bologna. Cesi, an ambitious, intelligent, and talented prelate, conceived the idea of producing a series of ten medals devoted to the commemoration of papal projects in Bologna. In this way the bishop not only celebrated the achievements of Pope Pius IV (1559–65), but also made certain that his own existence and activities were not lost on the pontiff.

Cesi accompanied the medals with a text describing each project which still exists in manuscript form in the Bibliotheca Ambrosiana, Milan. Tuttle meticulously describes each item in the manuscript and equates it with an existing medal. He then directly links the production of the medals with the Bolognese mintmaster at the time, Girolamo Faccioli (or Fagiuoli), a position he held from 1560 to 1573. Tuttle also recognizes the presence of another artist in two medals—the Fountain of Neptune (observe and reverse) and the Opera Mendicanti (obverse)—and suggests that this was the great sculptor Giovanni Bologna. Tuttle bases his argument on Giovanni's presence in Bologna, on his involvement in these monuments, and on what he sees as the superior quality of the two pieces.

Since it is difficult to perceive this quality, which Tuttle calls "superlative," the attribution carries very little weight.

Another paper that examines papel patronage is John Varriano's "Alexander VII, Bernini, and the Baroque Papal Medal." Varriano begins with a useful review of production methods in the papal mint, the reasons for striking medals, and a realistic assessment of their mediocre quality.

One of the most active papal medallic patrons was Alexander VII Chigi. A great builder, Alexander transformed the appearance of Rome and published this transformation through a series of medals. At the same time he was an avid numismatist, being concerned to an extraordinary degree with his collections of coins and medals and with the activities of the papal mint. One of his most important objectives was to improve the quality of its issues, and to this end on several occasions he called upon the talents of the great Gianlorenzo Bernini. Varriano notes that there exist four drawings by Bernini for one coin and three medals, as well as a print commemorating the issuing of a medal honoring Alexander VII, with a scene on the reverse of Androcles and the Lion that can also be attributed to Bernini. All these pieces were executed by either a die cutter such as the chief papal medalist, Gaspare Morone, or, in the case of the Androcles medal, a sculptor such as G. F. Travani.

Of great interest is the comparison between Bernini's drawings, which are superb, and the coins and medals struck from them. All that remains is the general design, the masterly tones of the wash drawings and the vibrant movements of the figures being lost in the translation to a die for striking.

The situation is somewhat different for the cast Androcles and the Lion medal, a preparatory drawing for which does not survive. Despite the fact that the quality of the medal as prepared by Travani is certainly not at the level of Bernini's work, it does possess the drama, complexity, spatial handling, and pictorial effects of baroque art. It is also in strong contrast to the usual small-scale, dry productions of the papal mint.

Evidence of the relationship between Alexander VII and Bernini as patron and artist is recorded in a diary kept by the pope which contains fifty entries pertaining to medals, some of which refer as well to Bernini. This is all valuable and intriguing material, and it is handled commendably by Varriano. He demonstrates that Bernini's important contribution to architectural reverses was their transformation into city views with the requisite *staffage* and the atmospheric effects already introduced by Johann Jakob Kornmann in 1648. This form of naturalism in the architectural reverses of medals was one of the most important innovations of Alexander VII and brought about some of the revitalization he had sought.

Papal architectural medals is also the subject of the article by Ingrid Weber of the Staatliche Münzsammlung, Munich. Titled "The Significance of Papal Medals for the Architectural History of Rome," the paper reviews the critical role played by numismatic evidence in the tracking of the history of many architectural projects and monuments in Rome, a role dating back to Roman coinage, whereon was often portrayed buildings, sculpture, and other monuments later damaged or destroyed. The popes continued this tradition with regular issues of coins and medals, chronicling their active participation in the growth of the city.

Weber concentrates on several key monuments, beginning with the Castel and Ponte S. Angelo, various stages in the construction and fortification of which are clearly illustrated on medallic reverses, beginning c. 1495 and ending in 1669.[19] She then reviews the history of the Capitoline Hill and its monuments, once again illustrating those medals that provide vital information about the unfolding of this program.

Finally, and inevitably, Weber examines the history of the basilica of St. Peter's and the evidence of its evolution preserved on medals. The entire article is a useful introduction to, and reminder of, the importance of numismatic evidence in art and architectural history, evidence that is particularly available in Rome for reasons already described.

If the portrait medal essentially has its origins in Italy, its form was very soon transported to other countries. This is nowhere more true than in France, where Italian artists produced medals for René d'Anjou in the 1460s. By the end of the century French artists were themselves issuing medals, as witness the large and handsome cast medal of Louis XII and Anne de Bretagne commissioned by the city of Lyon from a team of French artists. It is the relationship between France and Italy in the production of medals that is the subject of the paper by Mark Jones of the British Museum, "Medal-Making in France 1400–1650: The Italian Dimension." Jones wishes to determine whether medals produced in France during this very broad period are specifically French in character or merely provincial offshoots of what was being done in Italy.

This purpose is admirable, but its fulfillment appears to have been somewhat difficult. After the initial reference to early activity in France by Italian medalists, during which Jones makes the dreadful mistake of confusing the Nicholas de Florence, who was the brother-in-law of Jean Lepère, one of the artists involved in the casting of the medal of Louis XII and Anne de Bretagne, with Niccolo di Forzore Spinelli, called Niccolo Fiorentino, even illustrating the latter's medals of French subjects as being by the former. The paper continues with the misleading statement that most of the medals made in France in the early part of the sixteenth century were by Italian artists.

Jones then attempts to present a statistical analysis of the comparative volume of medal production in France and Italy during the period he is considering, but he qualifies this attempt with so many cautions that one wonders whether the exercise was worth undertaking. The graphs and maps that accompany the text give a pseudoscientific aura to the paper but actually demonstrate very little. Jones's conclusion is that at least until around 1550, medallic production in France was a provincial offshoot of Italian activity, and this seems to be an acceptable conclusion.

Jones then compares the basic imagery of French and Italian medals as seen in portraits combined with emblems and heraldry and attempts to understand what this might tell us about basic approaches to the medal. The questions the author asks are very important, and he makes a determined effort to answer them. Of particular interest is the examination of the distribution of both coins and medals in relation to their imagery and the materials used in their fabrication. Some of the discussion, however, seems muddled and incomplete.

Jones ends with a reference to Guillaume Dupré, who, building upon the dazzling work being done in Italy and having the spectacular relief portraits of Germain Pilon, whom Jones does not mention, as models, establishes himself as one of the greatest medalists in Europe and certainly dispels any notion about the provinciality of French medals.

In summary, *Italian Medals* is, as one would expect, a mixed bag, but one that is well worth the effort of exploring. The subject is one that has long needed the kind of attention it gets here from a group of scholars with a refreshing variety of approaches. It is to be hoped that this admirable effort will spawn many others.

Notes

1. G. F. Hill, *A Corpus of Italian Medals of the Renaissance Before Cellini*, 2 vols. (London, 1930); *Medals of the Renaissance*, revised and enlarged by Graham Pollard (London, 1978; first published, 1920).
2. Georg Habich, *Die deutschen Schaumünzen des XVI Jahrhunderts*, 5 vols. (Munich, 1929–34).
3. Two essential references are A. Armand, *Les Médailleurs italiens des XVe et XVIe siècles*, 2d rev. ed., 3 vols. (Paris, 1883–87); and Leonard Forrer, *Biographical Dictionary of Medallists*, 8 vols. (London, 1902–30).
4. G. F. Hill and Graham Pollard, *Renaissance Medals from the Samuel H. Kress Collection at the National Gallery of Art, New York* (London, 1967).
5. Graham Pollard, *Italian Renaissance Medals in the Museo Nazionale del Bargello*, 3 vols. (Florence, 1984–85).
6. Cesare Johnson and Rodolfo Martini, *Catalogo delle Medaglie. I. Secolo XV* (civiche raccolte: numismatiche) (Milan, 1986).

7. Mark Jones, *A Catalogue of the French Medals in the British Museum*, 2 vols. (London, 1982–88).
8. Hill, op. cit., 1978.
9. Although the letters are quite clear on the model, Avery reads the penultimate letter as "R" when it is actually "B." This is a mistake made often before. The reading of the inscription as "Barbara Ro(mana)" is thus incorrect. He also transcribes the surname as "Barbara" when it is clearly "Barbarae." It is curious that the illustration of this same model in Hill's *Medals of the Renaissance*, first published in 1920, does show the inscription as "RO." The model was then in the Max and Maurice Rosenheim Collection, which was sold in London in 1923. The model entered the Metropolitan Museum in 1936, as we have already indicated. Clearly, this beautiful object requires some further study.
10. Italics mine.
11. Fiorenza Vannel and Giussepe Toderi, *La Medaglia Barocca in Toscana* (Florence, 1987).
12. Cf. Richard E. Stone, "Antico and the Development of Bronze Casting in Italy at the End of the Quattrocento," *Metropolitan Museum Journal* 16 (New York, 1982): 87–116.
13. Cf. John Cunnally, *The Role of Greek and Roman Coins in the Art of the Italian Renaissance*, Ph.D. dissertation, University of Pennsylvania, Philadelphia, 1984. University Microfilms International, Ann Arbor, Michigan, 1987.
14. In his text Pollard gives a date of 1746 for the publication of the Mazzuchelli catalog. The correct dates, which he does cite in his notes (n. 32) are 1761 and 1763 for the two volumes. This may have been a typographical error, of which there are far too many throughout the book.
15. Hill and Pollard, op. cit., 1967, p. 19, nos. 73a, 74, 75.
16. It was in Padua as early as 1399 that medals were struck commemorating the liberation of the city by Francesco II, Novello, da Carrara, and showing on the obverses portraits *all'antica* of himself and his father, Francesco I, in imitation of Roman sestertii.
17. In one way or another this subject is addressed elsewhere in the volume under review in articles by Gorini, McCrory, and Pollard. See also Cunnally, op. cit., note 13.
18. Here again, this author appears to be unaware of Cunnally's (op. cit.) excellent dissertation.
19. In describing one of the medals of the Castel S. Angelo, Weber refers to the configuration of the tops of the walls as "pinnacles." The correct term is "crenellations."

Review Notices

Sandro Sticca, The *Planctus Mariae* and the Dramatic Tradition of the Middle Ages. Translated by Joseph R. Berrigan. The University of Georgia Press, 1988. Pp. xviii, 240.

The author of *The Latin Passion Play* (Albany, N.Y.: 1970) now presents a full-length study of an important element in that literary form, the *planctus* of Mary at the crucifixion of Jesus. Sticca presents a vast taxonomy of literary compositions of this type, showing how deeply rooted in the Greco-Latin tradition "are the vision and the idea of the *Virgo moerens*" (125). He develops a distinction between the *planctus*, with its "effort to capture the inward movements of the soul of the Virgin and to express them sorrowfully and tragically by the mournful lyricism of her own words," and the *compassio* of the Virgin, which is characterized by "an internalization of the Virgin's plaint and sorrow, which is purely descriptive" (85). This distinction, basically one between first-person monologue and narration, sometimes wavers in the course of the book, though the incorporation of the *compassio* in the form of intense lyrical presentations of the sorrowing Mother into the *planctus* in the setting of drama is made clear enough (e.g., 118, but cf. 125).

The fundamental conclusion of Sticca's analysis of his vast array of texts is that the *Planctus Mariae* does not constitute the source of the drama of the Passion. This of course assumes a fixed form for the *planctus,* a kind of fixity more often associated with liturgical than with purely literary productions, and Sticca acknowledges the difficulty of dealing with a multiform lament. He attempts to unify the *planctus* around recurring elements in it: "The *Planctus Mariae* invariably emphasizes the contrast of the logic of the maternal heart as it contemplates the awful intensity of the bloody drama of the Son upon the cross with the affirmation of the dogmatic elements of the Redemption, of which the *Planctus Mariae* represents nevertheless an ennobling spiritual crystallization" (71). "In them all, the *Planctus Mariae,* as a lyrical form, is always characterized by an essential and constant aesthetic orientation and by a precise spiritual objective: the articulation of the Mother's grief and affection, motivated only in part by the need to illustrate the physical and spiritual travail of the God-Man" (170–71). This is, of course, quite true. But it would be helpful in sorting out the many functions of the *planctus Mariae* to examine just whose need the "need to illustrate" is. The dramatic character of the Virgin, played by a cleric in a liturgical drama?

Or the poet's, out of personal piety or didactic intent? The programmatic directives of the church, whether local, diocesan, Franciscan, or, working under a rather overused concept in the book, the Zeitgeist? Such questions point to further work that can be done in this fascinating area where medieval literature, both lyric and dramatic, preaching, liturgy, art, and piety both corporate and individual meld together around such forms (if they indeed be stable forms) of *planctus* and *compassio*.

If the core of the book is devoted to examining the relationship of *planctus* to drama, there are also many pages which examine Mary as co-redemptrix with Christ. This seems to proceed from a state of Marian piety, to judge from the sources, often associated with the latter years of Pius XII and does not materially contribute to the purpose of the author, though some will find this aggregation of information to be of use. Much the same thing may be said of a chapter on the Marian cult and devotion, which does not seem fully integrated into the scope of the study. On the other hand, a chapter on the *planctus* of Mary and the Eastern tradition is a welcome expansion of our understanding of this genre. It would have been a very good idea to provide the reader with the Greek texts (or in some cases, the Syriac) rather than to rely on French translations (e.g., 22, 23), where the cultural bias of the translator needs to be discounted, as always in dealing with remote texts. Likewise, presenting the Latin translations from the *Patrologia Graeca* for Origen (33), George of Nicodemia (45ff.), and Simeon Metaphrastes (incorrectly called Simon here, 47ff.) leads to confusion; in many cases the original Greek (for, e.g., Simeon) is lost, but we are not told whether this is the case for texts quoted in this book. This is perhaps most vexing in the case of Jacob of Sarug (called "James" here) whose original Syriac works are presented in modern Latin translation, as are those of Ephraim the Syrian; the bibliography cites the six volumes of his *opera omnia* as "Rome, 1947," but this may be the six-volume edition, execrable to be sure, of the eighteenth century, three in Syriac and three in Greek. One cannot tell, nor can one learn the origin of the Latin translations cited. Romanos the Melodos is consistently cited in Latin, and the sole text printed in Greek is incorrect (34). In any event, it is certain that Ephraim did not live and work in Odessa, as claimed (35), but rather in Edessa.

It would be very interesting to learn just how the Greek (and Syriac!) texts were assimilated into the Latin consciousness. It seems likely that many of the compositions allegedly bearing the imprint of Greek sensibility were the work of pious people, often Franciscans, whose level of learning probably would not be up to dealing with languages other than Latin and their vernaculars. But Sticca does not go into this. He does examine the tension between Latin and vernacular expressions of lament, relying much on the three lines in the vernacular in the Montecassino Passion. This would have provided an opportunity to examine systematically the questions of social class, literacy versus orality, lay versus cleric, that surround these texts, their writers, and, even more important, the audiences envisioned for them.

Sticca is well aware of the many problems associated with studying a wealth of material from the patristic period to the Renaissance. His method is to stick to the pious aspects of the texts, to their emotive rather than their didactic function, and he may well be right to do so. He mentions in passing (118) the changing pictorial representations of Christ (without, however, noting that there is no parallel for this on the Greek side) as context for increasing realism in the *planctus*. One might have expected in this connection a discussion of Bernardine emphasis on the sacred humanity of Jesus, with its attendant implications for spirituality. As it stands, this study does not equip the reader to assess, for instance, differences in the *planctus Mariae* in a Cluniac versus a Franciscan setting, or in other social and religious contexts. All these texts are curiously flattened, foreshortened into their emotive baggage, and on that basis alone made comparable to one another. One would have thought that the emergence of courtly love would have changed both the means of apprehending the themes of the *planctus* and the kinds of *planctus* written in the ambience of courtly societies; there is, after all, the Provencal *planh*, with no religious preoccupation. The form exists in *Beowulf, Chanson de Roland,* and elsewhere, with reference to lamenting a lost leader and lover. Indeed, the inevitable question of the erotic aspects of these scenes of the Virgin receiving her lifeless son, taking him in her lap, kissing the wounds, smearing her face in his blood, and pleading for further time with her beloved (e.g., 112ff.) is nowhere addressed.

Eleven plates showing representations of the Crucifixion from early manuscripts and frescoes down to 1500 are included, but not mentioned by the text itself; they serve to present an increasingly animated Virgin and agonized victim. In view of the ample discussion of the Greek tradition, it might have been useful to illustrate how the Eastern church does not present Christ in agony on the cross but dead on the cross, and to assess the implications of this in the text as well as in the mute illustrations.

The Latin texts are virtually without mistake (though see e.g. 16, 42, etc.) There are occasional slips in consistence. For example (54), Paul the Deacon, of the eighth century, is asserted to have been the first in the Western world to refer to the Virgin as "mediatrix Dei ad homines," and on the following page we read, "It is true that the mediational role of Mary can be seen for the first time during the eleventh century." The

Acta Pilati are first dated as "the beginning of the fourth century . . . or, in any case, no later than the end of that century" (33) and later "generally attributed to the fifth or sixth century" (42). In following his sources, the writer apparently has not attempted to reconcile their differences of opinion. Other difficulties have probably arisen from the translation process. We are told of "the patristic tradition of Mary, extending over the first eight centuries of the Christian era" (50), of "Christian and Marian piety" (19). Names are not consistently presented; Justinus (Justin Martyr) appears at one point (51), and an eighth-century abbot appears in sonorous Italian as "Ambrogio Autperto" (54); the Opera del Duomo (136) is not "the musical archive of Florence."

This far-reaching study would have been improved, one might think, if methodological procedures and governing hypotheses and definitions had been sketched out at the beginning, rather than being allowed to bloom in the midst of textual presentations. A more rigorous adherence to the argument and a less exuberant flowering of *pietas* would also make the work tighter and its presentation more compelling. The thesis or problem that Sticca addresses is a real one, but it is all too often lost in the luxurious growth of his presentation. His work will doubtless impel others to further study. By gathering together such a repertory of texts and secondary sources Sticca has laid the groundwork for such an assessment of the *planctus* in its manifold shapes.

Charles Witke
The University of Michigan

Paul Hills, *The Light of Early Italian Painting*. New Haven and London: Yale University Press, 1987. Pp. 160. 84 illustrations; 32 color plates.

Significant studies in English on the development and use of linear perspective during the Italian Renaissance have long been available.[1] Now Paul Hills's thorough examination of the analogous effects of light upon Italian painting executed between 1250 to 1430 is a welcome contribution to an allied field. His book analyzes the Western notion of pictorial light, investigating its origins and evolution throughout this period. Hills wisely does not attempt a comprehensive survey of early Italian painting, but instead concentrates on major artists, particularly emphasizing the Florentine tradition of monumental frescoes begun by Giotto and continued in the work of Taddeo Gaddi through Masaccio. This focus on Tuscany, which can still be argued was the most artistically innovative region in Italy, provides a control for future comparisons with other Italian centers.

Applying modern research drawn from the psychology of perception, the subject is approached from various angles, thereby accomplishing Hills's desire to circumvent an interpretation based on a sequence of consecutive incidents. Thus, there are chapters that explore the etymology of optical terms and the theological character of late-medieval optics in conjunction with a contemporary artist's shop-practice handbook. Others show how different painting methods influenced the external representation of light across the picture plane, as opposed to light's illusionistic quality. Additional chapters assess Pietro Cavallini's role within the Roman mosaic tradition and pattern in fourteenth-century Sienese painting, especially in panels and subsequently in the pictures of the Marchigian painter Gentile da Fabriano. All this diverse material threatens to overwhelm; Hills avoids such a pitfall, however, through succinct, clear presentation.

Although he largely refrains from unnecessary conjecture, one of his objectives should be viewed cautiously. The discussion of three important late-thirteenth-century texts on optics, with the aim of securing some connection between their commentaries and trecento pictures, seeks a parallel rooted in theory which is rather contrived. I raise this issue because Hills, too, admits that it may be a "misleading undertaking." Although the fact that Roger Bacon, John Pecham, and Witelo had been at the papal court at Viterbo brings up an intriguing link vis-à-vis the Holy See, the extent to which these philosophers' opinions affected the new, discerning portrayal of light and color must remain speculative.

Such a reservation does not undermine the value of Hills's work. Elsewhere, specifically in the sections concerning pattern or the evolution of Florentine frescoes, astute observations abound. His suggestion that Sienese artists, like their Venetian counterparts, appropriated designs after those embellishing imported Oriental textiles due to Siena's lack of a native silk industry acknowledges a practical circumstance as one reason for the replication of intricate motifs. The selection of key pictures by Duccio, Simone Martini, and Pietro Lorenzetti to demonstrate the expansion of three-dimensional space through decorative patterns establishes a fundamental aesthetic peculiar to early-fourteenth-century Sienese painting which would persist for more than a century. Employment of gold punchwork and *sgraffito* technique, literally altering a picture's surface, underscores the inherent contradistinction between Sienese and coeval Florentine painting. Whereas Giotto's Scrovegni chapel frescoes in Padua were conceived with ingeniously modeled pictorial light creating the impression of penetrable space, Sienese artists preferred rich exterior effects.

Subsequent Florentine synthesis of luminous and spatial properties within a picture are considered against the background of Meiss's interpretation of the 1348 plague as dividing the fourteenth century into a progressive and retrogressive artistic phase.[2] Whether or not the reader agrees with the cause behind such a chronological development, the visual evidence introduced illustrates dramatic change. Taddeo Gaddi's early-1330s nocturnal fresco scenes along the altar wall of the Baroncelli chapel in Santa Croce, Florence exhibit an unprecedented understanding that darkness could be rendered by subtle gradations of shading as well as by symbolically handled torchlight. Yet his achievements had no immediate followers. Even the paintings executed throughout the 1380s and '90s by his son, Agnolo, favored, in contrast, a pastel palette whose pale hues reflect the architectural polychromy of Giotto's bell tower beside Florence Cathedral. This latter observation is just one instance where Hills perceptively notes the interdependence of one medium upon another.

His detailed analysis of the ornamental and monumental currents dominating Tuscan art next embraces the revolutionary descriptions of light that appeared in Florentine painting during the 1420s. Gentile da Fabriano, a foreigner, applied shining gold to enrich pictorial surfaces and so embodied the decorative tendency, while Masaccio revived the local Giottesque technique of situating forms in space by exploiting controlled, direct light. Although both artists refashioned the way pictures were illuminated, the analogy between Masaccio's painting and early-fifteenth-century humanism points out the growing dichotomy between the Christian and the classical within Florentine society. Time and later generations of painters did indeed prove that Masaccio best comprehended light's universal nature.

Hills has written a much-needed study whose purpose exceeds a quest for cast shadows in early Italian painting. Moreover, this book is well-produced. A list of treatises on color and fragments of painters' manuals, accompanied by a relevant bibliography, form a useful appendix. Even more important in a volume devoted to light and color are the inclusion of thirty-two good-quality color plates, many of them full-page illustrations. The ideas presented here offer new insights and ought to be required reading for anyone who is interested in the structure of Italian Renaissance painting.

Adrian S. Hoch
Florida State University

Notes

1. John White, *The Birth and Rebirth of Pictorial Space* (1st ed. London, 1957; 3d rev. ed. London, 1987) and Samuel Y. Edgerton, Jr., *The Renaissance Rediscovery of Linear Perspective* (New York, 1975).

2. Millard Meiss, *Painting in Florence and Siena After the Black Death The Arts, Religions and Society in the Mid-Fourteenth Century* (1st ed. Princeton, 1951; reprinted New York, 1973).

Giulio Busi, *Edizioni ebraiche del XVI secolo nelle biblioteche dell' Emilia Romagna*. Regione Emilia-Romagna. Istituto per i Beni Artistici Culturali e Naturali. Soprintendenza per i Beni Librari e Documentari. Emilia Romagna - Biblioteche Archivi, No. 5. Bologna: Edizioni Analisi, 1987. Pp. 222.

G. Busi's comprehensive catalog of sixteenth-century Hebrew works in libraries of Emilia Romagna derives its inspiration from two salutary developments in Italian scholarship: the massive effort undertaken by Italian libraries to catalog all of the country's rich written and printed cultural patrimony in a comprehensive, uniform, and up-to-date fashion; and the formation of the Associazione Italiana per lo Studio del Giudaismo, which has brought together scholars from diverse fields and given Jewish studies a respected academic voice in Italy.

This elegant volume is an admirable mark of the productive possibilities of that conjecture.

Some 1,500 volumes of Hebraica were examined, and 538 separate sixteenth-century titles were identified and listed with full bibliographic annotation. In addition, the work includes notes on five incunabula not registered in G. Tamani's *Gli incunaboli ebraici delle biblioteche d'Italia* (1981). Titles listed include works of Jews as well as of Christian Hebraists when these contain significant amounts of Hebrew text.

Twenty-four plates and comprehensive indices by title, place of publication, publisher, author/editor, former owner, and censor all add to the usefulness of the volume.

Through Busi's work, scholars everywhere, and especially those in Italy, gain access to the texts vital to their work. In addition, the catalog provides an important tool for those trying to trace the history of Hebrew book collecting and Hebrew studies in Italy, and hence to understand the cultural ambience of both Christian and Jewish learning since the late Renaissance.

Bernard Cooperman
Harvard University

Books Received

Abels, Richard P. *Lordship and Military Obligation in Anglo-Saxon England.* Berkeley: University of California Press, 1988. Pp. xii + 313. $39.95

Alford, John A., ed. *A Companion to Piers Plowman.* Berkeley: University of California Press, 1988. Pp. xii + 286. $32.50.

Alford, John A. *Piers Plowman: A Glossary of Legal Diction.* Wolfeboro, N.H.: D. S. Brewer, 1988. Pp. 170. $45.00.

Alter, Robert, and Frank Kermode, eds. *The Literary Guide to the Bible.* Cambridge: Harvard University Press, 1987. Pp. 678.

Anderson, David. *Before the Knight's Tale: Imitation of Classical Epic in Boccaccio's Teseida.* Philadelphia: University of Pennsylvania Press, 1988. Pp. 269. $29.95.

Augustinian Historical Institute. *Proceedings of the Patristic, Medieval and Renaissance Conference.* Vol. 11. Villanova: Villanova University Press, 1986. Pp. 186.

Baird-Lange, Lorrayne, and Hildegard Schnuttgen. *A Bibliography of Chaucer, 1974–1985.* Hamden: Archon Books, 1988. Pp. 344. $39.50.

The Barbarians. Ossining: Young Discovery Library, 1988. Pp. 37.

Barber, Paul. *Vampires, Burial, and Death: Folklore and Reality.* New Haven: Yale University Press, 1988. Pp. 236. $25.00.

Barnes, Robin Bruce. *Prophecy and Gnosis: Apocalypticism in the Wake of the Lutheran Reformation.* Stanford: Stanford University Press, 1988. Pp. 371. $39.50.

Baron, Hans. *In Search of Florentine Civic Humanism: Essays on the Transition from Medieval to Modern Thought.* 2 vols. Princeton: Princeton University Press, 1988. $59.00.

Baron, John H. *Chamber Music: A Research and Information Guide.* New York: Garland Publishing, Inc., 1987. Pp. 500. $62.00.

Beroul. *Tristran and Yseut: Old French Text With Facing English Translation.* Ed. by Guy R. Mermier. New York: Peter Lang, 1987. Pp. 266. $35.00.

Bloch, Herbert. *Monte Cassino in the Middle Ages.* 3 vols. Cambridge: Harvard University Press, 1986. Pp. 1530.

Blumenthal, Uta-Renate. *The Investiture Controversy: Church and Monarchy from the Ninth to the Twelfth Century.* Philadelphia: University of Pennsylvania Press, 1988. Pp. 191. $37.95.

Bodden, Mary-Catherine, ed. and trans. *The Old English Finding of the True Cross.* Wolfeboro, N.H.: D. S. Brewer, 1988. Pp. 132. $32.50.

Bremmer, H. Rolf, Jr. *The Fyve Wyttes.* Atlantic Highlands: Humanities Press International, 1987. Pp. 129. $70.00.

Brewer, Derek, ed. *Studies in Medieval English Romances: Some New Approaches.* Wolfeboro, N.H.: D. S. Brewer, 1988. Pp. 197. $45.00.

Bromiley, Geoffrey W., ed. *International Standard Bible Encyclopedia.* Vol. 4: Q–Z. Grand Rapids: William B. Eerdmans Publishing Company, 1988. Pp. 1210. $39.95.

Burgess, S. Glyn, and Anne Elizabeth Cobby. *The Pilgrimage of Charlemagne and Aucassin and Nicolette.* New York: Garland Publishing, Inc., 1988. Pp. 183. $29.00.

Campbell, Tony. *The Earliest Printed Maps: 1472–1500.* Berkeley: University of California Press, 1987. Pp. 244. $75.00.

Chance, Jane, and R. O. Wells, Jr., eds. *Mapping the Cosmos.* Houston: Rice University Press, 1985. Pp. 175.

Chaucer, Geoffrey. *The Legend of Good Women.* Trans. by Ann McMillan. Houston: Rice University Press, 1987. Pp. 179. $10.95.

Cobban, Allan B. *The Medieval English Universities: Oxford and Cambridge to c. 1500.* Berkeley: University of California Press, 1988. Pp. 465. $55.00.

Crociata, Mariano. *Umanesimo E Teologia in Agostino Steuco.* Rome: Citta Nuova Editrice, 1987. Pp. 252.

Dahlberg, Charles. *The Literature of Unlikeness.* Hanover: University Press of New England, 1988. Pp. 207. $30.00.

Davenport, W. A. *Chaucer: Complaint and Narrative.* Wolfeboro, N.H.: D. S. Brewer, 1988. Pp. 232. $53.00.

Davidson, H. R. Ellis. *Myths and Symbols in Pagan Europe: Early Scandinavian and Celtic Religions.* Syracuse: Syracuse University Press, 1988. Pp. 268. $28.00.

Davies, Peter V., and Angus J. Kennedy, eds. *Rewards and Punishment in the Arthurian Romances and Lyric Poetry of Mediaeval France.* Wolfeboro, N.H.: D. S. Brewer, 1988. Pp. 176. $57.50.

Davies, Wendy. *Small Worlds: The Village Community in Early Medieval Brittany.* Berkeley: University of California Press, 1988. Pp. 227. $30.00.

Day, John. *The Medieval Market Economy.* New York: Basil Blackwell, 1987. Pp. 232. $45.00.

Demaray, John G. *Dante and the Book of the Cosmos.* Transactions of the American Philosophical Society. Vol. 77, part 5, 1987. Philadelphia: American Philosophical Society, 1987. Pp. 114. $18.00.

Dominik, Mark. *Shakespeare-Middleton Collaborations.* Beaverton: Alioth Press, 1988. Pp. 173. $22.50.

Dronke, Peter, ed. *A History of Twelfth-Century Western Philosophy.* New York: Cambridge University Press, 1988. Pp. 495.

Earle, T. F. *The Muse Reborn: The Poetry of Antonio Ferreira.* Oxford: Clarendon Press, 1988. Pp. 187. $55.00.

Eco, Umberto. *Art and Beauty in the Middle Ages.* Trans. by Hugh Bredin. New Haven: Yale University Press, 1986. Pp. 131. $7.95.

Elliott, Alison Goddard. *Roads to Paradise: Reading the Lives of the Early Saints.* Hanover: University Press of New England, 1987. Pp. 244. $25.00.

L'epoque de la renaissance 1400–1600: L'avenement de l'esprit nouveau (1400– 1480). Vol. 1. Budapest: Akademiai Kiado, 1988. Pp. 594. $45.00.

Eriugena. *Periphyseon: The Division of Nature.* Trans. by I. P. Sheldon-Williams, revised by John J. O'Meara. Washington: Dumbarton Oaks, 1987. Pp. 722. $35.00.

Erler, Mary, and Maryanne Kowaleski, eds. *Women and Power in the Middle Ages.* Athens: University of Georgia Press, 1988. Pp. 277. $15.00.

Farthing, John L. *Thomas Aquinas and Gabriel Biel: Interpretations of St. Thomas Aquinas in German Nominalism on the Eve of the Reformation.* Durham: Duke University Press, 1988. Pp. 265. $22.50.

Field, Arthur. *The Origins of the Platonic Academy of Florence.* Princeton: Princeton University Press, 1988. Pp. 302. $47.50.

La "France Anglaise" au Moyen Age: Actes du 111e Congress National des Sociétés Savantes (Poitiers, 1986). Paris: Editions du Comite des Tranvaus Historiques et Scientifiques, 1988.

Goffen, Rona. *Spirituality in Conflict: Saint Francis and Giotto's Bardi Chapel.* University Park: The Pennsylvania State University Press, 1988. Pp. 142. $42.50.

Goldberg, Edward L. *After Vasari: History, Art, and Patronage in Late Medici Florence.* Princeton: Princeton University Press, 1988. Pp. 309. $49.50.

Gortein, S. T. *A Mediterranean Society. Vol. 5: The Individual: Portrait of a Mediterranean Personality of the High Middle Ages as Reflected in the Cairo Geniza.* Berkeley: University of California Press, 1988. Pp. 657.

Greenblatt, Stephen, ed. *Representing the English Renaissance.* Berkeley: University of California Press, 1988. Pp. xiii + 372. $42.00.

Greenblatt, Stephen. *Shakespearean Negotiations: The Circulation of Social Energy in Renaissance England.* Berkeley: University of California Press, 1988. Pp. 205. $20.00.

Grubb, James S. *Firstborn of Venice: Vicenza in the Early Renaissance State.* Baltimore: Johns Hopkins University Press, 1988. Pp. 238. $29.50.

Guillaume de Machaut. *The Judgment of the King of Navarre.* Ed. and trans. by R. Barton Palmer. New York: Garland Publishing, Inc., 1988. Pp. 217. $34.00.

Hartog, Francois. *The Mirror of Herodotus: The Representation of the Other in the Writing of History.* Trans. by Janet Lloyd. Berkeley: University of California Press, 1988. Pp. 386. $42.00.

Heffernan, Carol Falvo. *The Phoenix at the Fountain: Images of Women and*

Eternity in Lactantius's Carmen de Ave Phoenice and the Old English Phoenix. Newark: University of Delaware Press, 1988. Pp. 175. $27.50.

Herrera, Robert. *Lamps of Fire: Studies in Christian Mysticism.* Petersham, Mass.: St. Bede's Publications, 1986. Pp. 138. $7.95.

Hodges, Richard. *Primitive and Present Markets.* New York: Basil Blackwell, 1988. Pp. 175. $12.95.

Hollander, Robert. *Boccaccio's Last Fiction "Il Corbaccio."* Philadelphia: University of Pennsylvania Press, 1988. Pp. 86. $18.95.

Hooke, Dalla, ed. *Anglo-Saxon Settlements.* New York: Basil Blackwell, 1988. Pp. 319. $75.00.

Horowitz, Maryanne Cline, Anne J. Cruz, and Wendy A. Furman, eds. *Renaissance Rereadings: Intertext and Context.* Urbana: University of Illinois Press, 1988. Pp. 300. Paper: $12.50.

Iamartino, Giovanni. *Vizi capitali e pianeti in un sermone del Cinquecento inglese.* Milano: Pubblicazioni della University Cattolica, 1988. Pp. 149.

Imperatore, Giuliano. *Alla Madre Degli Dei: E Altri Discorsi.* Rome: Fondazione Lorenzo Valla, 1987. Pp. 351.

Jacquart, Danielle, and Claude Thomasset. *Sexuality and Medicine in the Middle Ages.* Trans. by Matthew Adamson. Princeton: Princeton University Press, 1988. Pp. 242. $35.00.

Jeffrey, David Lyle, trans. and ed. *The Law of Love: English Spirituality in the Age of Wyclif.* Grand Rapids: William B. Eerdmans Publishing Company, 1988. Pp. 404. $16.95.

Jordan, William Chester. *From Servitude to Freedom: Manumission in the Senonais in the Thirteenth Century.* Philadelphia: University of Pennsylvania Press, 1986. Pp. 149.

Karras, Ruth Mazo. *Slavery and Society in Medieval Scandinavia.* New Haven: Yale University Press, 1988. Pp. 309. $32.50.

Kaske, R. E. *Medieval Christian Literary Imagery: A Guide to Interpretation.* Toronto: University of Toronto Press, 1988. Pp. 247. $35.00.

Kay, Richard, ed. *The Broadview Book of Medieval Anecdotes.* Peterborough, Canada: Broadview Press, 1988. Pp. 366.

Kendrick, Laura. *Chaucerian Play: Comedy and Control in the Canterbury Tales.* Berkeley: University of California Press, 1988. Pp. xi + 215. $28.00.

Kendrick, Laura. *The Game of Love: Troubadour Wordplay.* Berkeley: University of California Press, 1988. Pp. 237. $32.50.

Kirshner, Julius, and Suzanne R. Wemple. *Women of the Medieval World: Essays in Honor of John H. Mundy.* New York: Basil Blackwell, 1985. Pp. 380. $15.95.

Koff, Leonard Michael. *Chaucer and the Art of Storytelling.* Berkeley: University of California Press, 1988. Pp. 298. $35.00.

Krstovic, Jelena, ed. *Classical and Medieval Literature Criticism.* Vol. 2. Detroit: Gale Research Inc., 1988. Pp. 508. $85.00.

Labriola, Albert C., and Edward Sichi, Jr., eds. *Milton's Legacy in the Arts.* University Park: Pennsylvania State University Press, 1988. Pp. 239. $24.95.

Lacy, Norris J., ed. *The Arthurian Encyclopedia.* New York: Garland Publishing, 1986. Pp. 649. $60.00.

Langland, William. *Piers Plowman: The A Version.* Ed. by George Kane. Berkeley: University of California Press, 1988. Pp. ix + 463. $115.00.

Langland, William. *Piers Plowman: The B Version.* Ed. by Talbot E. Donaldson and George Kane. Berkeley: University of California Press, 1988. Pp. vii + 681. $130.00.

Leacroft, Richard. *The Development of the English Playhouse.* New York: Methuen, 1988. Pp. 354. $49.95.

Lehmberg, Stanford E. *The Reformation of Cathedrals: Cathedrals in English Society, 1485–1603.* Princeton: Princeton University Press, 1988. Pp. 319. $49.95.

Link-Salinger, Ruth, ed. *A Straight Path: Studies in Medieval Philosophy and Culture.* Washington: Catholic University of America Press, 1988. Pp. 310. $35.00.

Long Ago in a Castle. Ossining: Young Discovery Library, 1988. Pp. 34.

Lopes, Fernao. *The English in Portugal 1367–87.* Trans. by Derek W. Lomax and R. J. Oakley. Warminster, England: Aris & Phillips Ltd., 1988. Pp. 368. $49.95.

Lynch, Kathryn L. *The High Medieval Dream Vision: Poetry, Philosophy, and Literary Form.* Stanford: Stanford University Press, 1988. Pp. 263. $35.00.

Martines, Lauro. *Power and Imaginations: City-States in Renaissance Italy.* Baltimore: Johns Hopkins University Press, 1988. Pp. 370. $12.95.

Miller, David Lee. *The Poem's Two Bodies: The Poetics of the 1590 Faerie Queen.* Princeton: Princeton University Press, 1988. Pp. 297. $29.50.

Minnis, A. J. *Medieval Theory of Authorship: Scholastic Literary Attitudes in the Later Middle Ages.* 2d ed. Philadelphia: University of Pennsylvania Press, 1988. Pp. 323. $16.95.

Moore, R. I. *The Formation of a Persecuting Society: Power and Deviance in Western Europe, 950–1250.* Oxford: Basil Blackwell, 1987. Pp. 168. $27.50.

Morabito, Raffaele, ed. *Diddrezioni: Griselda I.* Rome: Japadre Editore, 1988. Pp. 123.

Newman, Charlotte A. *The Anglo-Norman Nobility in the Reign of Henry I: the Second Generation.* Philadelphia: University of Pennsylvania Press, 1988. Pp. 243. $40.00.

Noakes, Susan. *Timely Reading: Between Exegesis and Interpretation.* Ithaca: Cornell University Press, 1988. Pp. 249. $29.95.

Noffke, Suzanne, O. P., trans. *The Letters of St. Catherine of Siena.* Vol. 1. Binghamton: Medieval & Renaissance Text & Studies, 1988. Pp. 450. $28.00.

Nordenfalk, Carl. *Early Medieval Book Illumination.* New York: Rizzoli International Publications Inc., 1988. Pp. 145. $25.00.

Norman, Joanne S. *Metamorphoses of an Allegory: The Iconography of the Psychomachia in Medieval Art.* New York: Peter Lang, 1988. Pp. 353. $52.50.

Oakley, Francis. *The Medieval Experience: Foundations of Western Cultural Singularity.* Toronto: University of Toronto Press, 1988. Pp. 228. $9.95.

O'Callaghan, Joseph F. *The Cortes of Castile-Leon 1188–1350.* Philadelphia: University of Pennsylvania Press, 1989. Pp. 265. $39.95.

Ochino, Bernardino. *Seven Dialogues.* Trans. by Rita Belladona. Ottawa: Dovehouse Editions, 1988. Pp. 96. $12.50.

Orgel, Stephen, ed. *The Renaissance Imagination: Important Literary and Theatrical Texts from the Late Middle Ages Through the Seventeenth Century.* New York: Garland Publishing, Inc., 1987. Pp. 207. $40.00.

Orgelfinger, Gail, ed. *The Hystorye of Olyuer of Castylle.* New York: Garland Publishing, Inc., 1988. Pp. 258. $37.00.

Paden, William D., trans. *The Medieval Pastourelle.* 2 vols. New York: Garland Publishing, Inc., 1987. $100.00

Papuli, G., ed. *Bollettino Di Storia Della Filosofia Dell 'Universita' Degli Studi Di Lecce.* Vol. 8. Lecce: Edizioni Milella, 1987. Pp. 431.

Peck, Russell A. *Chaucer's Romaunt of the Rose and Boece, Treatise on the Astrolabe, Equatories of the Planetis, Lost Works, and Chaucerian Apocrypha: An Annotated Bibliography 1900 to 1985.* Toronto: University of Toronto Press, 1988. Pp. 402. $60.00.

Person, James E., ed. *Literature Criticism from 1400 to 1800.* Vol. 8. Detroit: Gale Research Inc. Pp. 542. $95.00.

Pickles, J. D., and J. L. Dawson, eds. *A Concordance to John Gower's Confessio Amantis.* Wolfeboro, N.H.: D. S. Brewer, 1987. Pp. 1124. $95.00.

Pollard, Graham, ed. *Studies in the History of Art: Italian Medals.* Vol. 21. Hanover: University Press of New England, 1987. Pp. 299. $35.00.

Poupard, Dennis, and Jelena O. Krustovic, eds. *Classical and Medieval Literature Criticism.* Detroit: Gale Research Company, 1988. Pp. 607. $80.00.

Powers, James F. *A Society Organized for War: The Iberian Municipal Militias in the Central Middle Ages, 1000–1284.* Berkeley: University of California Press, 1988. Pp. 365. $45.00.

Prestwich, Michael. *Edward I.* Berkeley: University of California Press, 1988. Pp. 618. $29.95.

Radding, Charles M. *The Origins of Medieval Jurisprudence: Pavia and Bologna 850–1150.* New Haven: Yale University Press, 1988. Pp. 258. $25.00.

Reilly, Bernard F. *The Kingdom of Leon–Castilla Under King Alfonso VI 1065–1109.* Princeton: Princeton University Press, 1988. Pp. 406. $54.50.

Renoir, Alain. *A Key to Old Poems: The Oral-Formulaic Approach to the Interpretation of West-Germanic Verse.* University Park: Pennsylvania State University Press, 1988. Pp. 224. $32.00.

Romano, Dennis. *Patricians and Popolani: The Social Foundations of the Venetian Renaissance State.* Baltimore: Johns Hopkins University Press, 1987. Pp. 220. $25.00.

Rossabi, Morris. *Khubilai Khan: His Life and Times.* Berkeley: University of California Press, 1988. Pp. 332. $25.00.

Rowe, Donald W. *Through Nature to Eternity: Chaucer's Legend of Good Women.* Lincoln and London: University of Nebraska Press, 1988. Pp. 218. $22.95.

Schlueter, Paul, and June Schlueter, eds. *An Encyclopedia of British Women Writers.* New York: Garland Publishing, Inc., 1988. Pp. 516. $75.00.

Schmidt, A. V. C. *The Clerkly Maker: Langland's Poetic Art.* Wolfeboro, N.H.: D. S. Brewer, 1987. Pp. 158. $42.00.

Scully, Terence, ed. *The Viandier of Taillevent.* Ottawa: University of Ottawa Press. Pp. 361. $29.95.

Seebass, Tilman, ed. *Imago Musaicae IV.* Durham: Duke University Press, 1987. Pp. 366. $55.00.

Shapiro, Michael, and Marianne Shapiro. *Figuration in Verbal Art.* Princeton: Princeton University Press, 1988. Pp. 286. $37.50.

Shuger, Debora K. *Sacred Rhetoric: The Christian Grand Style in the English Renaissance.* Princeton: Princeton University Press, 1988. Pp. 289. $32.50.

Skrynnikov, Ruslan G. *Time of Troubles: Russia in Crisis 1604–1618.* Ed. and trans. by Hugh F. Graham. Gulf Breeze: Academic International Press, 1988. Pp. 325.

Societe Internationale pour l'etude de la Philosophie Medievale, ed. *Bulletin* (29e annee 1987). Louvain-la-nerve: Secretariat de la S. I. E. P. M. Chemin d'Aristote 1, 1987. Pp. 311.

Soloviev, Sergei M. *History of Russia, Vol. 14: The Time of Trouble: Boris Godunov and False Dmitry.* Ed. and trans. by Edward G. Orchard. Gulf Breeze: Academic International Press, 1988. Pp. 171. $30.00.

Spearing, A. C. *Readings in Medieval Poetry.* Cambridge: Cambridge University Press, 1987. Pp. 270.

Spillenger, Paul, et al., eds. *Envoi: A Review Journal of Medieval Literature.* Vol. 1, No. 1 Spring/Summer. New York: AMS Press, 1988. Pp. 265.

Sticca, Sandro. *The Planctus Mariae in the Dramatic Tradition of the Middle Ages.* Trans. by Joseph R. Berrigan. Athens and London: University of Georgia Press, 1988. Pp. 239. $35.00.

Straw, Carole. *Gregory the Great: Perfection in Imperfection.* Berkeley: University of California Press, 1988. Pp. 295. $35.00.

Tabuteau, Emily Zack. *Transfers of Property in Eleventh-Century Norman Law.* Chapel Hill: University of North Carolina Press, 1988. Pp. 445. $49.95.

Thrupp, Sylvia L. *Change in Medieval Society: Medieval Academy Reprints for Teaching.* Toronto: University of Toronto Press, 1988. Pp. 324. $12.95.

Tierney, Brian. *The Crisis of Church and State 1050–1300, with Selected Documents.* Toronto: University of Toronto Press, 1988. Pp. 212. $8.95.

Treadgold, Warren. *The Byzantine Revival, 780–842.* Stanford: Stanford University Press, 1988. Pp. 504. $49.50.

Trexler, C. Richard. *The Christian at Prayer: An Illustrated Prayer Manual Attributed to Peter the Chanter (d. 1197).* Binghamton: Medieval and Renaissance Texts and Studies, 1987. Pp. 260.

Turner, Ralph V. *Men Raised from the Dust: Administrative Service and Upward Mobility in Angevin England.* Philadelphia: University of Pennsylvania Press, 1988. Pp. 218.

Von Simson, Otto. *The Gothic Cathedral: Origins of Gothic Architecture & the Medieval Concept of Order.* 3d ed. Princeton: Princeton University Press, 1988. Pp. 282. $12.95.

Walker, Julia M., ed. *Milton and the Idea of Woman.* Urbana: University of Illinois Press, 1988. Pp. 263. $27.50.

Wallace, David. *Chaucer and the Early Writings of Boccaccio.* Wolfeboro, N.H.: D. S. Brewer, 1985. Pp. 209. $54.00.

Wasserman, Julian N., and Lois Roney, eds. *Sign, Sentence, Discourse: Language in Medieval Thought.* Syracuse: Syracuse University Press, 1988. Pp. 318. $18.95.

Waugh, Scott L. *The Lordship of England: Royal Wardships and Marriages in English Society and Politics 1217–1327.* Princeton: Princeton University Press, 1988. Pp. 327. $44.50.

Weever, de Jacqueline. *Chaucer Name Dictionary: A Guide to Astrological, Biblical, Historical, Literary, and Mythological Names in the Works of Geoffrey Chaucer.* New York: Garland Publishing, Inc., 1988. Pp. 451. $50.00.

White, Hugh. *Nature and Salvation in Piers Plowman.* Wolfeboro, N.H.: St. Edmundsbury Press, 1988. Pp. 128. $45.00.

White, Stephen D. *Custon, Kinship, and Gifts to Saints: The Laudatio Parentum in Western France, 1050–1150.* Chapel Hill: University of North Carolina Press, 1988. Pp. 313. $29.95.

Wolfram, Herwig. *History of the Goths.* Trans. by Thomas J. Dunlap. Berkeley: University of California Press, 1988. Pp. 613. $39.95.